Fountas&Pinnell
CLASSROOM™
System Guide

Irene C. Fountas

Gay Su Pinnell

HEINEMANN
Portsmouth, NH

GRADE 4

Heinemann
361 Hanover Street
Portsmouth, NH 03801-3912
www.heinemann.com

Offices and agents throughout the world

Library of Congress Cataloging-in-Publication Data is on file.
ISBN: 978-0-325-11191-9

Editor: Debra Doorack
Production: Angel Lepore
Cover design: Suzanne Heiser, Kelly Goodwin, Kelsey Roy
Interior designs: Monica Ann Crigler
Typesetter: Technologies 'N Typography, Inc.
Manufacturing: Deanna Richardson, Erin St. Hilaire

Printed in the United States of America on acid-free paper
1 2 3 4 5 VP 23 22 21 20 19

August 2019 Printing

CONTENTS

Welcome to
Fountas & Pinnell Classroom™

As a teacher of literacy, you transform the lives of the students in your classroom. You create in students the knowledge and ability to make sense of ideas—simple and complex, current and ancient, big and small, entertaining and provocative—and to contribute new ideas through their own expressions of language. Equipped with this knowledge and ability, students have the potential and capacity to lead lives full of wonder and discovery. Why? Because they have the knowledge and ability to *transform* their thinking by absorbing, critiquing, and sharing ideas orally and through print.

Whether you are teaching prekindergarteners to recognize individual letters in their names or you are teaching sixth graders to recognize bias in the language of a persuasive text, your work is demanding, challenging, and at times altogether frustrating. But your work as a teacher of literacy is also worthwhile and genuinely important because of the lasting impact you can make on students' lives.

> *Your work as a teacher of literacy is worthwhile and important because it tranforms the lives of students.*

FIGURE 1–1

For nearly twenty-five years, we have been honored to partner with you in this transformative work. As we have visited your classrooms, taught our own classes, led seminars, and developed the professional books, intervention systems, assessments, and classroom resources that make up *Fountas & Pinnell Literacy*, we have had the opportunity and pleasure to talk to you about high-impact literacy instruction. We asked:

▶ What does it look like in the classroom?

▶ What types of student and teacher materials are needed to implement it?

▶ What kinds of professional learning resources are needed to support it?

As we learned from you, literacy instruction is most effective when it takes place within a classroom community of readers and writers. In this lively community, students are reading, thinking about, talking about, and writing about a wide range of beautiful, engaging texts; students' curiosity drives authentic inquiry that builds a deep understanding of their world; and all parts of the literacy curriculum are thoughtfully connected to best support the learning needs of each student.

This coherent system of literacy education became the vision for *Fountas & Pinnell Classroom*™ for prekindergarten through grade 6. The system relies on responsive teaching using an inquiry-rich, multitext approach. As a system, *Fountas & Pinnell Classroom* stands apart from "reading programs" in its fidelity to the following principles:

▶ **Coherence.** As a coherent system, each instructional context in *Fountas & Pinnell Classroom* is reciprocally connected to the others, improving student outcomes and creating equitable literacy opportunities for the whole school. In a coherent system, the messages are clear. School makes sense to students.

▶ **Responsive teaching.** The moment-to-moment instructional decisions that you make based on your observations and analysis of students' learning behaviors are honored and supported by *Fountas & Pinnell Classroom*. In this system, you teach individual readers, not a book or a program. Consider each lesson a menu of instructional options from which you select and tailor to best support the learners in your classroom. If you can, think of *Fountas & Pinnell Classroom* as a system of materials and resources that allows you to operationalize the vision and goals of responsive teaching—teaching that *responds* to the needs, capabilities, and interests of each individual student.

▶ **Student inquiry.** Students are curious. *Fountas & Pinnell Classroom* allows students' curiosity to propel authentic learning and discovery. As students think across texts and choose their own books to read, they pursue lines of inquiry that interest and engage them as learners, building content knowledge of different topics and themes across a range of disciplines.

▶ **Multitext approach.** Books, and lots of them, are at the heart of *Fountas & Pinnell Classroom*: exciting books to stir students' imagination, beautifully crafted books to enhance students' language and knowledge of story, challenging books to lift every reader, and diverse books to expand readers' life experiences and knowledge of their world. Every title is carefully crafted or selected to support an instructional context. Every title has a purpose.

- **Language-rich.** When students talk, they communicate and refine their ideas, reveal their understandings and perspectives, and make meaning from texts and experiences. Talk is thinking, on display, and is the foundation for written language. Therefore, text-based interactive speaking is an essential component of each instructional context in *Fountas & Pinnell Classroom*.

- **Teacher expertise.** Whether you are a new teacher or one with years of classroom experience, *Fountas & Pinnell Classroom* both relies upon and contributes to your expertise as a teacher. Your knowledge informs responsive teaching; the extensive professional learning tools woven into the system strengthen your practice. Implementing *Fountas & Pinnell Classroom* is, at once, a commitment to value your skillfulness as a literacy teacher and a commitment to elevate your expertise.

Underlying these principles are a unifying Vision and a set of Core Values upon which *Fountas & Pinnell Literacy,* including *Fountas & Pinnell Classroom,* is built. We believe these Core Values are essential to meaningful and effective literacy learning for all students. As you explore the Core Values on the next several pages, you're likely to find that you already share some of them, perhaps using one or more to guide the decisions you make as a teacher. We designed *Fountas & Pinnell Classroom* as a system through which you can "teach into" all of these Core Values. Our hope is that, as you begin to implement *Fountas & Pinnell Classroom,* you find each instructional context is an opportunity for a deeper commitment to and a greater expression of these Core Values in *your* classroom and in your transformative work as a teacher of literacy.

Fountas & Pinnell Classroom is a system through which you can "teach into" the Core Values on the following pages.

FIGURE 1-2 *Fourth graders enjoying a book during interactive read-aloud*

Our Vision and Core Values

The schools we envision recognize every student's right to grow up literate as a member of a dynamic learning community that values the richness of linguistic, ethnic, and cultural diversity. Members of the school community are treated and treat others with empathy, kindness, and respect. Students are motivated to investigate new ideas that fuel intellectual curiosity and act as powerful agents in their own learning. Because students are fully engaged and feel a sense of joy in their own learning, they achieve a higher level of literacy. Through dynamic literacy education that exemplifies the beliefs and core values described on the following pages, students come to understand their physical, social, and emotional world and their roles as informed global citizens—hallmarks of the literate lives they can lead.

Schools are places where **students**—

1

Act as members of a cohesive learning community that sustains their literacy growth and success.

2

Engage in authentic inquiry within and beyond the classroom walls to ignite their intellectual curiosity and expand their knowledge of the world and of others.

3

Believe in themselves and their own ability to acquire and use language and literacy for learning and enjoyment.

Schools are places where **students**—

Read, think about, talk about, and write about relevant content that engages their hearts and minds every day.

Read, think about, talk about, and write about texts that are culturally sensitive, reflect the diversity in our world, and vary in genre, content, and perspective.

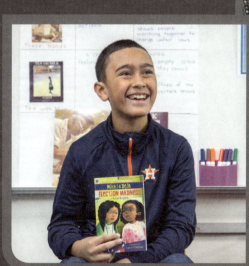

6

Implement a coherent set of evidence-based instructional practices in whole-class, small-group, and individual contexts.

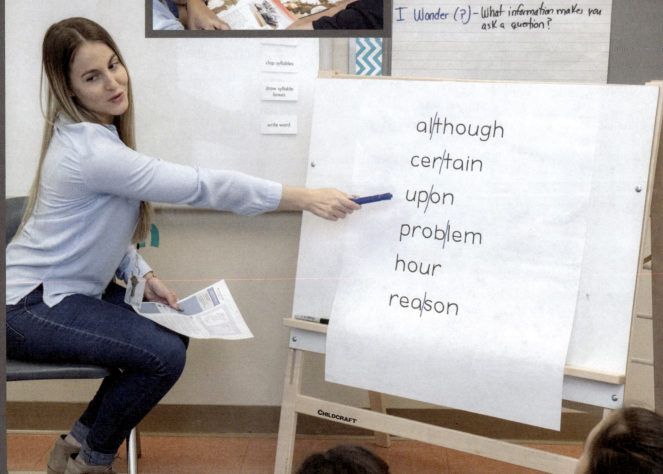

7

Make expert instructional decisions based on evidence gained from systematic observation and ongoing assessment data.

8

Work as a team to take collective responsibility for the high achievement of every student in a widely diverse population.

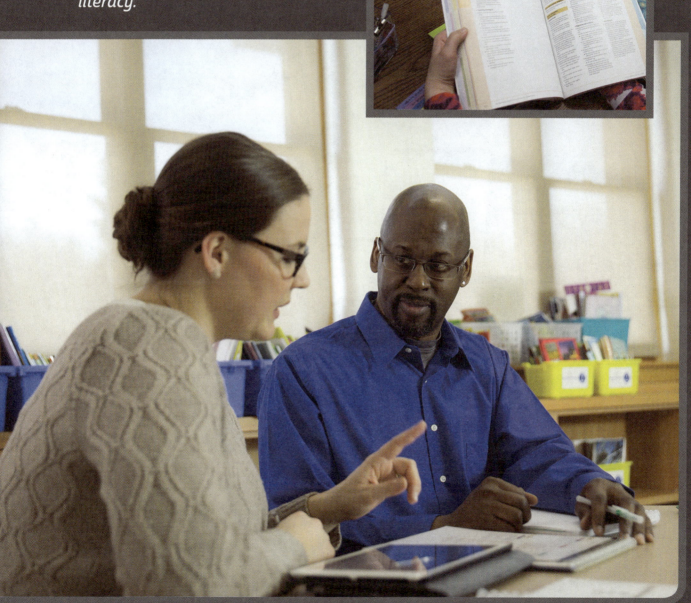

9

Act as members of a community with a common vision, common goals, common language, and a strong belief that their work can transform students' lives through literacy.

10

Demonstrate an unwavering commitment to their own professional learning and to supporting the learning of their colleagues and team members.

Your Materials and Resources

FOUNTAS & PINNELL CLASSROOM™ is organized into seven instructional contexts, with designed and explicit links between contexts. Resources for each context may include books, lesson folders, conferring cards, discussion cards, or minilessons, as well as online resources and other supporting materials for a systematic and cohesive approach to literacy instruction. The system is designed to support whole-class, small-group, and individual learning opportunities (Figure 2–1). As you organize your classroom, use the information in this section to sort and arrange your materials and resources.

FOUNTAS & PINNELL CLASSROOM INSTRUCTIONAL CONTEXTS

Whole Class	Small Groups	Individuals
IRA Interactive Read-Aloud	**GR** Guided Reading	**IR** Independent Reading (and Conferring)
SR Shared and Performance Reading	**BC** Book Clubs	**PWS** Phonics and Word Study (Apply)
RML Reading Minilessons	**PWS** Phonics and Word Study (Apply)	
PWS Phonics and Word Study (Teach and Share)		

FIGURE 2–1 Fountas & Pinnell Classroom *Instructional Contexts*

SYSTEM GUIDE

Provides an overview of *Fountas & Pinnell Classroom* with suggestions for organizing your classroom, planning your instruction, implementing each instructional context, and assessing your students' learning.

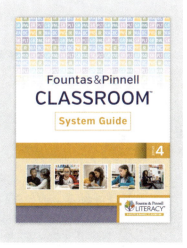

Fountas & Pinnell Classroom™ System Guide, Grade 4

IRA Interactive Read-Aloud

A whole-class activity in which you select a book to read aloud to your class, engaging students in authentic discussion about the text. Books are organized into text sets that spark inquiry-based learning.

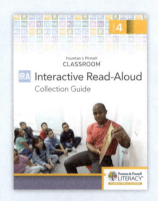

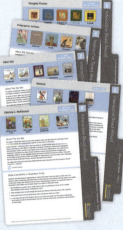

Fountas & Pinnell Classroom™ Interactive Read-Aloud Collection Guide, Grade 4

120 Interactive Read-Aloud Books, organized into 25 text sets

25 text set cards, including Inquiry Overview Cards, Author and Illustrator Study Cards, and Genre Study Cards

120 Interactive Read-Aloud Lessons

SR Shared and Performance Reading

A whole-class or small-group activity in which students read aloud or perform from an enlarged or projected text, giving them the opportunity to engage in reading texts they would not be able to read independently.

Books from other *Fountas & Pinnell Classroom* instructional contexts can be used for shared and performance reading. See pages 85–88 for a list of particularly appropriate books.

Several books from the *Fountas & Pinnell Classroom, Grade 4, Guided Reading Collection* contain ready-to-use readers' theater scripts for students to read and perform.

Activities involving shared or performance reading are included in many interactive read-aloud, guided reading, and book club lessons in *Fountas & Pinnell Classroom*.

Guided Reading

A small group of students reads a challenging text at their instructional reading level as you demonstrate, prompt for, or reinforce effective reading behaviors, providing students an opportunity to apply what they have learned how to do as readers.

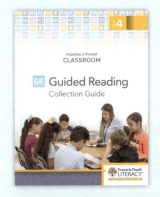

Fountas & Pinnell Classroom™ Guided Reading Collection Guide, Grade 4

180 Guided Reading Books, levels N–V, six copies of each title

188* Guided Reading Lessons
*There are more lessons than books because we provide lessons for each book in a two-way text.

Independent Reading

Students read texts of their choice independently, allowing them to enjoy books, practice the reading process, and share their thinking about the books they are reading.

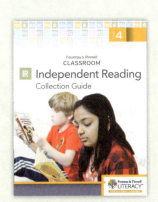

Fountas & Pinnell Classroom™ Independent Reading Collection Guide, Grade 4

200 Independent Reading Books

200 Independent Reading Conferring Cards, plus genre-based prompting cards

Book Clubs

A small-group activity in which students choose a book to read from a limited set of titles and then come together for a discussion that expands their thinking about texts.

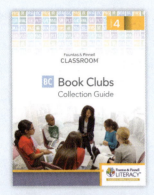

Fountas & Pinnell Classroom™ Book Clubs Collection Guide, Grade 4

48 Book Club books organized into eight text sets, with six copies of each title

12 Inquiry Overview Cards, one for each text set

48 Book Club Discussion Cards

Reading Minilessons

Brief, whole-class lessons on the topics of management, literary analysis, skills and strategies, and writing about reading.

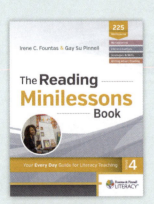

The Reading Minilessons Book, Grade 4, containing 225 minilessons

Phonics and Word Study Lessons

Brief lessons for whole-group instruction that help students attend to, learn about, and efficiently solve words.

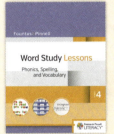

Fountas & Pinnell Word Study Lessons: Phonics, Spelling, and Vocabulary, Grade 4, containing 105 lessons, many generative to use with more examples

Fountas & Pinnell Word Study Ready Resources

Online Resources

The Fountas & Pinnell Comprehensive Phonics, Spelling, and Word Study Guide

Lesson Folders

Fountas & Pinnell Online Resources

A range of resources organized to support your teaching, including a video library, instructional context lessons, recording forms, and more.

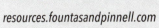

resources.fountasandpinnell.com

Required Resources (available separately)

The following tools and resources are required to ensure a successful implementation of *Fountas & Pinnell Classroom*.

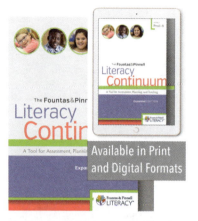

The Fountas & Pinnell Literacy Continuum: A Tool for Assessment, Planning, and Teaching, Expanded Edition

Guided Reading: Responsive Teaching Across the Grades, Second Edition

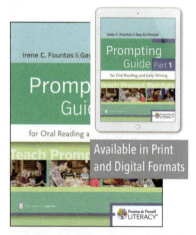

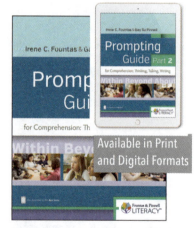

Fountas & Pinnell Prompting Guide, Part 1, for Oral Reading and Early Writing

Fountas & Pinnell Prompting Guide, Part 2, for Comprehension: Thinking, Talking, and Writing

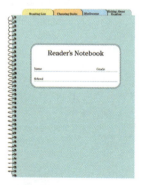

Fountas & Pinnell Reader's Notebook, Grades 2–4

Additional Resources (available separately)

Strengthen and support your teaching with these additional *Fountas & Pinnell Literacy* resources.

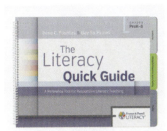

The Literacy Quick Guide

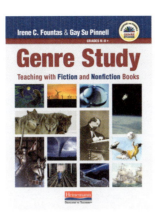

The Fountas & Pinnell Genre Study

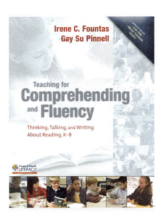

Teaching for Comprehending and Fluency

Fountas & Pinnell Genre Prompting Guide for Fiction

Fountas & Pinnell Genre Prompting Guide for Nonfiction, Poetry, and Test Taking

Fountas & Pinnell Benchmark Assessment System 2

Digital Resources

Online Data Management System

Fountas & Pinnell Reading Record App

Organizing Your Classroom

THE CLASSROOM IS A place of joy, activity, and continuous inquiry. This bright, busy space accommodates a wide variety of learning tools and resources that are essential to a community of readers and writers: pencils, markers, and crayons; computers and tablets; an extensive collection of engaging books, both big and small; paints, scissors, glue sticks, and other art supplies; math manipulatives; natural and mechanical objects for hands-on inquiry; the *Reader's Notebook,* book bags, and book boxes; writing supplies and book-making tools; charts and displays of students' collective and individual work; and much more. In an organized classroom, all tools and resources have a place and are accessible so students can work efficiently and grow in self-regulation.

A group of fourth graders will enter this rich environment needing to learn the rhythms of the school day, the routines of your classroom, and the many resources available to them as they begin to take responsibility for their literacy learning. You'll want to establish a predictable schedule and clear expectations for each part of the day and area of the classroom. Students can then focus on thinking, talking, reading, writing, listening, and discovering.

Creating a calm, structured, and predictable classroom environment requires intentional planning. It requires *organization.* An uncluttered and organized classroom increases students' independence and sense of agency as active learners. As importantly, it gives you more time for teaching. A teacher who feels organized feels in control.

Fountas & Pinnell Classroom is designed as a coherent, organized system, because a well-planned literacy experience, implemented with responsive teaching, is the most effective way to advance students' learning. As you begin to arrange your classroom to teach with *Fountas & Pinnell Classroom,* consider how your space and materials work together to enhance learning in different instructional contexts.

An organized classroom increases students' independence and sense of agency as active learners.

FIGURE 3–1 *An inviting and organized place for curling up with a good book*

Learning Spaces

As you plan the layout of your classroom, consider how to incorporate three types of learning spaces: an area for whole-group instruction and gatherings; an area for small-group instruction and discussions; and areas for students to work independently. Designating spaces for these distinct instructional purposes and specific learning activities helps increase the efficiency and effectiveness of your teaching and promotes students' learning:

▶ All books, lessons, materials, and resources specific to an instructional context are located where your teaching occurs, simplifying your lesson preparation and allowing you to respond flexibly to students' learning needs without having to interrupt the flow of instruction.

▶ General supplies are stocked in a central area, giving students a sense of agency and control over their learning.

▶ Students know what to do and what is expected of them within each learning space, reinforcing classroom routines and fostering productive learning behaviors.

The instructional contexts of *Fountas & Pinnell Classroom* are designed to work within these three learning spaces, as described in Figure 3–3. Interactive Read-Aloud, Reading Minilessons, and Shared and Performance Reading are usually whole-class activities conducted in the whole-group meeting area. Guided Reading occurs at a table in the small-group area, while Book Club meetings ideally take place in a circle of chairs pulled together for this purpose. Independent Reading can take place in a designated independent work area, such as a classroom reading nook with comfortable seating or at students' tables. Word Study Lessons may be delivered to the whole class in the meeting area or sometimes to small groups at a table, while the corresponding application activities will take place at independent work tables.

FIGURE 3–2 *A book club meets in a circle of chairs while other students work quietly at surrounding tables.*

THREE TYPES OF LEARNING SPACES

	Whole-Group Area	Small-Group Area	Independent Work Areas
Description	An area with enough space for all students to sit comfortably on the floor without touching each other.	A quiet corner of the room containing a round or horseshoe table situated so that you can easily monitor students in other areas of the room.	Students perform independent work at their tables.
Purpose	■ Whole-class meetings ■ Read-alouds ■ Minilessons	■ Small-group reading instruction ■ Small-group writing instruction	■ Choice reading ■ Writing in the *Reader's Notebook* ■ Application of learning from whole- and small-group lessons
***Fountas & Pinnell Classroom* Instructional Contexts**	■ Interactive Read-Aloud ■ Shared Reading ■ Reading Minilessons ■ Phonics and Word Study (Teach and Share)	■ Guided Reading ■ Book Clubs ■ Phonics and Word Study (Apply)	■ Independent Reading (and Conferring) ■ Phonics and Word Study (Apply)
Essential and Helpful Materials and Resources	■ Large, colorful rug ■ Teacher's chair ■ Two easels, one for group writing and one for enlarged texts ■ Big books, poetry charts, or other enlarged texts ■ Long pointer ■ Chart paper and markers ■ Pocket chart ■ Sticky notes ■ Highlighter tape ■ Masking card ■ Greek and Latin Roots charts ■ Student-generated anchor charts for reading, writing, and word study ■ White correction tape	■ Plastic caddy, basket, or tub ■ Leveled books and lessons ■ Records of students' reading ■ Paper and writing materials ■ Thin markers and pencils ■ Easel with chart paper ■ Blank word cards ■ White correction tape	■ Wide variety of books in the classroom library ■ Writing in the *Reader's Notebook*

FIGURE 3–3 *Three types of learning spaces*

Arranging Your Classroom

As you implement *Fountas & Pinnell Classroom* in your classroom, you will be creating a warm and inviting yet functional space that supports the classroom community. While classrooms vary in size and shape, consider the following suggestions (Figure 3–4) as you arrange your classroom for effective teaching and learning.

Organizing for Independent Reading Choose a place in your classroom to create a classroom library. Shelves that accommodate book bins are ideal. Bins are organized by genre, topic, author, and interest for easy access and browsing by students. Organize the Conferring Cards in your resource area, so that you can quickly pull the appropriate cards to support your conferences with individual readers.

Organizing for Reading Minilessons Many of your lessons on management, skills, strategies, and literary analysis will flow from observations you make during interactive read-aloud and conferring with students during independent reading. Designate wall space near the meeting area to display anchor charts with principles that students are currently learning and applying.

Organizing for Shared Reading Accommodate students so that every student can see the enlarged texts. Store texts and tools nearby for easy access.

Texts:

• fiction and nonfiction books

• poems

• reader's theater scripts

• plays

• speeches

• primary source documents

• projected texts

Tools:

• easel

• plain pointer

• highlighter tape

• whiteboard

• markers

• sticky notes

• computer and screen, or document camera, to project an image or text

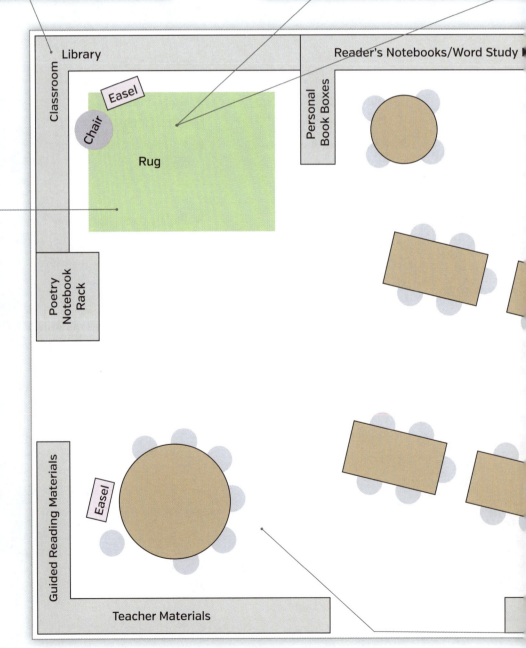

FIGURE 3–4 *Layout of an intermediate classroom*

IRA

Organizing for Interactive Read-Aloud Interactive read-aloud takes place in the whole-class meeting area of your classroom. It is ideal to have a bright rug or natural barriers, such as bookshelves, to mark the area. Students sit on the floor or in a circle of chairs, so arrange your chair and an easel to give all students an unobstructed view. As you finish with a book, you can move it to a bin in the classroom library or display it on the easel or bookshelves, offering students the opportunity to choose to read it independently. Keep interactive read-aloud lessons, books, and supplies in your resource area for easy access.

PWS

Organizing for Word Study Lessons When you present phonics and word study lessons, you will need word cards, a whiteboard, whiteboard markers, and chart paper. Store your book of lessons and Ready Resources in your resource area to streamline planning and the gathering of materials.

anipulatives/Writing Materials

Tablets

Computers

Math Manipulatives

/Social Studies Materials

BC

Organizing for Book Clubs Book clubs can take place anywhere in your classroom where there is room for small groups of students to sit in a circle and discuss books together. They can sit on chairs or the floor. Designate a shelf in your resource area where you can store the books and Discussion Cards together for easy access.

GR

Organizing for Guided Reading Your guided reading area is best located in an area of the classroom that accommodates a table large enough to seat four to six students and yourself. A kidney-shaped table is ideal. Arrange the table so you sit facing the students and classroom, allowing you to monitor the students working independently. Ideally, the lessons and books are arranged by level on shelves behind your small-group table, allowing you to easily retrieve and return instructional materials.

Sharing Materials and Resources

If you are sharing parts of *Fountas & Pinnell Classroom* with other teachers, find a space that is easily accessible to all of you to store the shared books, materials, and resources. Together, create a plan for how to share the resources so that you do not all need them at the same time.

Learn More

For more ideas on managing effective independent work, read *Guided Reading: Responsive Teaching Across the Grades*, Chapter 23.

A final thought: Your classroom's physical space and the placement, accessibility, and use of materials show what you value as a teacher. Design a classroom that reflects your values and also makes students feel it is their place of learning.

FIGURE 3–5 *The classroom library is a great place for book clubs to meet in chairs or on the floor.*

Planning Your Year

So much is accomplished in the school year. Beyond learning important academic skills—among them reading, writing, listening, and speaking—students grow more confident, self-determined, and considerate of others. They use their imagination and creativity to expand their conceptual understanding, problem-solving ability, and critical thinking. They begin to take responsibility for their own learning, following lines of inquiry and exploring various disciplinary topics that matter to them as individuals. They develop a perception of themselves as growing learners, who read and write for authentic purposes not only in their classroom but throughout their lives.

Yet, it's challenging to create a classroom community in which these academic, behavioral, social, and emotional accomplishments occur in a typical school year. Thoughtful planning is needed.

As you plan your year, consider the length of your instructional day. The suggestions on page 30 will help you arrange priority instructional actions. A predictable daily structure enables students to work independently and confidently with each other—in essence, helping them achieve self-regulation—while allowing you to teach individuals and small groups. Next, determine the routines and transitions that you will use consistently in your classroom. Think about the practices that worked well during the previous school year: will you carry them forward, improve upon them, or replace one or more with new ideas? The beginning of the school year is the best time to establish classroom routines and expectations. The ideas on page 33 will help you get started creating a workable, consistent schedule and classroom routines. Your plans for the school year will ensure predictability and stability for your classroom community of learners.

Your plans for the school year will ensure predictability and stability for your classroom community of learners.

FIGURE 4–1 *Colleagues gather to discuss plans for the school year.*

Literacy Opportunities

As you plan your year, consider the length of your instructional day. How much time does your daily schedule allow for language and literacy teaching? Within your daily schedule, what is the best way to organize your instructional time to prioritize responsive teaching? The following time allotments (Figure 4–2) provide suggestions for using the instructional contexts of *Fountas & Pinnell Classroom* within your classroom. The instructional contexts do not have to be conducted in this order; you will want to arrange these to fit your own classroom schedule. If you do not have 3 or more hours for literacy during the full-day schedule, consider shorter time frames or alternating the literacy opportunities.

GRADE 4: SUGGESTED TIME FRAMES FOR LITERACY OPPORTUNITIES

Instructional Context	Activity Options	Minutes Each Day
GROUP MEETING	Bring the classroom community together to introduce/discuss the day and set goals.	5
INTERACTIVE READ-ALOUD LESSON and/or SHARED AND PERFORMANCE READING	■ Teacher reads aloud a book from a text set, and students share their thinking. The text experience often leads to writing about reading in the *Reader's Notebook*. ■ Teacher engages students in shared reading using enlarged and projected texts. The text experience often leads to shared writing. Science and social studies topics and themes are integrated into the Interactive Read-Aloud and Shared Reading lessons.	25
BREAK		
READING MINILESSON	■ Teacher provides an explicit minilesson for students to apply to their independent reading and writing about reading/drawing.	10
SMALL-GROUP INSTRUCTION INDEPENDENT LITERACY WORK	■ Teacher meets with about three Guided Reading groups each day. ■ Teacher initiates Book Clubs as appropriate, and they meet about once per month. ■ Students engage in: • Independent reading • Writing about reading in the *Reader's Notebook*	60
GROUP SHARE	Gather students together to reflect on and share learning.	5
BREAK		
PHONICS AND WORD STUDY LESSON	■ Teacher provides an explicit, inquiry-based lesson on a word study principle that students can apply to reading and writing. Students work individually, with partners, or in small groups to apply their understanding of the principle.	30
WRITERS' WORKSHOP	Teacher provides an explicit minilesson and then supports individual students as they work on their own writing or convenes a guided writing group.	60
	TOTAL: 3 hours and 15 minutes	

FIGURE 4–2 *Suggested time frames for literacy opportunities in a fourth-grade classroom*

Fountas & Pinnell Classroom System Guide, Grade 4

You may find it helpful to create blocks of instructional time on cards or sticky notes and move them around "fixed" times, such as lunch and specials, until you have a workable daily schedule that both expresses your values and accounts for all constraints on your time. Once you've created an effective, smooth schedule, as much as possible, *follow it every day* so that your students experience predictability and a rhythm to the day.

FIGURE 4–3 *Fourth graders write about reading during independent literacy work.*

Getting Started

The First Eight Weeks

The culture of a classroom is often very different from any environment that students have experienced outside of school. In the classroom, students have to learn how to work together to become a community of learners. New routines and higher expectations can be unsettling at first. That is why a specialized plan for the first eight weeks of school is critical to establishing a productive and positive classroom community. During those first few weeks, students seek structure and are willing and prepared to behave in the new ways that you, and their new learning community, expect.

The calendar in Figure 4–5 provides suggestions for creating a successful "getting-started" period with *Fountas & Pinnell Classroom*. Minilessons from *The Reading Minilessons Book* that you may find helpful as you establish procedures and routines are identified by a special bullet (■) and umbrella numbers. Milestones in other instructional contexts are also identified by special bullets.

The Reading Minilessons Book, Grade 4

FIGURE 4–4 *Students feel free to share their opinions in a positive and supportive classroom community.*

FIRST EIGHT WEEKS CALENDAR

Week	Suggestions for Working with Students
1	■ Establish morning meeting and routines. ■ ■ Introduce **Interactive Read-Aloud** and **Shared Reading.** ■ Engage students in a series of lessons on respect, behavior, and classroom norms using **Management Umbrella 1:** Being a Respectful Member of the Classroom Community. ■ Have students help organize the classroom library according to topics and genres. ■ Help students learn how to select books to read and return them to the classroom library.
2	■ Teach students the guidelines and routines for Reader's Workshop. ■ Begin conferring with students during **Independent Reading.** ■ **Management Umbrella 2:** Getting Started with Independent Reading. ■ Involve students in Shared Writing. ■ Show students that they can choose books from a variety of fiction and nonfiction genres. ■ **Writing About Reading Umbrella 1:** Introducing a reader's notebook. ■ When students are involved in independent literacy work, conduct assessment conferences.
3	■ Continue to read aloud and use shared reading and shared writing to establish the learning community and build up common reading materials and mentor texts for writing. ■ Teach students how to turn and talk to each other in response to reading. ■ Teach students the guidelines and routines for Writers' Workshop. ■ Help students understand that there are a variety of topics they can write about. ■ Begin **Phonics, Spelling, and Word Study** lessons. ■ Complete individual assessments and form tentative guided reading groups to begin in week 4.
4	■ **Management Umbrella 3:** Living a Reading Life. ■ Teach students to remember their thinking to prepare for writing in a reader's notebook. ■ Teach students how to make book recommendations to others. ■ Teach students ways of responding to text through talk to support writing in a reader's notebook. ■ Begin **Guided Reading** groups with your lowest groups. Help students learn the routines of the lesson. ■ Teach students the guidelines and routines for independent reading and writing while you are meeting with guided reading groups.
5–6	■ Meet with all guided reading groups. ■ **Writing About Reading Umbrella 2:** Using a reader's notebook. ■ **Writing About Reading Umbrella 3:** Writing Letters to Share Thinking About Books. ■ **Literacy Analysis Umbrella 13:** Studying Memoir. ■ **Literacy Analysis Umbrella 5:** Understanding Fiction and Nonfiction Genres.
7–8	■ Continue to monitor independent work and help students self-assess and problem-solve as needed. ■ **Literacy Analysis Umbrella 2:** Getting Started with Book Clubs. ■ **Writing About Reading Umbrella 3:** Writing Letters to Share Thinking About Books. ■ **Literacy Analysis Umbrella 1:** Studying Authors and Their Process.

FIGURE 4–5 *First Eight weeks calendar*

Teaching Routines and Transitions

A routine is a set of actions or steps that you repeat for accomplishing something. The key to teaching students to make good choices and to "automating" continuous learning in your classroom is to establish and teach routines for each activity. A few simple routines that are used frequently and with consistency will make a big impact in your classroom.

Establishing routines for your readers' workshop will increase student productivity, reduce interruptions to your teaching time, and create a calm work atmosphere in the classroom. From the beginning of the year, establish expectations and routines for independent reading and writing about reading in the *Reader's Notebook*. As students work independently, you will be available to meet with guided reading groups and confer individually with students.

Planning for Instructional Contexts: Sequence of Books

We have provided a recommended sequence of texts for three instructional contexts in *Fountas & Pinnell Classroom*: Interactive Read-Aloud, Guided Reading, and Book Clubs. As you plan your year, consider how the text sequence of these instructional contexts may impact your instructional plans:

IRA **Interactive Read-Aloud** books are organized into text sets that are in a recommended sequence based on typical instructional emphases and the likely needs of a classroom community throughout the school year.

GR **Guided Reading** books are organized by text level. We have taken into account the ten characteristics of text in providing the recommended sequence, though you may decide to reorder or skip a book. It is important to note that you may not need to use all the books at any given level. During Guided Reading, you will need to use books at a higher level as soon as the readers need more challenge, even if the students have not read every book at the current level. *The Literacy Continuum* will be essential in supporting you as you make these decisions.

BC **Book Club** text sets are in a recommended sequence and are related to the text sets in Interactive Read-Aloud, focusing on genres, authors, themes, or topics that are common to both instructional contexts.

There is no sequence of books for Independent Reading, because students select books to read based on their individual interests. In grade 4 Shared Reading often consists of readers' theater or choral reading connected to Interactive Read-Aloud and Guided Reading. But you will provide support and guidance for productive choices through book talks, minilessons, and quick individual conferences.

Collaborating with Parents and Caregivers

The students in your classroom will benefit from communication and collaboration between home and school. As you begin to plan your year, we encourage you to think about ways to actively engage parents and caregivers in the literacy lives of their children. You may find that some parents are not comfortable approaching you or the school and that some parents are unsure about how to support their children in their learning. Finding effective and creative ways to engage all parents and caregivers is likely to be a yearlong endeavor, but the benefits for the students in your class are immense.

In Online Resources, we have provided a sample letter that you may wish to send to parents and caregivers at the beginning of the school year (Figure 4–6). The letter, which is available in several languages, explains what a literacy-rich classroom looks like and offers suggestions for how parents and caregivers can support their children's literacy development at home. Consider this letter a template that you can adapt to reflect your values and priorities for the school year.

Date

Dear Parents and Caregivers,

I would like to take this opportunity to welcome your child to our classroom. It is going to be an exciting year of exploration and learning. Your child is part of a classroom community that explores new interests, collaborates, thinks and talks about new understandings, and reads and writes every day. Your child is on a journey that will lead to increased literacy learning through reading, writing, listening and speaking across every part of the school day.

Over the course of the year, your child will read, think about, and write about a lot of different books for a variety of purposes. Some books I will read aloud to the class to spark children's ability to think deeply about books. The whole class will read other books and poems together as a shared experience. Children will read some books in a small group to allow me to provide individualized instruction for your child. Children will also have the opportunity to choose books based on their interests and read those books independently, giving them time to practice all that they are learning about reading. Your child may respond to all of these different books through talking and writing.

Your child will experience books at many different reading levels throughout the course of the day. Some books will be above the level at which your child typically reads independently. I will read these books aloud, or the class will read them together. Your child will also read books that are challenging, with my support and instruction. These books are essential for lifting your child's ability to read. Your child will also be reading books independently. Your child may choose to read books that are easy, just right, or even somewhat challenging for them. The important thing is for children to experience many different books—including picture books, chapter books, poetry collections, and engaging nonfiction books—throughout their day. All reading will contribute to the growth your child will experience this year.

Your child will also write every day for enjoyment and to learn how to use his voice to communicate his thinking with clarity. We will write for a variety of real purposes for many different audiences.

As parents and caregivers, you are a critical part of your child's literacy development. Here are some ways that you can support your child:

- Ask your child to tell you the plot or the big, important messages in books they are reading at home.
- Encourage your child to read a variety of books at home, including picture books, chapter books, poetry, and nonfiction books.
- Talk about books together.
- Go to the library with your child and be sure to check out some books yourself.
- Encourage your child to memorize and recite favorite poems.
- Have your child write for authentic purposes (shopping lists, journal entries, email messages to family members, how-to instructions for younger siblings, etc.)
- Talk frequently about current events and topics of interest to your child.
- Encourage your child to substitute screen time for reading time or outdoor activities as often as possible.
- Let your child see you read.

All these activities support your child's developing literacy skills.

I look forward to the journey our class will take together this year. Your child is an important member of this learning community. If I can be of any help or answer any questions you may have, please feel free to contact me. Thank you in advance for all your support this year.

Sincerely,

Teacher Name

FIGURE 4–6 *Sample letter to parents and caregivers*

There are opportunities throughout *Fountas & Pinnell Classroom* to engage parents and caregivers. For example, some of the suggested projects for exploration on the Interactive Read-Aloud Inquiry Overview Cards encourage parent and caregiver participation, and each Word Study lesson concludes with activities for extending students' learning at home. You will find many more suggested activities to be completed at home, as well as ideas for parents to participate in activities in school and suggested ways to tap into home cultures and traditions. Parents and caregivers are also encouraged to discuss the books their children bring home to read. You may want to invite parents and caregivers into the classroom throughout the year for special literacy occasions, such as:

- Listening to their children participate in a Readers' Theater
- A reading celebration in which parents and caregivers listen to their children read or they read to their children
- Watching a simple skit or play the students have written and performed
- Viewing the drawings, writings, or projects their children created in response to reading

As you actively and creatively engage parents and caregivers in the literacy lives of their children, each child and family know that their traditions and cultures are honored and the collaborative partnership between home and school is valued.

Planning Your Week

To help you plan a week of literacy opportunities across the instructional contexts of *Fountas & Pinnell Classroom,* we have provided a downloadable Weekly Lesson Plan in Online Resources (Figure 4–7).

FIGURE 4–7 *Weekly Lesson Plan*

Using *The Literacy Continuum*

SOME JOURNEYS ARE BEST made with a map, either paper or electronic. A map can help you plan your trip, inform you about landmarks and other notable sights along the way, suggest new routes when you hit a roadblock, and allow you to retrace your path to understand how you got from your starting point to your destination. Implementing a cohesive literacy system in your classroom is one such journey that deserves and requires a map. For *Fountas & Pinnell Classroom*, your map is *The Fountas & Pinnell Literacy Continuum: A Tool for Assessment, Planning, and Teaching*, also available electronically.

The Literacy Continuum is a tool that you will consult regularly. It will help you think about, plan for, and reflect on the literacy instruction you provide to individuals, small groups, and your whole class. Refer to the continuum as you plan your lessons, identify specific teaching goals, observe the students in your classroom, and assess the effectiveness of your teaching and the extent of students' learning.

The Literacy Continuum serves as the curriculum underlying *Fountas & Pinnell Classroom*. It creates coherence across classrooms and grade levels within your school. You will immediately notice, however, that the continuum is not prescriptive. It doesn't dictate a static scope and sequence of lessons. Rather, the continuum is *descriptive:* it describes, with precision, the characteristics of texts and the observable behaviors and understandings of proficient readers, writers, and language users that you may choose to notice, teach, and support. Your decisions are based on the strengths and needs of your students. The continuum is the foundational tool for informed, systematic, responsive teaching of literacy. As you and your colleagues consult *The Literacy Continuum* to teach for the same behaviors and understandings and use a common language, your students will benefit from the coherence.

> *As you and your colleagues teach for the same behaviors and understandings and use common language, your students will benefit from the coherence.*

Content of the Continuum

AS YOU BECOME FAMILIAR with *The Literacy Continuum*, you will notice that it describes text characteristics and learning goals for prekindergarten through grade 8 across eight different continua (Figure 5–2). Each of these continua focuses on a different aspect of the language and literacy instructional design presented in *Guided Reading: Responsive Teaching Across the Grades,* and each contributes substantially—in different but complementary ways—to students' conceptual growth and development of reading, writing, and language processes. Taken together, the eight continua present a broad picture of the learning that takes place during these important years of school.

As you implement each instructional context of *Fountas & Pinnell Classroom*, you will regularly ask: *What are my students showing that they know and can do?* A thoughtful, informed response to that question will guide the moment-to-moment instructional decisions that you make. Becoming well acquainted with the various continua, especially the grade 4 descriptions, will guide your responsive teaching within each instructional context.

The continuum comes with an important caveat, which you know well as a teacher of literacy: the progress of the students in your classroom is not an even, lock-step process. Students learn as they have opportunities and give attention in different ways and at different times. A student might make tremendous gains in one area while seeming to almost "stand still" in another. Sometimes new learning inspires a reconsideration of existing learning. Learning over time is "messy"; it depends on experience, attention, and motivation.

As you utilize the continuum, you will want to apply the expectations that are described flexibly, keeping in mind the individual learners in your classroom as you select goals that are specific and appropriate for their needs. Often you will find wide variations in literacy experiences among individual students. If you find that some students are taking on literacy learning at a slower pace, you may need to refer to the grade 3 continuum. If you find other students have vast experience with texts, you may wish to consult the grade 5 continuum. Your thoughtful use of this tool will allow you to identify appropriate goals and intervene in precise ways to help students gain control of new behaviors and understandings.

Text Characteristics and Complexity

BUILDING ON THE FOUNDATIONAL skills and strategic actions developed in earlier grades, students in grade 4 are ready for books that open doors to further learning and allow them to explore and think deeply about new ideas, to critically analyze content, and to construct meaning to expand their horizons. Accordingly, the *Fountas & Pinnell Literacy Continuum* describes successively more demanding texts that grow in complexity. The categories of these demands may be similar, but the specific challenges are constantly increasing.

By fourth grade students encounter multidimensional characters who represent a variety of perspectives and experiences—reflecting in a more nuanced way the diversity and complexity of human experience. Plots have more episodes and may not be resolved in predictable or simple ways. Big ideas or messages in stories often are not explicit and may require inference on the part of the reader. Students also encounter themes, ideas, and topics that are outside their own experience, requiring them to consider perspectives and cultures beyond their own. Some texts may require background knowledge and understanding of historical events, time periods, and people. Finally, more complex books provide more frequent opportunities for students to engage critically and analytically with the text, deepening their understanding of writer's craft.

Naturally, more demanding texts create new instructional demands as well. For example, with some books you may want to spend more time on the introduction, providing just enough additional support to enable readers to take on the more complex text. The particulars of that support will depend on the specific challenges of the text but may include closer attention to difficult vocabulary, unfamiliar text structures, themes and ideas beyond students' own experience, or required background knowledge. During interactive read-aloud, you might support readers by building in more frequent stopping points for clarification, spreading the read-aloud over more than one session, or allowing for more in-depth discussion of characters and plots in fiction or of graphics and other text features in nonfiction. Minilessons also provide opportunities to support students in using integrated systems of strategic actions for thinking within, beyond, and about many different types of texts at many levels of complexity. Finally, you will find suggestions for ways to support your students' reading of difficult texts in many of the lessons provided in *Fountas & Pinnell Classroom*.

Using *The Literacy Continuum*

In side columns throughout the *System Guide,* you will find specific suggestions for using *The Literacy Continuum* to support your planning and teaching of each instructional context.

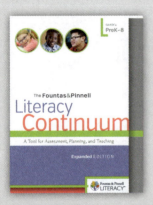

THE FOUNTAS & PINNELL LITERACY CONTINUUM

Continuum	Brief Definition	Description of the Continuum
Interactive Read-Aloud and Literature Discussion	Students engage in discussion with one another about a text that they have heard read aloud or one they have read independently.	▪ Year by year, grades PreK–8 ▪ Genres appropriate to grades PreK–8 ▪ Specific behaviors and understandings that are evidence of thinking within, beyond, and about the text
Shared and Performance Reading	Students read together or take roles in reading a shared text. They reflect the meaning of the text with their voices.	▪ Year by year, grades PreK–8 ▪ Genres appropriate to grades PreK–8 ▪ Specific behaviors and understandings that are evidence of thinking within, beyond, and about the text
Writing About Reading	Students extend their understanding of a text through a variety of writing genres and sometimes with illustrations.	▪ Year by year, grades PreK–8 ▪ Genres/forms for writing about reading appropriate to grades PreK–8 ▪ Specific evidence in the writing that reflects thinking within, beyond, and about the text
Writing	Students compose and write their own examples of a variety of genres, written for varying purposes and audiences.	▪ Year by year, grades PreK–8 ▪ Genres/forms for writing appropriate to grades PreK–8 ▪ Aspects of craft, conventions, and process that are evident in students' writing, grades PreK–8
Oral and Visual Communication	Students present their ideas through oral discussion and presentation.	▪ Year by year, grades PreK–8 ▪ Specific behaviors and understandings related to listening and speaking, presentation
Technological Communication	Students learn effective ways of communicating and searching for information through technology; they learn to think critically about information and sources.	▪ Year by year, grades PreK–8 ▪ Specific behaviors and understandings related to effective and ethical uses of technology
Phonics, Spelling, and Word Study	Students learn about the relationships of letters to sounds as well as the structure and meaning of words to help them in reading and spelling.	▪ Year by year, grades PreK–8, with emphasis on word study by grade 4 ▪ Specific behaviors and understandings in nine areas of understanding related to letters, sounds, and words and how they work in reading and spelling
Guided Reading	Students read a teacher-selected text in a small group; the teacher provides explicit teaching and support for reading increasingly challenging texts.	▪ Level by level, A to Z ▪ Genres appropriate to grades PreK–8 ▪ Specific behaviors and understandings that are evidence of thinking within, beyond, and about the text ▪ Specific suggestions for word work (drawn from the Phonics, Spelling, and Word Study continuum)

FIGURE 5–2 *The Fountas & Pinnell Literacy Continuum*

Using the Continuum in Instructional Contexts

YOU MAY FIND THE following suggestions and ideas for using *The Literacy Continuum* within each context helpful as you plan, teach, observe, and reflect.

IRA BC Interactive Read-Aloud and Book Clubs

In selecting texts and teaching goals for interactive read-aloud and book clubs, you will be considering both the characteristics of texts and opportunities for new learning on pages 56–65.

During interactive read-aloud and book clubs, students talk about books. When **selecting texts** for interactive read-aloud, consider the high level of support you will need to provide to students to help them process and think about the text. The amount of support you provide during book clubs will vary by book and over the course of the year—more support at the beginning and less at the end.

Red bullets show new text characteristics introduced at grade 4; texts with these characteristics may require extra attention.

The continuum describes the **characteristics of texts** suitable for interactive read-aloud and book clubs in grade 4. The books for interactive read-aloud and book clubs in *Fountas & Pinnell Classroom* reflect these characteristics. You may also use these characteristics when choosing books to add to your own collection.

GRADE **4**

INTERACTIVE READ-ALOUD AND LITERATURE DISCUSSION

Selecting Texts Characteristics of Texts for Reading Aloud and Discussion

Interactive Read-Aloud and Literature Discussion

GENRE

▸ **Fiction**
- Realistic fiction
- Historical fiction
- Traditional literature: e.g., folktale, tall tale, fairy tale (including fractured fairy tale), fable
- More complex fantasy including science fiction
- Hybrid text
- Special types of fiction: e.g., mystery; adventure story; animal story; family, friends, and school story; humorous story; sports story

▸ **Nonfiction**
- Expository nonfiction
- Narrative nonfiction
- Biography
- Autobiography
- Memoir
- Procedural text
- Persuasive text
- Hybrid text

FORMS
- Series books
- Picture books
- Chapter books, some with sequels
- Poems
- Poetry collections
- Plays
- Types of poetry: lyrical poetry, free verse, limerick, haiku, narrative poetry, ballad, epic/saga, concrete poetry
- Letters, diary and journal entries
- Short stories
- Photo essays, news articles, and feature articles

TEXT STRUCTURE
- Narratives with straightforward structure and multiple episodes that may be more elaborated
- Stories with complex plot and multiple problems
- Some texts with variations in structure: e.g., story-within-a-story, flashback
- Longer stories with multiple plots

- Some books with chapters connected to a single plot
- Some collections of short stories related to an overarching theme and with plots that intertwine
- Informational texts related to a larger topic with subtopics
- Underlying structural patterns: description, cause and effect, chronological sequence, temporal sequence (e.g., life cycles, how-to books), categorization, compare and contrast, problem and solution, question and answer
- Informational texts with clearly defined structure and categories and subcategories, some defined by headings and sections
- Simple biographical and historical texts with narrative structure
- Informational texts with some examples of simple argument and persuasion

CONTENT
- Content that is appropriate for students' cognitive development, social and emotional maturity, and life experience
- Content that engages students' intellectual curiosity and emotions
- Content that promotes inquiry and investigation
- Content that requires prior knowledge and invites extended discussion
- Familiar topics that are authentic and relevant: e.g., animals, family relationships, friendship, sports, music, neighborhoods, nutrition, weather and seasons, maps, plants
- More sophisticated, subtle humor: e.g., characters with humorous traits, surprising outcomes, humorous comparisons
- Content that reinforces and expands a student's experience and knowledge of self and the world
- Topics that may be beyond most students' immediate experiences: e.g., systems of the human body (circulatory, respiratory, endocrine); domestic and wild animals; environments such as ocean, desert, rainforest, mountains, village, city, farm; rocks and minerals; energy; magnetism; customs and beliefs in different cultures; government; economics
- Content that reflects a wide range of settings, languages, and cultures

- Content related to historical periods, circumstances, and places
- Some content linked to specific areas of study as described by the school curriculum or standards
- Characters, settings, and events that could exist in contemporary life or in another historical period
- More complex characters, settings, and events that occur in fantasy
- Content that reflects increasing understanding of the physical and social world: e.g., health, social studies, science, mathematics, arts

THEMES AND IDEAS
- Themes reflecting important human challenges and social issues: e.g., self and self-esteem, popularity, bullying, sportsmanship, transition to adolescence, life cycles, survival, interconnectedness of humans and the environment, social justice, social awareness and responsibility
- Many books with multiple ideas, some requiring inference to understand
- Ideas close to students' experience: e.g., becoming independent, family relationships, peer relationships, valuing change in self and others, empathizing with others, valuing differences, working with others to accomplish goals, connecting past and future, recognizing individual responsibility for the environment, overcoming challenges

LANGUAGE AND LITERARY FEATURES
- Elements of traditional literature and modern fantasy: e.g., the supernatural; imaginary and otherworldly creatures; gods and goddesses; talking animals, toys, and dolls; heroic characters; technology or scientific advances; time travel; aliens or outer space
- Basic motifs of traditional literature and modern fantasy: e.g., struggle between good and evil, magic, secondary or alternative worlds, the hero's quest, special character types, fantastic or magical objects, wishes, trickery, transformations
- Predictable story outcomes typical of traditional literature: e.g., clever overcomes power, good defeats evil

FIGURE 5–3 The Literacy Continuum, *page 56*

Curriculum goals are included for both **fiction and nonfiction texts.**

Selecting Goals Behaviors and Understandings to Notice, Teach, and Support *(cont.)*

Interactive Read-Aloud and Literature Discussion

NONFICTION TEXTS *(continued)*

Organization

- ● Follow and understand nonfiction texts with clearly defined overall structure and simple categories
- ● Be aware when the teacher is reading bulleted or numbered lists
- ● Notice and understand information in texts that are organized in categories (expository)
- ● Understand the use of headings and subheadings
- ● Use headings and subheadings to search for and use information
- ■ Notice primary and secondary sources of information when embedded in a text
- ■ Understand that a nonfiction text can be expository or narrative in structure
- ■ Notice the organization of a nonfiction text, distinguishing between expository and narrative structure
- ■ Notice a nonfiction writer's use of narrative text structure in biography and narrative nonfiction
- ■ Recognize and understand a writer's use of underlying text structures: e.g., categorical, description, sequence (chronological, temporal), compare and contrast, cause and effect, problem and solution, question and answer, combination
- ■ Notice a nonfiction writer's use of categories and subcategories to organize an informational text
- ■ Understand when a writer is telling information in a sequence (chronological order)
- ■ Understand that a writer can tell about something that usually happens in the same order (temporal sequence) and something that happens in time order (chronological sequence)
- ■ Notice a nonfiction writer's use of organizational tools: e.g., title, table of contents, heading, subheading, sidebar

Topic

- ◆ Show curiosity about topics encountered in nonfiction texts and actively work to learn more about them
- ◆ Think across nonfiction texts to construct knowledge of a topic
- ◆ Think across texts to compare and expand understanding of content and ideas from academic disciplines: e.g., social responsibility, environment, climate, history, social and geological history, cultural groups

- ◆ Infer the importance of a topic of a nonfiction text
- ◆ Infer the writer's attitude toward a topic
- ◆ Recognize that a wide variety of informational texts may be about a wide range of diverse places, languages, and cultures
- ◆ Recognize that informational texts may present a larger topic with many subtopics
- ◆ Infer a writer's purpose in a nonfiction text
- ◆ Extend understanding to nonfiction topics and content that are beyond most students' immediate experience: e.g., systems of the human body (circulatory, respiratory, endocrine); domestic and wild animals; environments such as ocean, desert, rainforest, mountains, village, city, farm; rocks and minerals; energy; magnetism; customs and beliefs in different cultures; government; economics
- ■ Understand that a writer is presenting related facts about a single topic
- ■ Hypothesize the writer's reasons for choosing a topic and infer how the writer feels about a topic

Messages and Main Ideas

- ● Follow arguments in a persuasive text
- ◆ Understand that there can be different interpretations of the meanings of a text
- ◆ Make connections among the content and ideas in nonfiction texts: e.g., animals, pets, families, sports, the five senses, nutrition and food, school, neighborhood, weather and seasons, machines, plants
- ◆ Understand the relationships among ideas and content in an expository nonfiction text (larger topic with subtopics)
- ◆ Connect the information in nonfiction books to disciplinary studies
- ◆ Infer the significance of nonfiction content to their own lives
- ◆ Infer the larger ideas and messages in a nonfiction text
- ■ Understand themes and ideas that are mature issues and require experience to interpret
- ■ Understand that a nonfiction writer has one or more messages or big (main) ideas
- ■ Distinguish fact from opinion

Possible curriculum goals are described in terms of **behaviors and understandings** to notice, teach, and support.

While **red bullets** indicate new goals for grade 4, keep in mind that all of the goals are important. In fourth grade, students are challenged to apply each behavior or understanding to more complex texts.

The **shape of the bullet** indicates actions for thinking *within, beyond,* or *about* the text.

- ● Thinking ***Within*** the Text
- ◆ Thinking ***Beyond*** the Text
- ■ Thinking ***About*** the Text

Interactive Read-Aloud and Literature Discussion

INTERACTIVE READ-ALOUD AND LITERATURE DISCUSSION

FIGURE 5–4 The Literacy Continuum, *page 63*

SR Shared and Performance Reading

On pages 136–141, the continuum provides guidance for choosing appropriate texts and selecting specific learning goals for shared reading.

> To support you in **selecting texts** for shared and performance reading, the descriptions are organized according to ten characteristics of texts. As you choose texts to use in shared reading, you will want to keep these characteristics in mind.

> **Red bullets** indicate new text characteristics introduced at grade 4. Texts with these characteristics may require extra attention during a lesson.

GRADE **4**

SHARED AND PERFORMANCE READING

Selecting Texts Characteristics of Texts for Sharing and Performing

Shared and Performance Reading

GENRE

▶ **Fiction**
- Realistic fiction
- Historical fiction
- Traditional literature: e.g., folktale, tall tale, fairy tale, fractured fairy tale, fable
- More complex fantasy including science fiction
- Hybrid texts
- Special types of fiction: e.g., mystery; adventure story; animal story; family, friends, and school story; humorous story; sports story

▶ **Nonfiction**
- Expository nonfiction
- Narrative nonfiction
- Biography
- Autobiography
- Memoir
- Procedural texts
- Persuasive texts
- Hybrid texts

FORMS
- Poetry (much unrhymed) on many topics of various types: e.g., lyrical poetry, free verse, narrative poetry, limerick, haiku, ballad, concrete poetry
- Rhymes and songs from many cultures
- Individual poetry collections
- Plays
- Readers' theater scripts, some designed by students
- Picture books
- Excerpts from chapter books, series books
- Letters, diaries, and journal entries
- Texts produced through shared writing
- Short stories
- Photo essays, news articles, and feature articles

TEXT STRUCTURE
- Narratives with straightforward structure but multiple episodes
- Excerpts that highlight particular literary features: e.g., description, turning point in a narrative, figurative language, dialogue, persuasive language

- A few fiction texts with variations in narrative structure: e.g., story-within-a-story, flashback
- Informational texts with examples of simple argument and persuasion
- Short excerpts or scripts drawn from longer texts in a variety of genres and text structures
- Underlying structural patterns: description, temporal sequence, question and answer, cause and effect, chronological sequence, compare and contrast, problem and solution, categorization
- Poems that may have narrative structure or reflect the organizational patterns of various types of poetry

CONTENT
- Content that is appropriate for students' cognitive development, emotional maturity, and life experience
- Content that engages intellectual curiosity and emotions
- Content that nurtures the imagination
- Topics important to preadolescents: e.g., sibling rivalry, friendship, growing up, family problems, and conflicts
- Language and word play related to concepts or parts of speech: e.g., alliteration, assonance, onomatopoetic words
- Humor conveyed through playful or created language
- Content that reinforces and expands a student's experience and knowledge of self and the world
- A few topics that may be beyond students' immediate experiences
- Content that reflects a wide range of settings, languages, and cultures
- Some content linked to specific areas of study as described by the school curriculum or standards
- Characters, settings, and events that could exist in contemporary life or in history
- Characters and settings that occur in fantasy
- People, settings, and events in biographical texts that could exist in contemporary life or in history
- Content that reflects understanding of the physical and social world

THEMES AND IDEAS
- More sophisticated interpretation of themes reflecting everyday life: e.g., self, family relationships, friendship, imagination, feelings, bravery, cleverness, wisdom, wonders of nature, cultural sensitivity, multiple and diverse views, how things are made, how things work
- Themes, emotions, sensory experiences, inspiring ideas expressed through poetry
- More complex ideas requiring inference, sometimes expressed through the language of poetry
- More sophisticated interpretation of ideas close to students' experience: e.g., expressing feelings, sharing with others, valuing differences, taking different perspectives, cooperating, helping, caring for others, standing up for what is right, belonging, problem solving, working hard, being brave or clever or wise, appreciating the sounds of language, noticing and appreciating nature, caring for the world

LANGUAGE AND LITERARY FEATURES
- Descriptive language conveying sensory experiences and a range of human feelings
- Descriptive and figurative language that is important to understanding the content: imagery, metaphor, simile, personification, hyperbole
- Some texts and poems with basic or obvious symbolism used to convey larger meaning
- Poetic language
- Sensory imagery expressed in poetry
- Rhythm and repetition of words and language patterns, as well as rhymes
- Settings distant in time and place from students' own experiences
- Language and events that convey an emotional atmosphere (mood) in a text, affecting how the reader feels
- Both realistic and fantastic settings, events, and characters
- Excerpts from some longer texts with one or more subplots
- Main characters and supporting characters, some with multiple dimensions, especially in plays
- Characters revealed through dialogue and behavior, especially in plays

136   *The Fountas & Pinnell Literacy Continuum, Grades PreK–8*

FIGURE 5–5 The Literacy Continuum, *page 136*

While **red bullets** indicate new goals for grade 4, keep in mind that all of the goals are important. At grade 4, students are challenged to apply each behavior or understanding to more complex texts.

Curriculum goals are included for both **fiction and nonfiction texts**.

Selecting Goals Behaviors and Understandings to Notice, Teach, and Support (cont.)

Shared and Performance Reading

FICTION AND NONFICTION TEXTS (continued)

■ Use some academic language to talk about genres: e.g., *fiction, folktale, fairy tale, fractured fairy tale, fable, tall tale, adventure story, animal story, family, friends, and school story, humorous story, realistic fiction, traditional literature, historical fiction, fantasy; nonfiction, informational text, informational book, factual text, personal memory story, biography, autobiography, narrative nonfiction, memoir, procedural text, persuasive text*

■ Use some academic language to talk about forms: e.g., *picture book, wordless picture book, label book, ABC book, counting book, poem, poetry, nursery rhyme, rhyme, song, poetry collection, series book, chapter book, play, letter, sequel, limerick, haiku, concrete poetry, short story, diary entry, journal entry, news article, feature article*

■ Use some academic language to talk about literary features: e.g., *beginning, ending, problem, character, solution, main character, question and answer, topic, events, character change, message, dialogue, description, time order, setting, main idea, comparison and contrast, flashback, conflict, resolution, theme, descriptive language, simile, cause and effect, categorization, persuasive language*

■ Use some academic language to talk about plays and performance: e.g., *line, speech, scene, act, actor, actress, role, part, hero, villain, playwright*

■ Use some academic language to talk about book and print features: e.g., *front cover, back cover, title, author, illustrator, page, text, illustration, photograph, label, table of contents, acknowledgments, chapter, section, heading, drawing, caption, map, chapter title, dedication, author's note, illustrator's note, section, diagram, glossary, endpapers, sidebar, book jacket, subheading, chart, graph, timeline, index*

Book and Print Features

● Search for information in illustrations and in book and print features in an enlargement of a nonfiction text: e.g., drawing, photograph, map with legend or key, scale, diagram, infographic, cutaway; title, table of contents, chapter title, heading, subheading, sidebar, call-out

● Use illustrations (when applicable) to monitor and correct reading

● Shift attention from one part of a page layout to another to gather information: e.g., body text; drawing, photograph, map, diagram, infographic; label, caption, legend, key, scale, cutaway, sidebar, call-out

◆ Make connections between the body of the text and illustrations

◆ Make connections between text, illustrations, and book and print features: e.g., body text; drawing, photograph, map, diagram, infographic; label, caption, legend, key, scale, cutaway; title, table of contents, chapter title, heading, subheading, sidebar, call-out

● Notice and learn new ways to present information in nonfiction texts using illustrations and book and print features

◆ Infer information from nonfiction illustrations and book and print features

■ Talk about illustrations and book and print features and evaluate whether they help readers understand information and add interest

Possible curriculum goals are described in terms of **behaviors and understandings** to notice, teach, and support.

SHARED AND PERFORMANCE READING

As you plan your teaching, identify systems of strategic actions that readers use in thinking *within, beyond,* and *about* the text, as designated by the **shape of the bullet.**

● Thinking *Within* the Text   ◆ Thinking *Beyond* the Text   ■ Thinking *About* the Text

FIGURE 5–6 The Literacy Continuum, *page 141*

GR Guided Reading

This section of the continuum is organized by text levels, rather than grade levels. As you form guided reading groups, consult the continuum to learn about the characteristics of readers and texts at each level.

This section provides a brief description of what you may find generally true of **readers at a particular level.** While no one description is true of all readers, understanding general expectations of readers at a level can help you select books and provide appropriate support to individuals and groups. Remember that *books* are leveled; *readers* are not.

Studying the **text characteristics** of books at a given level will provide a good inventory of the challenges readers will meet across that level. All original texts, the guided reading books in *Fountas & Pinnell Classroom* were meticulously crafted and edited to reflect the characteristics at each level. Students read a variety of texts for different purposes.

LEVEL **R**

Readers at Level

At level R, readers automatically read and understand a very wide range of genres, including a variety of special types of realistic and historical fiction, biographical texts, narrative and expository nonfiction, persuasive texts, and hybrid texts that blend more than one genre in a coherent whole. They read short and longer forms. Fiction narratives are straightforward but have complex problems with many episodes and multidimensional characters who develop and change over time. They experience some variation in narrative structure (for example, flashbacks or change in narrators). As readers, they encounter perspectives different from their own as well as settings and people far distant in time and space. They can process sentences (some with more than twenty words) that contain prepositional phrases, introductory clauses, and lists of nouns, verbs, or adjectives. They solve new vocabulary words, some defined in the text and others unexplained. Most reading is silent, but all dimensions of fluency in oral reading are well established. Readers are challenged by many longer descriptive words and by content specific and technical words that require using embedded definitions, background knowledge, and understanding of text features such as headings, subheadings, and call-outs. They can take apart multisyllable words and use a full range of word-solving skills. They read and understand texts in a variety of layouts as well as fonts and print characteristics and consistently search for information in illustrations and increasingly complex graphics.

Selecting Texts Characteristics of Texts at **Level R**

GENRE

▶ **Fiction**
- Realistic fiction
- Historical fiction
- Traditional literature (folktale, fairy tale, fable)
- More complex fantasy including science fiction
- Hybrid texts
- Special types of fiction: e.g., mystery; adventure story; sports story; animal story; family, friends, and school story; humorous story

▶ **Nonfiction**
- Expository nonfiction
- Narrative nonfiction
- Biography
- Autobiography
- Memoir
- Procedural texts
- Persuasive texts
- Hybrid texts

FORMS
- Series books
- Picture books
- Chapter books

- Chapter books with sequels
- Plays
- Readers' theater scripts
- Graphic texts
- Letters, diaries, journal entries
- Short stories
- Photo essays and news articles

TEXT STRUCTURE

- Narrative texts with straightforward structure and multiple episodes that may be more elaborated
- Embedded forms (e.g., letters, directions, journal entries, emails) within narrative and expository structures
- Variations in structure: e.g., story-within-a-story, simple flashback
- Books with chapters connected to a single plot
- Some collections of short stories related to an overarching theme
- Nonfiction books divided into sections, and some with subsections
- Underlying structural patterns: description, cause and effect, chronological sequence, temporal sequence, comparison and contrast, problem and solution, question and answer

CONTENT

- Content interesting to and relevant for the reader
- Some books with little or no picture support for content: e.g., chapter books
- Much content that requires accessing prior knowledge
- Content that requires the reader to take on perspectives from diverse cultures and bring cultural knowledge to understanding
- Most texts with new content that will engage and interest readers and expand knowledge: e.g., travel, experience with other cultures, adventures in science, survival
- Settings in some texts that require content knowledge of disciplines: e.g., history, geography, culture, language
- Most content that goes beyond students' immediate experience
- Much content that requires the reader to search for information in graphics: e.g., maps, charts, diagrams, illustrated drawings, labeled photographs

GUIDED READING

LEVEL

530   *The Fountas & Pinnell Literacy Continuum, Grades PreK–8*

FIGURE 5–7 The Literacy Continuum, *page 530*

Fountas & Pinnell Classroom System Guide, Grade 4

LEVEL **R**

Selecting Goals Behaviors and Understandings to Notice, Teach, and Support

THINKING ***WITHIN*** THE TEXT

SEARCHING FOR AND USING INFORMATION

- Sustain searching for information over a text (usually under forty-eight pages) and/or in a chapter book with as many as 2,500 + words
- Search for information across chapters connected to a single plot
- Search for information and language that states or implies the larger message(s) of the text
- Search for information in texts where print wraps around sidebars, pictures, and other graphics
- Use background knowledge to search for and understand information about settings, geographical areas, history, economics
- Use organizational tools to search for information: e.g., title, table of contents, chapter title, heading, subheading, sidebar, call-out
- Use text resources to search for information: e.g., acknowledgments, author's note, pronunciation guide, glossary
- Sustain searching over some longer sentences with more than twenty words, and multiple clauses and phrases
- Search for information in sentences that vary in length, structure, and punctuation based on text complexity
- Search for information in sentences with variation in placement of subject, verb, adjectives, and adverbs
- Search for information in sentences with nouns, verbs, adjectives, and adverbs in a series, divided by commas
- Search for and understand information presented in a variety of ways: e.g., simple dialogue, dialogue with pronouns, split dialogue, assigned and sometimes unassigned dialogue, dialogue among multiple characters, some long stretches of dialogue, direct dialogue
- Search for and understand information over some long stretches of dialogue with multiple characters talking
- Use the chronological order within multiple episodes to search for and use information
- Notice and use punctuation marks: e.g., period, comma, question mark, exclamation mark, parentheses, quotation marks, hyphen, dash, ellipses
- Search for and use information from a wide variety of illustrations or graphics
- Search for and use information in texts with variety in placement of the body of a text, sidebars, and graphics
- Search for information in a variety of graphics (photos, drawings with labels and captions, diagrams, maps)

MONITORING AND SELF-CORRECTING

- Use multiple sources of information (visual information in print, meaning/pictures, graphics, language structure) to monitor and self-correct
- Self-correct covertly prior to or after error, with little overt self-correction
- Closely monitor understanding of texts using knowledge of a wide range of fiction genres: e.g., realistic fiction, historical fiction, traditional literature (folktale, fairy tale, fable, myth, legend, epic, ballad), fantasy including science fiction, hybrid text
- Closely monitor understanding of texts using knowledge of a wide range of forms: e.g., poems, plays, graphic texts, letters, diaries, journal entries, short stories
- Use understanding of plot, setting, and character to monitor and correct reading
- Use awareness of narrative structure and the attributes of multidimensional characters that change to self-monitor and self-correct
- Use content knowledge of the topic of a text to self-monitor and self-correct
- Use knowledge of nonfiction genres to monitor understanding of a text: e.g., expository nonfiction, narrative nonfiction, biography, autobiography, memoir, procedural text, persuasive text
- Use information from graphics (e.g., maps, diagrams, charts, photos, illustrations) to self-monitor reading

SOLVING WORDS

▸ **Reading Words**

- Recognize a large number of high-frequency words and other multisyllable words rapidly and automatically
- Solve multisyllable words by taking them apart using syllables
- Read the full range of regular and irregular plurals
- Identify spelling patterns within multisyllable words to solve them
- Read some multisyllable words with complex letter-sound relationships
- Read a wide range of contractions, possessives, compound words, adjectives, adverbs, comparatives, common and complex connectives
- Notice parts of words and connect them to other words to solve them

GUIDED READING

LEVEL R

Guided Reading 533

FIGURE 5–8 The Literacy Continuum, *page* 533

The heart of the Guided Reading continuum is a description of the expectations for readers at each level. As you plan your lesson for each group, you will want to identify **behaviors and understandings** to notice, teach, and support. As in the other continua, the descriptions are organized into the systems of strategic actions that readers use when thinking *within, beyond,* and *about* a text. Your selection of goals will be based on the knowledge you gain from ongoing observations and reading records.

As they process texts, readers are constantly applying knowledge of phonemes and graphemes and phonics and word study principles. An important component of a guided reading lesson is some brief but focused attention to words and how they work. At the end of the Selecting Goals section, you will find a list of suggested **word study activities** from which you can select and tailor to the specific demands of a text and the needs of particular group of readers.

IR Independent Reading

You may find that you need to consult the Guided Reading and Interactive Read-Aloud sections of the continuum to identify goals for different types and levels of text. To help students extend their understanding and provide evidence of their thinking, you will want to have students occasionally write about their reading. While appropriate to use with other instructional contexts as well, writing about reading can be especially informative in independent reading because you have not taken part in students' selection or reading of a particular book.

Selecting Genres and Forms

Writing About Reading

Even in the intermediate grades, teaching students to write about reading means more than simply "assigning" the particular task or form. You can explain how to do something (for example, creating a new graphic organizer), but you can't count on students' using it effectively if they have never seen good models. Use modeled writing if something is very new to students or you expect a higher level of articulation. Explain your thinking conversationally and then write it, or show a piece of writing that you have prepared previously. Have students highlight examples of specific statements you want them to notice—for instance, main ideas and details, specific examples, or statements of the writer's message. You can use shared writing to involve students in the coconstruction of a piece of writing about reading; here, they use everything they know and share their understandings, but they are freed from the mechanical task of writing, and they have your support in composition. Here again, they can analyze the piece to mark the specific language they used. Then, you can turn the task over to students to use independently in their own writing about reading. Students will be building a repertoire of ways they can write about reading, but you will always be providing demonstrations to increase their view of how to express their thinking. Keep in mind these behaviors represent the outcomes of a year of instruction, so they are goals to work toward.

The forms of writing that are appropriate for students to write at grade 4 are listed by genre. You may wish to demonstrate each form for students through modeled or shared writing.

FUNCTIONAL WRITING

▶ **Notes and Sketches**

- Sketches or drawings that represent a text and provide a basis for discussion or writing
- Notes (about setting, events in a story, characters, memorable words or phrases) on sticky notes, Thinkmarks, and in a Reader's Notebook to support memory for later use in discussion or writing
- Notes that record interesting information, details, language, or examples of the writer's craft as shown by quotes from a text
- Labels and legends for illustrations such as drawings, photographs, and maps related to a text
- Lists of books (completed or abandoned) with title, author, genre, one-word responses to the book, and dates read

▶ **Graphic Organizers**

- Webs that connect information within a text or across texts (organization, character traits, settings, problems)
- Webs that represent the organization of a text
- Charts that show the way a text is organized: description, temporal sequence, question and answer, cause and effect, chronological sequence, compare and contrast, problem and solution
- Story maps that record title, author, setting, plot events, characters, problem, and resolution

- Graphic organizers supporting genre study including examples of books, noticings from inquiry, and working definitions of genres
- Graphic organizers showing embedded genres within hybrid texts
- Grids that show analysis of a text
- Columns to show comparisons

▶ **Letters About Reading**

- Letters to other readers or to authors and illustrators including dialogue letters in a Reader's Notebook

▶ **Short Writes**

- Short Writes stating a prediction, opinion, or any interesting aspect of the text
- Character sketch

▶ **Longer Responses**

- Double-column entry with a phrase, sentence, quote from the text, or question in left column and room for reader's thinking on the right
- Longer responses in a Reader's Notebook expanding on thinking from notes, sketches, Short Writes, or graphic organizers

NARRATIVE WRITING

▶ **Summaries**

- Plot summaries containing a brief statement of the message, theme, or "take" on a topic, setting, the story problem, turning point, and resolution

- Story maps that record title, author, setting, plot events, episodes, characters, problem, and resolution

▶ **Writing for Dramatic Purposes**

- Scripts for readers' theater

▶ **Cartoons/Storyboards**

- Cartoons or comics that present a story or information
- Storyboards that represent significant events in a text

INFORMATIONAL WRITING

▶ **Reports**

- Short reports giving information from one or more texts
- Reports using of illustrations (e.g., photo and/or drawing with label or caption; diagram, cutaway; map with legend or key, scale), organizational tools (e.g., title, table of contents, chapter title, heading, subheading, sidebar, callout), and text resources (e.g., acknowledgments, author's note, references)

▶ **Outlines**

- Lists of headings and subheadings that reflect the organization of a text

▶ **How-to Articles**

- Directions sometimes illustrated with drawings showing a sequence of actions based on a text
- How-to articles requiring the writer to do research

WRITING ABOUT READING

FIGURE 5–9 The Literacy Continuum, *page 191*

Curriculum goals are included for both **fiction and nonfiction texts**.

Selecting Goals Behaviors and Understandings to Notice, Teach, and Support

Writing About Reading

FICTION TEXTS

General

- Notice, comment on, and actively work to acquire new vocabulary, including technical words, and intentionally use it in writing about reading
- Explore definitions of new words from texts, including figurative uses, by writing about them
- Use vocabulary typical of everyday oral language to talk and write about reading (Tier 1) and understand some words that appear in the language of mature users and in written texts (Tier 2)
- Use common (simple) connectives that are frequently used in oral language (words, phrases that clarify relationships and ideas): e.g., *and, but, so, because, before, after*
- Use some sophisticated connectives (words that link ideas and clarify meaning) that are used in written texts but do not appear often in everyday oral language: e.g., *although, however, meantime, meanwhile, moreover, otherwise, therefore, though, unless, until, whenever, yet*
- Use some Tier 3 vocabulary that is specialized and related to scientific domains in writing about reading
- Understand and draw information for writing from the purpose of the dedication, author's note, and acknowledgments
- Record the titles, authors, and genres of books to recommend
- Record in Reader's Notebook the titles, authors, illustrators, and genre of texts read, and the dates read
- Draw or sketch to represent or remember the content of a text and provide a basis for discussion or writing
- Remember information or details from a text to independently produce lists, simple sequences of action, and directions
- Compose notes, lists, letters, or statements to remember important information about a text
- Make notes about the need to clarify information (questions, confusions)
- Make notes about a text as evidence to support opinions and statements in discussion and writing
- Revisit texts for ideas or to check details when writing or drawing
- Provide evidence from the text or from personal experience to support written statements about a text
- Represent a longer series of events from a text through drawing and writing
- Write summaries that reflect literal understanding of a text
- Select and include appropriate and important details when writing a summary of a text
- Reference page numbers from a text in writing about important information

- Reread writing to check on meaning, accuracy, and clarity of expression
- Show connections between the setting, characters, and events of a text and their own personal experiences
- Draw and write about connections between the ideas in texts and their own life experiences
- Relate important information/ideas within a text or to other texts
- Write about connections among texts by topic, theme, major ideas, authors' styles, and genres
- Draw and write about something in students' lives prompted by characters or events in a story
- Notice and write about the importance of ideas relevant to their world: sharing, caring for others, doing your job, helping your family, taking care of self, staying healthy, caring for the world or environment, valuing differences, expressing feelings, empathizing with others
- Provide evidence from the text or from personal experience to support written statements about a text
- Write about a wide range of predictions based on evidence from the text
- Write predictions for story outcomes and use evidence from the text to support predictions
- Predict what will happen next in a story or at the end of the story and support the prediction with evidence
- Provide details that are important to understanding the story problem, the setting, and the characters
- Make notes and write longer responses to indicate acquisition of new information and ideas from a text
- Write an interpretation of a story, a nonfiction text, or of illustrations understanding that there can be more than one interpretation
- Use texts as resources for words, phrases, and ideas for writing
- Write statements that reflect understanding of both the text body and the graphics or illustrations and how the two are integrated
- Notice and write about decorative or informative illustrations and/or print outside the body of the text (peritext)
- Write about the meaning of a text's dedication, acknowledgments, author's note, glossary, index
- Write about why an author might choose to write a story or write about a topic
- Write to explore the writer's purpose and stance toward a story
- Notice and write about the characteristics of fiction genres: e.g., realistic fiction, historical fiction, folktale, tall tale, fairy tale, fable, fantasy, and some special types of fiction (adventure story, animal story, humorous story, family, friends, and school story)

While **red bullets** indicate new goals for grade 4, keep in mind that all of the goals are important. At grade 4, students are challenged to apply each behavior or understanding to the writing of more complex texts.

Behaviors and understandings to notice, teach, and support as students think *within, beyond,* and *about* the text are specified by the shape of the bullet. Remember that genres and forms are demonstrated and constructed through the use of modeled and shared writing, as well as reading minilessons, *before* students are expected to produce them independently.

- Thinking **Within** the Text   ♦ Thinking **Beyond** the Text   ■ Thinking **About** the Text

WRITING ABOUT READING

FIGURE 5–10 The Literacy Continuum, *page 193*

RML Reading Minilessons

Reading minilessons allow you to teach to a specific need that you've identified in your class. The topic of the minilesson and its category (management, literary analysis, strategies and skills, or writing about reading) will determine which section of the continuum will be most helpful.

PWS Phonics, Spelling, and Word Study

Consult pages 378–382 to help you identify and select goals for phonics, spelling, and word study.

The continuum is drawn from the longer continuum published in *The Fountas & Pinnell Comprehensive Phonics, Spelling, and Word Study Guide*. In both tools, you will find specific principles related to nine areas of learning. In grade 4, **six areas of learning** are considered important: letter-sound relationships, spelling patterns, high-frequency words, word meaning/vocabulary, word structure, and word-solving actions.

While **red bullets** indicate new goals for grade 4, keep in mind that all of the goals are important. At grade 4, students are challenged to apply each behavior or understanding to words and connected text of greater length and complexity.

GRADE **4**

PHONICS, SPELLING, AND WORD STUDY

Selecting Goals Behaviors and Understandings to Notice, Teach, and Support (cont.)

Phonics, Spelling, and Word Study

WORD MEANING/ VOCABULARY (continued)

▶ **Word Origins** (continued)

■ Understand and discuss the concept of Greek roots and recognize their use in determining the meaning of some English words: e.g., *aer, arch, aster, astr, astro, bio, chron, cycl, dem, geo, gram, graph, hydr, hydro, log, mega, meter, micro, ology, phon, photo, pod, pol, poli, polis, scop, scope, tele, therm*

WORD STRUCTURE

▶ **Syllables**

■ Hear, say, clap, and identify syllables in words with three or more syllables: e.g., *fish/er/man, par/a/graph; el/e/va/tor, un/u/su/al, wat/er/mel/on*

■ Recognize and use open syllables–syllables that end with a single vowel, which usually represents a long vowel sound: e.g., *o/pen, pi/lot, ti/ger*

■ Recognize and use closed syllables– syllables that end with a consonant and usually have a short vowel sound: e.g., *can/dle, fif/teen, mod/ern*

■ Recognize and use r-influenced syllables– syllables that contain one or two vowels followed by the letter r: e.g., *a/part/ment, dirt/y, for/get, four/teen, gar/bage, prair/ie*

■ Recognize and use vowel combination syllables–syllables that contain two or more letters together that represent one vowel sound: e.g., *be/tween, en/joy, mid/night*

■ Recognize and use VCe syllables–syllables that contain a (long) vowel followed by a consonant and then silent e: e.g., *be/side, eve/ning, in/vite, lone/ly, stam/pede, state/ment*

■ Recognize and use consonant + le syllables–syllables that contain a consonant followed by the letters le: e.g., *a/ble, ea/gle, scram/ble, tem/ple*

■ Recognize and use syllables in words with the VCCV pattern (syllable juncture): e.g., *ber/ry, both/er, dis/may, hel/met*

■ Recognize and use syllables in words with the VCCCV pattern (syllable juncture): e.g., *emp/ty, hun/dred, king/dom, mon/ster*

■ Recognize and use syllables in words with the VV pattern: e.g., *gi/ant, ru/in*

▶ **Compound Words**

■ Recognize and use compound words that have frequently used component words: e.g., *somebody, someday, somehow, someone, someplace, something, sometime, somewhat, somewhere*

■ Recognize and use compound words that have common parts: e.g., *campfire, firefighter, firehouse, fireplace, firewood, wildfire*

▶ **Contractions**

■ Recognize and use contractions with have: e.g., *I've, we've, you've, they've*

■ Recognize and use contractions with had or would: e.g., *I'd, we'd, you'd, he'd, she'd, they'd*

▶ **Plurals**

■ Recognize and use plurals that add -es to words that end with a consonant and y after changing the y to i: e.g., *countries, jellies, rubies*

■ Recognize and use plurals that add -es to words after changing the final f or fe to v: e.g., *knives, scarves, wolves*

■ Recognize and use irregular plurals that change the spelling of the word: e.g., *goose/ geese, mouse/mice, ox/oxen, woman/women*

■ Recognize and use irregular plurals that are the same as the singular form of the word: e.g., *deer, moose, salmon, sheep*

■ Recognize and use plurals that add -s to words that end with o: e.g., *pianos, rodeos*

■ Recognize and use plurals that add -es to words that end with a consonant and o: e.g., *echoes, heroes*

▶ **Possessives**

■ Recognize and use possessives that add an apostrophe and s to singular nouns (including proper nouns) that end with s to show ownership: e.g., *princess's closet, Texas's flag, harness's buckle*

■ Recognize and use possessives that add an apostrophe to plural nouns that end with s to show ownership: e.g., *girls' disappointment, woodpeckers' clatter*

■ Recognize and use possessives that add an apostrophe and s to irregular plural nouns to show ownership: e.g., *oxen's strength, women's jackets*

▶ **Suffixes**

■ Understand and talk about the concept of a suffix

■ Understand and talk about the fact that several basic rules govern the spelling of words with suffixes: e.g.,

♦ For many words, there are no spelling changes when adding a suffix: e.g., *run/runs, bright/brighter/brightest, final/finally, teach/teacher*

♦ For words that end with silent e, usually drop the e when adding a suffix that begins with a vowel, but usually keep the e when adding a suffix that begins with a consonant: e.g., *live/living but live/lives, fierce/fiercer/fiercest, please/pleasant but grace/graceful*

♦ For one-syllable words that end with a single vowel and one consonant, usually double the final consonant when adding a suffix that begins with a vowel, but usually do not double the final consonant when adding a suffix that begins with a consonant: e.g., *grin/grinning but grin/ grins, sad/sadder/saddest, flat/flatten, beg/beggar but fit/fitness*

♦ For multisyllable words with an unaccented final syllable that ends with a single vowel and one consonant, usually do not double the final consonant when adding a suffix: e.g., *visit/visited, slender/ slenderer, develop/developer*

♦ For words that end with a consonant and y, usually change the y to i and add the suffix, but for words that end with a vowel and y, usually keep the y and add the suffix: e.g., *copy/copied but enjoy/enjoyed*

▶ **Suffixes: Inflectional Endings**

■ Recognize and use the ending -ing with multisyllable verbs with an accented last syllable when forming the present participle of a verb: e.g., *remind/reminding, enjoy/enjoying*

FIGURE 5–11 The Literacy Continuum, *page 380*

Instructional Contexts

"USE THE RIGHT TOOL for the job." This common-sense adage applies to many situations: hanging a picture on the wall, changing the spark plug on a lawnmower, or piping icing on a cake. It's no less true in your classroom. Texts are the tools of your craft. The goal is to continuously select the right texts for the many precise jobs that are required to sustain and expand students' literacy learning. A helpful way to think about those jobs, and the texts needed to accomplish them, is in terms of instructional contexts. An *instructional context* is a structure for teaching a select grouping of students for a particular instructional purpose using a specific type of text.

Fountas & Pinnell Classroom consists of seven instructional contexts, within which you provide teaching to the whole class, small groups, or individuals (Figure 6–1). Each context has a specific instructional purpose, with texts, lessons, conferring cards, and discussion cards to support your teaching and students' learning. While each context has a specific purpose, the instructional contexts in *Fountas & Pinnell Classroom* have also been designed to connect with and build upon each other in a cohesive manner across the school year.

Texts are the tools of your craft.

FOUNTAS & PINNELL CLASSROOM INSTRUCTIONAL CONTEXTS

Whole Class	Small Groups	Individuals
IRA Interactive Read-Aloud	**GR** Guided Reading	**IR** Independent Reading (and Conferring)
SR Shared Reading	**BC** Book Clubs	**PWS** Phonics and Word Study (Apply)
RML Reading Minilessons	**PWS** Phonics and Word Study (Apply)	
PWS Phonics and Word Study (Teach and Share)		

FIGURE 6–1 *There are seven instructional contexts in Fountas & Pinnell Classroom, each one serving a different purpose.*

In this section of the *System Guide,* you will find detailed information about each instructional context:

▶ A list of texts, organized according to the specific instructional context. For example, texts for Interactive Read-Aloud are organized by texts sets, while texts for Guided Reading are organized by level.

▶ A walkthrough of the instructional design, with a description of the features and support in the lesson folders, conferring cards, discussion cards, and minilessons.

▶ Ideas, effective instructional practices, and language for putting each context into action in your classroom.

▶ Notes on assessing student learning within each context.

▶ Resources where you can learn more about each context.

Systems of Strategic Actions

When students read, they use in-the-head systems of strategic actions to process texts, flexibly integrating many different kinds of information in order to make meaning. These systems are displayed as a wheel (Figure 6–2) to express how proficient readers use all of the actions simultaneously in a smoothly orchestrated way. The twelve strategic actions are clustered into three categories that encompass how readers make meaning from text: Thinking Within the Text, Thinking Beyond the Text, and Thinking About the Text.

Each instructional context of *Fountas & Pinnell Classroom* is designed to teach and support students as they build a robust text-processing system. By learning to integrate these strategic actions flexibly through the various instructional contexts, students are able to successfully interact with texts of increasing challenge and complexity.

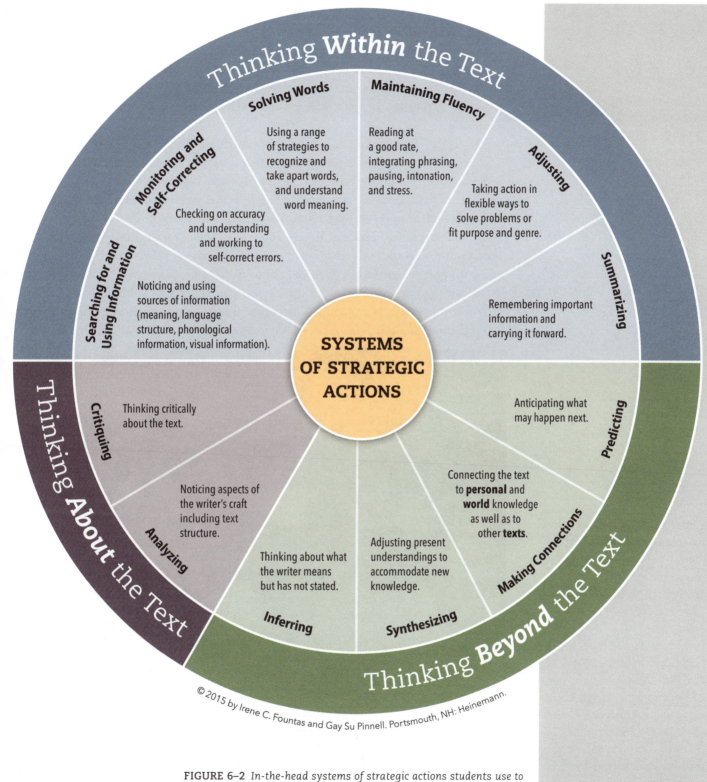

Thinking **Within** the Text

Solving Words
Using a range of strategies to recognize and take apart words, and understand word meaning.

Maintaining Fluency
Reading at a good rate, integrating phrasing, pausing, intonation, and stress.

Monitoring and Self-Correcting
Checking on accuracy and understanding and working to self-correct errors.

Adjusting
Taking action in flexible ways to solve problems or fit purpose and genre.

Searching for and Using Information
Noticing and using sources of information (meaning, language structure, phonological information, visual information).

Summarizing
Remembering important information and carrying it forward.

SYSTEMS OF STRATEGIC ACTIONS

Thinking **About** the Text

Critiquing
Thinking critically about the text.

Predicting
Anticipating what may happen next.

Analyzing
Noticing aspects of the writer's craft including text structure.

Making Connections
Connecting the text to **personal** and **world** knowledge as well as to other **texts**.

Inferring
Thinking about what the writer means but has not stated.

Synthesizing
Adjusting present understandings to accommodate new knowledge.

Thinking **Beyond** the Text

FIGURE 6–2 *In-the-head systems of strategic actions students use to process text*

Each instructional context is anchored by texts and talk. Through talking about texts, students can:

▸ Express ideas
▸ Expand language
▸ Ask questions
▸ Build understanding

Five Keys to Thoughtful Talk

Students' talk about reading reveals and expands their thinking. A set of learned behaviors and talk structures provide rich opportunities for deep thinking about texts. Consider these ways to build a culture of thoughtful talk in your classroom.

1. Help students understand that reading is thinking and that when they talk, they share their thinking.
2. Teach students to turn and talk effectively with each other.
3. Give students wait time, and guide them to give others wait time as well.
4. Demonstrate the use of language that fosters participation and respect for others' thinking and also promotes building on the ideas of others.
5. Set the norm that everyone listens attentively and respectfully to each other.

Importance of Language in the Classroom

Strong, literacy-rich classrooms are joyful, busy places where students—through language—develop relationships, explore ideas, negotiate decisions, and expand their imagination, language, vocabulary, and content knowledge. Students discover the world through inquiry and exploration. As active and curious learners, they are constantly exploring, solving problems, and, in the process, using language to share their ideas.

While they listen to and talk about stories and react to the new and interesting facts they discover about the world, students are also building a framework for understanding new information. As they interact with others, they are learning the structure or "grammar" of language. Through their experiences and books, they add daily to their oral vocabularies. As they interact with others, they learn the "rules" of conversation and how to talk about (and attend to) the same topic for a period of time. As they talk, they begin to see how ideas are related to each other and learn how to sustain attention and curiosity.

Because language is critical for student learning about the world and for acquiring the behaviors and understandings of literacy, it is infused with literacy learning throughout each instructional context of *Fountas & Pinnell Classroom*.

FIGURE 6–3 *Fourth graders sharing ideas with their book club and with partners*

Interactive Read-Aloud

INTERACTIVE READ-ALOUD IS THE foundation for instruction in your classroom. Usually a whole-class activity, interactive read-aloud is a dedicated instructional time in which you read aloud to students a text you have selected for their enjoyment. Most of your selections are age-appropriate picture books, so as you turn the book toward students, they can notice the illustrations or text features. These picture books have sophisticated language and mature themes as well as complex art. However, because students do not have to visually process the print—that is, they do not have to decode the words, attend to punctuation, etc.—they can give their full attention to engaging other key systems of strategic actions, such as predicting and inferring. Importantly, this instructional context is designed to be interactive, which means that the text that you read aloud is the basis for rich discussion among your students. You identify places in the text to pause and invite students to turn and talk with a partner or respond to the whole group.

Even as new read-alouds are introduced, a text often becomes an old favorite as it is read multiple times in subsequent days for enjoyment and to give attention to various aspects of craft. And because the interactive read-aloud texts in *Fountas & Pinnell Classroom* are organized into text sets, students can also make connections among ideas and notice parallels in the craft of writing and illustration across multiple texts. In every way except decoding the words, they are processing the text—interpreting it, responding to it, connecting it to texts with similar themes, and using it as a mentor for analyzing and writing. So while students are not "reading" the text during interactive read-aloud, the careful thinking and talking that they are doing about the text makes this instructional context a vital, essential, and enjoyable part of the school day.

At a Glance

During Interactive Read-Aloud, the teacher reads aloud a selected text to students, occasionally and selectively pausing for discussion.

- Whole-class teaching
- Texts may be beyond the instructional reading level of some students
- Students are listening and can see illustrations
- Text-based discussion helps students construct meaning and expand vocabulary and language
- Often, favorite texts are reread
- Texts or parts of texts are reread and revisited for extended discussion or response and as a basis for minilessons in reading and writing

FIGURE IRA 1 *Teacher and students during an interactive read-aloud*

Texts for Interactive Read-Aloud

THE FOUNTAS & PINNELL CLASSROOM collection of interactive read-aloud texts is ___ ___xt sets that reflect a global perspective, with a diversity of char-___ ___es, and topics. Each text set contains four to six high-quality ___books that were selected because students will love them and ___ety of authors and illustrators, topics, genres, themes, and text ___of texts has been carefully curated around a connecting idea, ___dy of a particular author, illustrator, or genre.

___tion and nonfiction genre that are usually familiar to fifth ___ve read-aloud text collection for grade four features traditional ___plex fantasy including some science fiction, and poetry. Many ___are longer and have more complex plots and themes. The non-___ more sophisticated but grade-appropriate content and a wider ___es.

___ead-aloud texts below are in a recommended sequence based ___al emphases and the likely needs of a classroom community ___ol year. However, as you discover your students' needs and interests, you may wish to present the text sets in a different order or even mix and match texts from different sets to create new collections.

Note: Books marked with SR provide opportunities for shared or performance reading.

Months 1–2

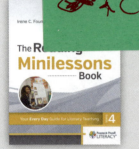

Building C___

The miniless___
Minilessons ___
Interactive R___
as the basis ___
modeling. Yo___
introduce ce___
upcoming mi___
plan to prese___

TEXT SET Friendship

Essential Question *What does it mean to be a good friend?*

Title	Author	Genre
The Other Side	Woodson, Jacqueline	Fiction
Better Than You	Ludwig, Trudy	Fiction
The Dunderheads	Fleischman, Paul	Fiction
Snook Alone	Nelson, Marilyn	Fiction
Mangoes, Mischief, and Tales of Friendship: Stories from India	Soundar, Chitra	Fiction

54   *Fountas & Pinnell Classroom System Guide, Grade 4*

TEXT SET Figuring Out Who You Are

Essential Question *Why is it important to always be yourself?*

Title		Author	Genre
	A Boy and a Jaguar	Rabinowitz, Alan	Nonfiction
	Heroes	Mochizuki, Ken	Fiction
	La Mariposa	Jimenez, Francisco	Fiction
	The Junkyard Wonders	Polacco, Patricia	Fiction
	The Gold-Threaded Dress	Marsden, Carolyn	Fiction

TEXT SET Empathy

Essential Question *How can feeling understood make a difference to someone?*

Title		Author	Genre
	The Boy and the Whale	Gerstein, Mordicai	Fiction
	A Symphony of Whales	Schuch, Steve	Fiction
	Step Right Up: How Doc and Jim Key Taught the World About Kindness	Bowman, Donna Janell	Nonfiction
	The Crane Wife Japanese Tale Unit 1	Bodkin, Odds	Fiction

TEXT SET Memoir · Genre Study

Essential Question *What is the writer's reason for writing?*

Title	Author	Genre
The Scraps Book: Notes from a Colorful Life	Ehlert, Lois	Nonfiction
Play Ball!	Posada, Jorge & Burleigh, Robert	Nonfiction
The Upside Down Boy	Herrera, Juan Felipe	Nonfiction
Twelve Kinds of Ice	Obed, Ellen Bryan	Nonfiction

TEXT SET Allen Say · Author/Illustrator Study

Essential Question *How does an author make decisions to interest readers?*

Title	Author	Genre
The Bicycle Man	Say, Allen	Fiction
The Lost Lake	Say, Allen	Fiction
Tea with Milk	Say, Allen	Fiction
The Sign Painter	Say, Allen	Fiction
Kamishibai Man	Say, Allen	Fiction

TEXT SET Craft — Illustration Study

Essential Question *How does an illustrator make decisions to interest readers?*

Title	Author	Genre
Gecko	Huber, Raymond	Hybrid
Dingo	Saxby, Claire	Hybrid
Giant Squid	Fleming, Candace	Nonfiction
Eye to Eye: How Animals See the World	Jenkins, Steve	Nonfiction
Magnificent Birds	Walker Books	Nonfiction

TEXT SET Floyd Cooper — Illustrator Study

Essential Question *How does an illustrator use art to interest readers?*

Title	Author	Genre
Meet Danitra Brown	Grimes, Nikki	Fiction
Ma Dear's Aprons	McKissack, Patricia	Fiction
Ruth and the Green Book	Ramsey, Calvin Alexander	Fiction
These Hands	Mason, Margaret H.	Fiction
A Dance Like Starlight: One Ballerina's Dream	Dempsey, Kristy	Fiction

SR

TEXT SET Biography: Artists

Essential Question *Why is creativity important for the individual? For the culture?*

Title	Author	Genre
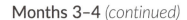 Mary Cassatt: Extraordinary Impressionist Painter	Herkert, Barbara	Nonfiction
Radiant Child: The Story of Young Artist Jean-Michel Basquiat	Steptoe, Javaka	Nonfiction
Me, Frida	Novesky, Amy	Nonfiction
Action Jackson	Greenberg, Jan & Sandra Jordan	Nonfiction
The East-West House: Noguchi's Childhood in Japan	Hale, Christy	Nonfiction

TEXT SET Telling a Story with Photos

Essential Question *How do authors and illustrators make decisions to interest readers?*

Title	Author	Genre
Wolf Island	Read, Nicholas	Nonfiction
A Bear's Life	Read, Nicholas	Nonfiction
The Seal Garden	Read, Nicholas	Nonfiction
A Little Book of Sloth	Cooke, Lucy	Nonfiction
Face to Face with Whales	Nicklin, Flip & Linda	Nonfiction

IRA

TEXT SET Douglas Florian

Author/ Illustrator Study

Essential Question *How does an author make decisions to interest readers?*

Title	Author	Genre
Insectlopedia	Florian, Douglas	Fiction
Mammalabilia	Florian, Douglas	Fiction
Lizards, Frogs, and Polliwogs	Florian, Douglas	Fiction
On the Wing	Florian, Douglas	Fiction
In the Swim	Florian, Douglas	Fiction

TEXT SET Poetry   Genre Study

Essential Question *What is the writer's reason for writing?*

Title	Author	Genre
The Barefoot Book of Earth Poems *Unit 1*	Nicholls, Judith. Ed.	Fiction
Shape Me a Rhyme: Nature's Forms in Poetry	Yolen, Jane	Nonfiction
On the Wing	Elliott, David	Nonfiction
A Place to Start a Family: Poems About Creatures That Build	Harrison, David L.	Nonfiction
What Are You Glad About? What Are You Mad About?	Viorst, Judith	Fiction

TEXT SET Historical Fiction   Genre Study

Essential Question *What is the writer's reason for writing?*

Title	Author	Genre
Uncle Jed's Barbershop	Mitchell, Margaree King	Fiction
The Glorious Flight: Across the Channel with Louis Blériot	Provensen, Alice & Martin	Fiction
The Buffalo Storm	Applegate, Katherine	Fiction
The Houdini Box	Selznick, Brian	Fiction
Crow Call	Lowry, Lois	Fiction
Dad, Jackie, and Me	Uhlberg, Myron	Fiction

TEXT SET Exploring Identity

Essential Question *How do you become the person you want to be?*

Title		Author	Genre
	The Royal Bee	Park, Frances & Ginger	Fiction
	Imagine	Herrera, Juan Felipe	Nonfiction
	Crown: An Ode to the Fresh Cut	Barnes, Derrick	Fiction
	Be Water, My Friend: The Early Years of Bruce Lee	Mochizuki, Ken	Nonfiction
	Rickshaw Girl	Perkins, Mitali	Fiction

TEXT SET Perseverance

Essential Question *Why is it important to persevere when you are faced with a challenge?*

Title		Author	Genre
	Rescue & Jessica: A Life-Changing Friendship	Kensky, Jessica & Patrick Downes	Fiction
	Strong to the Hoop	Coy, John	Fiction
	King for a Day	Khan, Rukhsana	Fiction
	Razia's Ray of Hope: One Girl's Dream of an Education	Suneby, Elizabeth	Nonfiction
	Barbed Wire Baseball: How One Man Brought Hope to the Japanese Internment Camps of WWII	Moss, Marissa	Nonfiction

TEXT SET Biography: Individuals Making a Difference `Genre Study`

Essential Question *What is the writer's reason for writing?*

Title	Author	Genre
Fly High: The Story of Bessie Coleman	Borden, Louise & Mary Kay Kroeger	Nonfiction
Six Dots: A Story of Young Louis Braille	Bryant, Jen	Nonfiction
Farmer Will Allen and the Growing Table	Martin, Jacqueline Briggs	Nonfiction
The Secret Kingdom: Nek Chand, a Changing India, and a Hidden World of Art	Rosenstock, Barb	Nonfiction

FIGURE IRA 2 *Fourth graders enjoying an interactive read-aloud*

TEXT SET Taking Action, Making Change

Essential Question *Why is it important to take action when you see that something is wrong?*

Title	Author	Genre
Follow the Moon Home: A Tale of One Idea, Twenty Kids, and a Hundred Sea Turtles	Cousteau, Philippe & Deborah Hopkinson	Fiction
The Promise	Davies, Nicola	Fiction
Emmanuel's Dream: The True Story of Emmanuel Ofosu Yeboah	Thompson, Laurie Ann	Nonfiction
Brothers in Hope: The Story of the Lost Boys of Sudan	Williams, Mary	Fiction
One Hen: How One Small Loan Made a Big Difference	Milway, Katie Smith	Fiction

TEXT SET Innovative Thinking and Creative Problem Solving

Essential Question *Why do people have a responsibility to try to right things that are wrong?*

Title	Author	Genre
Ivan: The Remarkable True Story of the Shopping Mall Gorilla	Applegate, Katherine	Nonfiction
Hands Around the Library: Protecting Egypt's Treasured Books	Roth, Susan & Karen Leggett Abouraya	Nonfiction
One Plastic Bag: Isatou Ceesay and the Recycling Women of the Gambia	Paul, Miranda	Nonfiction
Parrots over Puerto Rico	Roth, Susan L. & Cindy Trumbore	Nonfiction

TEXT SET: VANISHING CULTURES | Series Study

Essential Question *Why is it important to understand the challenges that other cultures face?*

Title		Author	Genre
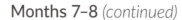	*Sahara*	Reynolds, Jan	Nonfiction
	Himalaya	Reynolds, Jan	Nonfiction
	Amazon Basin	Reynolds, Jan	Nonfiction
	Frozen Land	Reynolds, Jan	Nonfiction
	Far North	Reynolds, Jan	Nonfiction

TEXT SET Coping with Loss

Essential Question *How does loss affect people's lives?*

Title		Author	Genre
	The Dam	Almond, David	Fiction
	Dad's Camera	Watkins, Ross	Fiction
	Eight Days: A Story of Haiti	Danticat, Edwidge	Fiction
	Hachiko Waits	Newman, Leslea	Fiction

TEXT SET The Idea of Home		

Essential Question *Why is it important to have a place that feels like home?*

Title	Author	Genre
The Lotus Seed	Garland, Sherry	Fiction
Red Butterfly: How a Princess Smuggled the Secret of Silk Out of China	Noyes, Deborah	Fiction
Grandfather's Journey	Say, Allen	Fiction
My Name Is Sangoel	Williams, Karen Lynn & Khadra Mohammed	Fiction

TEXT SET What It Means to Be a Family

Essential Question *What is special about being in a family?*

Title		Author	Genre
	Jalapeño Bagels	Wing, Natasha	Fiction
	In Our Mothers' House	Polacco, Patricia	Fiction
	The Matchbox Diary	Fleischman, Paul	Fiction
	Buffalo Bird Girl: A Hidatsa Story	Nelson, S. D.	Nonfiction
	Journey	MacLachlan, Patricia	Fiction

TEXT SET Patricia McKissack

Author/ Illustrator Study

Essential Question *How does an author make decisions to interest readers?*

Title		Author	Genre
	A Million Fish...More or Less	McKissack, Patricia	Fiction
	Goin' Someplace Special	McKissack, Patricia	Fiction
	The Honest-to-Goodness Truth	McKissack, Patricia	Fiction
	Stitchin' and Pullin': A Gee's Bend Quilt	McKissack, Patricia	Fiction

TEXT SET Fantasy   Genre Study

Essential Question *What makes fantasy fun to read?*

Title	Author	Genre
Weslandia	Fleischman, Paul	Fiction
Night of the Gargoyles	Bunting, Eve	Fiction
The Wolves in the Walls	Gaimon, Neil	Fiction
The Field Guide (The Spiderwick Chronicles, Book 1)	DiTerlizzi, Tony & Holly Black	Fiction
Tuck Everlasting	Babbitt, Natalie	Fiction

TEXT SET Fairy Tales   Genre Study

Essential Question *Why are fairy tales important to people?*

Title	Author	Genre
The Twelve Dancing Princesses	Isadora, Rachel	Fiction
Beauty and the Beast	Brett, Jan	Fiction
The Dragon Prince: A Chinese Beauty and the Beast Tale	Yep, Laurence	Fiction
Rumpelstiltskin	Zelinsky, Paul O.	Fiction
Brave Red, Smart Frog: A New Book of Old Tales	Jenkins, Emily	Fiction

TEXT SET Cinderella Stories

Essential Question *What choices does the writer make when writing?*

Title	Author	Genre
The Rough-Face Girl	Martin, Rafe	Fiction
Sootface: An Ojibwa Cinderella Story	San Souci, Robert D.	Fiction
Cendrillon: A Caribbean Cinderella	San Souci, Robert D.	Fiction
Domitila: A Cinderella Tale from the Mexican Tradition	Coburn, Jewell Reinhart	Fiction
The Persian Cinderella	Climo, Shirley	Fiction
Yeh-Shen: A Cinderella Story from China	Ai-Ling, Louie	Fiction

FIGURE IRA 3 *Fourth graders turn and talk to a partner during an interactive read-aloud.*

Instructional Design for Interactive Read-Aloud

Inquiry Overview Cards

Fountas & Pinnell Classroom includes an Inquiry Overview Card for each thematically related text set. The cards are designed to help you prepare to use the books in a particular set, as well as introduce some of the thinking that students will do as they engage with the texts. See Figure IRA 4 A–B for an overview.

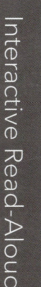

Empathy

The Boy and the Whale • A Symphony of Whales • Step Right Up • The Crane Wife

About This Text Set

Empathy is the ability to understand and share the feelings of others. The characters or subjects in these books attempt to do just that, motivated by a desire to help and an ability to put others' needs before their own. The messages in these books reflect the idea that if you can understand the suffering of another person or creature, you will take action to help them. Students will make connections to their own experiences with helping others, or to simply treating others with kindness.

You might also include the following additional books and resources from the *Fountas & Pinnell Classroom™* collection.

 A Boy and a Jaguar   *Ivan*   *Uncle Willie and the Soup Kitchen*

 Mr. Lincoln's Way   *Freedom Summer*

Thinking Across Books

While reading the books in this text set, help students make connections across the set, and facilitate ways of learning and finding out more about empathy.

- What are the problems the characters face in these books and how are they similar to one another?
- What do the characters' choices tell about each of them?
- How do the characters in each of these books change by the end of each story?

Essential Question and Big Ideas

Engage students by keeping this essential question and these big ideas in mind as you read and talk about the texts in this set. Be sure to use language appropriate for the grade level. This question can also be explored through a variety of inquiry projects, including the suggested projects on the next page.

Why is it important to try to understand the feelings of others? → **It can make a difference to someone if they feel understood.** → If you understand what someone is going through, you might be able to help them.

↓

Understanding how others feel can give you a new perspective.

Interactive Read-Aloud

Empathy Grade 4

An **overview** of the text set explains how the books in the set are connected and suggests titles from other sets or instructional contexts that you may want to include.

By **thinking across books**, students expand their ability to notice patterns, discuss similarities and differences, make connections to their own lives, and synthesize evidence from several sources.

An **essential question** helps students think about underlying themes and big ideas and make connections among ideas presented in the books they are hearing and discussing.

FIGURE IRA 4 A *An example of an Inquiry Overview Card*

Projects for Exploration are designed to help students bring together what they have learned and explore a topic in more depth. Based on your schedule and your students' interests, you can decide which project(s) you would like to do and at what point during the text set you would like students to complete the project. Some projects are best completed at the end of a text set, while other projects can be done as you read through a text set.

Empathy Grade 4

Interactive Read-Aloud

IRA

Asking open-ended questions about the big ideas addressed by the texts can help students identify lines of inquiry they might like to research and explore.

Fountas & Pinnell LITERACY
FOUNTAS & PINNELL CLASSROOM

Learning Through Exploration and Investigation

Asking Questions

Think about the essential question and big ideas on the previous page in order to formulate some questions that will help guide students in identifying projects for further exploration of the essential question.

| What are some different ways you can try to understand how someone is feeling? | How do you feel when others help you or try to understand what you're going through? | What can you learn by understanding how others feel? |

Suggested Projects for Exploration

The following are suggested projects for students to further explore the questions and big ideas related to the books in this text set. If students work in groups, you will need to meet with each group to support their investigation.

Practicing Empathy

For the next week, encourage students to practice empathy when dealing with others. Talk about some of the ways that you can try to understand someone else's feelings or experiences, and how this can change the way you relate to them. Encourage students to think about a situation they could respond to with empathy or kindness. Ask: "What kind of action could you take in this situation?" "How does your response make a difference or change your understanding of the situation?" Continue to meet and talk as a class about ways to practice empathy.

Problem-Solving With Compassion

To encourage further learning, invite the class to divide into two groups to create a short theatrical performance about responding to situations, both small and large, with kindness. Similar to the books they've read, students should create a problem to solve while demonstrating compassionate character traits. Encourage the students to brainstorm as a group before writing the script together. After students have practiced their plays, they can perform them for the class. Invite the audience to provide feedback in relation to the play's illustration of empathy.

Making a Difference Through Empathy

Invite students to research some local charitable organizations or nonprofits. When they find an organization that they are interested in (or feel a personal connection to), encourage students to think of ways that they might be able to help that organization. Some examples might be: making cards for a children's hospital, holding a fundraiser, making informative posters, writing letters to people in government, or another student-identified action.

Reflecting on Local Heroes

Come together as a group and talk about the different ways that the characters in these books responded to different situations with kindness and empathy. Discuss how their actions impacted the lives of the people and animals in these stories. Have students think about the many different opportunities they have to practice empathy or respond to a given situation with kindness. Why is this important? How have their own lives been impacted by the kindness of others? Encourage students to explore the idea of celebrating the lives or actions of "unsung heroes" in their community. Invite them to share this person's kind actions through a medium of their choice.

FIGURE IRA 4 B *An example of an Inquiry Overview Card*

Genre and Author Study Cards

Text sets that focus on genre studies and author/illustrator studies are supported by inquiry cards featuring the steps in the study process and characteristics of the genre or information about the author or illustrator. Figure IRA 5 A–B provides an overview of the instructional support that you can utilize as you present a study-based text set.

An **overview** of the text set explains how the books in the set are connected and suggests titles from other instructional contexts that you may want to include.

A consistent set of **steps** guides students through an inquiry-based study of a particular genre or author/illustrator. Through this procedure, students actively construct a deep understanding of a genre or author/illustrator that they can carry forward into experiences with other texts.

Allen Say

Author/Illustrator Study

IRA Interactive Read-Aloud

 The Bicycle Man

 The Lost Lake

 Tea with Milk

 The Sign Painter

Kamishibai Man

About This Text Set

For author or illustrator study, be sure that students think and talk about the meaning of each text before looking for characteristics specific to this author or illustrator.

An artist at heart, Allen Say dabbled in a variety of art-related training and professions before finding his true calling writing and illustrating children's books. Say's books often reflect his and his family members' experiences growing up in and living in Japan. His love of landscapes, Japanese culture, and life experiences strongly influence his stories and illustrations.

You might also include the following additional book by Allen Say from the *Fountas & Pinnell Classroom*™ collection.

 Grandfather's Journey

Steps in an Author or Illustrator Study

Students will need plenty of opportunity to explore the texts in this set–both on their own or in groups or pairs, and during read-aloud time. As they become more familiar with the steps in an author or illustrator study, they will learn how to notice characteristics common to a particular author or illustrator's work. Below are the basic steps in an author or illustrator study.

1. Take students on a quick "tour" of the books in this set, pointing out some of the notable characteristics of the author or illustrator's work.

2. Allow students time to look through the books and discuss what they notice with a partner.

3. Read each book in the set aloud to the class and discuss what you notice.

4. After you have read all of the books in the set, as well as any others by this author or illustrator, have students analyze characteristics that are common to the texts, and list the characteristics on chart paper.

Author/Illustrator Study: Allen Say Grade 4

FIGURE IRA 5 A *An example of a Genre Study Card*

As students talk about the **characteristics** of a genre or of an author or illustrator's craft that they have noticed, they refine and extend their thinking. Observations shared by the classroom community can be recorded through shared or independent writing.

Students collaborate to create a **working definition** of a genre or description of a trait exhibited through the work of an author or illustrator. Through this inquiry-based process, students experience a strong sense of agency as they take ownership of their understanding.

Learning Through Inquiry

Characteristics of the Author or Illustrator's Work

After reading and discussing all of the books in this set, draw out and list what students have noticed across the texts. Use shared writing to help them generate a list of characteristics common to all of the books. You might want to list the characteristics they notice all of the time and the characteristics they notice often.

Allen Say

Noticings:

Always:

- His illustrations show the setting of the story, detailing the time, place, and culture.
- He uses earth tones in his illustrations.
- He uses watercolor.
- He focuses on Japanese and Japanese-American characters and culture.

Often:

- He uses details about his own life, family history, and Japanese history to illustrate and tell the story.
- His illustrations feature landscapes.
- His stories take place in the past.
- His stories are set in Japan.

Author/Illustrator Study: Allen Say Grade 4

Interactive Read-Aloud

IRA

IRA3823

FIGURE IRA 5 B *An example of a Genre Study Card*

Lesson Folders

Fountas & Pinnell Classroom includes a four-page Lesson Folder for each interactive read-aloud text. Lessons can also be downloaded from Online Resources. The lessons, which are carefully planned to expand students' thinking across the year, provide an extensive menu of ideas and language to spark discussion. Figure IRA 6 A–D provides an overview of the features and instructional support that you can utilize as you plan and present an interactive read-aloud lesson.

Book information includes a list of other texts in the text set, in their suggested order.

You Will Need

- *The Crane Wife*
- Paper and pencils (optional)
- Poster paper, poster paints, and markers (optional)

Book	*The Crane Wife*
Grade	4
Retold by	Odds Bodkin
Illustrator	Gennady Spirin
Genre	Fiction/Folktale
Text Set	Empathy

- *The Boy and the Whale*
- *A Symphony of Whales*
- *Step Right Up: How Doc and Jim Key Taught the World About Kindness*
- *The Crane Wife*

Interactive Read-Aloud

Materials you will need to prepare for and present the lesson. Most are included with *Fountas & Pinnell Classroom*, as well as a few common items available at most schools.

Summary

Osamu is a lonely sail maker who longs for a wife. One stormy night, he finds an injured crane and nurses it back to health. Later, a lovely woman appears at his door, and Osamu and the woman fall in love and marry. When Osamu learns that his wife can make magical sails, he demands more and more sails—until he loses his beloved wife.

Messages

It is important to appreciate the beautiful things in your life and not keep seeking more. Kindness is repaid with kindness; greed is repaid with sorrow.

Messages help you encourage students to articulate and reinforce the universal or "big ideas" of the text.

 ### Goals

Think about the reading behaviors and understandings your students control. Refer to *The Fountas & Pinnell Literacy Continuum* for Grade 4 Interactive Read-Aloud and select appropriate goals. You may want to consider these:

Inquiry
- Identify characteristics of folktales.
- Discuss the cultural significance of the illustrations.

Comprehension
- Make predictions about story events.
- Notice character changes that occur in Osamu.
- Use information from the beginning of the story to interpret later events.
- Infer and understand the moral lessons about kindness and greed in a traditional folktale.

Communication
- Connect ideas in the text to ideas in other texts.
- Discuss how one event in the story builds on another.

Vocabulary
- Use some academic language to talk about literary features (e.g., *character, message, setting*).
- Acquire new vocabulary from text and graphics (e.g., *loom, crane, shuttle*).

Teaching goals for the lesson align with *The Fountas & Pinnell Literacy Continuum*. Choose or modify goals that match the learning needs of your students and will lead them forward in their ability to process and talk about texts.

About This Book

GENRE FOCUS This Japanese folktale is about a poor sail maker who longs for a wife. As in many folktales, kindness is rewarded and greed is punished.

HOW THE BOOK WORKS The folktale is told in third-person narrative form. The story takes place over an undetermined period, with the passage of time marked by words such as "Time passed." The text is superimposed on full-page illustrations that contribute to the mood of the story, with the white cranes in the illustrations standing out against a muted background.

SOCIAL STUDIES CONNECTION Culture This book exposes students to the traditional Japanese appreciation of nature and family, while the expressive art done in a Japanese style shows scenes of medieval Japan.

IMPORTANT TEXT CHARACTERISTICS

- A mix of simple and complex sentences
- Some use of Tier 2 vocabulary (e.g., *caressing, pelting, emerged*)
- Page-blanketing, framed illustrations, usually two-page spreads done in watercolor and gouache

A description of the book's **genre, structure, and important characteristics**, which you may want to draw students' attention to before or after reading

1

FIGURE IRA 6 A *An example of an Interactive Read-Aloud lesson*

IRA

Suggestions for briefly **introducing the book** to pique student interest and engage their thinking about the text

Suggested stopping points that you may want to use during your **reading of the text** to engage student thinking

Discussion suggestions for extending student thinking within, beyond, and about the text

---

Numbering Book Pages

Begin numbering this book on the left-hand page that begins "Once, in ancient Japan . . ." and end with the left-hand page that begins "Never again did . . ." for a total of 27 pages.

Supporting English Learners

Support students' understanding of concepts and vocabulary.

- Explain unfamiliar words, such as *stunned, delicate,* and *shivering.*
- Help students understand the concept of weaving and words associated with weaving, such as *loom, warp, weft, shuttle.*

 Prompting Guide, Part 2 Refer to pages 19 and 44 as needed

Supporting English Learners

Support students' discussion of the text.

- If needed, rephrase the second question. *How did Osamu change during the story?*

 Prompting Guide, Part 2 Refer to pages 23 and 45 as needed

Introduce the Text

Consider the strengths and needs of your students and the demands of the text as you introduce and read the book. Examples to invite thinking are provided. Make the introduction and reading interactive, allowing time for students to share their thoughts (indicated by ●).

■ *Folktales are simple stories that are told over and over again. The folktale I'm going to read you today is from Japan. It is called* The Crane Wife *by Odds Bodkin.* Display the illustration on page 5, pointing out the man and the crane. *The story begins when a poor man who lives alone is kind to a wounded crane.*

Read the Text

Stop a few times to invite thinking and a brief conversation. Students may turn and talk in pairs or threes. Some stopping points and quick comments are suggested below.

■ After page 5: *Osamu is kind to the crane and nurses it back to health. What do you think might happen because of his kindness?* Have students turn and talk with a partner.

■ After page 9: *What are you thinking about Yukiko?* ● *Where do you think she came from?*

■ After page 17: *Yukiko weaves another sail and it exhausts her. Why do you think she's exhausted?* ● *What do you think will happen at the end of another six months?*

■ After page 22, as you display the illustration on pages 23 to 24: *What happened? Why does Osamu see a crane weaving?* ● *Have your feelings about Osamu changed? Talk with a partner about it.*

■ After page 27: *Do you think Osamu would change anything if he could go back in time?* ● *If so, what do you think he would change?* Have students turn and talk with a partner.

Discuss the Text

Invite students to share their thinking about the book. Some prompts to support discussion are suggested below.

■ *How is Osamu rewarded for his kind treatment of the crane at the beginning of the story?*
■ *How did Osamu change over the course of the story?*
■ *What would you say is the most important lesson in this folktale?*

Guide students toward the key understandings of the text. Some key understandings students may express are:

Thinking *Within* the Text

- Osamu is a lonely, poor sail maker.
- He nurses an injured crane back to health.
- Later, a beautiful woman appears at his door. He marries her.
- When they don't have enough to eat, Yukiko twice weaves a magic sail.
- After Osamu demands that Yukiko weave a third sail, she is unable to complete it and flies off.

Thinking *Beyond* the Text

- The crane turns into a woman who repays Osamu's kindness with love.
- When Yukiko weaves a sail, a part of her is woven into the sail.
- Osamu changes from valuing love and companionship to valuing gold.
- The tale has a bigger message about the importance of treating others well.

Thinking *About* the Text

- *The Crane Wife* is a Japanese folktale with a simple plot and message.
- Full-page watercolor illustrations provide a dreamlike quality to the story.
- Vague references to the passage of time give the story a timelessness.

FIGURE IRA 6 B *An example of an Interactive Read-Aloud lesson*

Suggestions for **responding to the text**, which may include art activities, shared and independent writing, drama, exploring specific elements of craft, investigative projects, and cross-curricular connections

Respond to the Text

Below are suggestions for ways to enhance students' appreciation and interpretation of the text.

INDEPENDENT WRITING Reread pages 18–21. *How does Osamu change when he learns he can have a lifetime's gold in exchange for one more sail?* ● *Imagine you are able to give him advice after he hears the captain's offer but before he runs home to Yukiko. What would you say?* ● Ask students to write in the reader's notebook what they would advise Osamu to do.

SOCIAL STUDIES Page through the book and point out different settings in the text as students jot down notes and sketch a rough map. Have them include Osamu's house on the hilltop, the marsh, the village, and the harbor. In small groups, students should compare sketches and discuss how each location relates to the others. Then distribute poster paper for the groups to create final maps. Display the maps in your classroom or in the hallway.

READERS' THEATER Have students work in groups of three to write a script showing what might have happened if Osamu had turned down the wealthy ship captain's offer. Students can write the script with three characters: Osamu, the ship captain, and Yukiko. How would the ship captain have responded? What plan might Osamu and Yukiko have made to earn enough money on which to live? After writing the scene, have students read it aloud with expression in front of the class.

Supporting English Learners

Support students' participation in the independent writing activity.

● Make sure students understand the meanings of *advice* and *advise*.

● Provide an oral sentence frame for students, such as *I would tell Osamu _____ because _____*.

● Have students use their oral sentence frame for their writing.

The Crane Wife Grade 4

Suggestions for modifying or scaffolding instruction to **support English learners** in processing the text, using language to participate in discussions, and benefiting from the teaching

Supporting English Learners

Support students' participation in the readers' theater activity.

● Group native English speakers with English learners.

● Have students discuss the script before writing.

● Provide oral sentence frames (e.g., *Osamu says _____. The ship captain answers _____. Yukiko and Osamu plan _____*.).

● Have students use the oral sentence frames to help them with their scripts.

● Demonstrate reading a script aloud with expression. Have students repeat after you.

FIGURE IRA 6 C *An example of an Interactive Read-Aloud lesson*

Suggestions for **rereading and revisiting the text** to deepen comprehension of the text's meaning, build and extend vocabulary, and notice additional aspects of the writer's craft or features of the book

Extend text analysis, attend to vocabulary, and make personal connections. As you discuss books and present lessons, you will be able to share information and students will benefit from the opportunity to think deeply about the text with others. The teacher guides the discussion skillfully.

The Crane Wife · Grade 4

Supporting English Learners

Support students' comprehension and language.

- Use the illustration on page 8 to support students' understanding of the concept of bowing.
- Provide an oral sentence frame for students for page 13, such as *I can tell what the sail is made of because _____.*
- Have partners discuss the illustration on pages 23–24. Provide an oral sentence frame, such as *Yukiko is _____ because _____.*

Prompting Guide, Part 2
Refer to pages 37 and 47 as needed

Reread and Revisit the Text

You may want to revisit the whole book or parts of the book on the same day, or on subsequent days, so that students can notice more about the text and illustrations.

Comprehension and Language

- Reread pages 1–2. *At the beginning of the story, Osamu compares the cranes to sails. How are cranes and sails connected later in the story?* ● *How are the cranes' wings like sails?*
- Reread page 8. *When the woman first steps inside Osamu's house, Osamu bows. In Japan, bowing is a way of greeting or showing respect. When have you seen someone bow?*
- Reread page 13. *The sail is strong but very light, and the wind is woven into it. Think about the comparison Osamu makes at the beginning of the book. What kind of clue does this give you about what the sail is made of?*
- Revisit pages 23–24. *The illustrator shows you what is happening to Yukiko as she tries to weave the third sail. Talk to a partner about what you see in the illustration.*

Vocabulary

- Reread the first paragraph on page 18. *How does the context help you understand the meaning of restless?* Help students identify the suffix *-less* and explain how it changes the meaning of the word *rest.*
- Reread the fourth paragraph on page 22 and display the illustration on pages 23–24. *How do this illustration and the words help you understand how a loom and shuttle weave fabric?* ● If possible, display a picture or video of a person using a loom and shuttle to weave, and compare it to what is happening in the illustration.

Book and Print Features

- Revisit pages 1–2. *Some of the language on these pages is in italic type. The author uses italic type to show that a character is thinking something but not saying it aloud.*
- Go back to the illustrations on pages 9–10, 17–18, and 21–22, and reread the text. *What happens in the story on these pages?* ● *Why do you think the illustrator illustrated the pages the same way?*

Suggestions for **making connections** to other texts in *Fountas & Pinnell Classroom* or to texts that students may already know that are related by topic or theme

Connect to Other Books (Text Sets)

If you have read other, similar books or other books in this text set, help students make connections between them.

- Display the covers of the other books in this text set that you have read to the class. *How do the characters and subjects in each of the books in this set show the importance of empathy, or thinking of others' feelings?* ● *Which character or person do you think showed the most kindness?*
- *The settings in the books in this text set are all very different. Which did you most enjoy reading about?* ● *Which setting is most like the place where you live?*

Prompting Guide, Part 2
Refer to pages 35 and 43 as needed

Assess the Learning

Observe students to find evidence that they can:

- identify characteristics of folktales.
- make predictions about story events.
- analyze how the illustrations support the text.
- connect ideas between texts.
- understand the bigger message in *The Crane Wife.*

Specific behaviors and understandings to observe, based on the lesson goals, as you **assess student learning** during and after an interactive read-aloud lesson

IRA3817

Fountas & Pinnell
LITERACY™
FOUNTAS & PINNELL CLASSROOM

FIGURE IRA 6 D *An example of an Interactive Read-Aloud lesson*

Putting Interactive Read-Aloud into Action

INTERACTIVE READ-ALOUD PROMOTES THE joy of reading, expands students' vocabulary and language, and increases their ability to think, talk, and write about texts in ways that fully engage their interest. As you put this instructional context into action in your classroom, the following practices, tools, and language may be helpful.

Making the Most of Interactive Read-Aloud

Interactive read-aloud can be a highlight of every day. Use the suggestions and practices in Figure IRA 7 to make the most of this enjoyable experience.

Before Reading	During Reading	After Reading
■ Read and analyze the text. ■ Read the suggested introduction in the lesson, and tailor it to engage your students' interest and/or introduce them to an aspect of the text that may be confusing. ■ Notice the suggested stopping points in the lesson. On stick-on notes, write the questions or prompts you select to use. Place the notes in the book at the appropriate places to pause and invite discussion. ■ Introduce the book to the students.	■ Read the text aloud in an engaging manner. For long books with lots of text features, you may not be able to read every chapter, sidebar, or caption. Choose those that most directly support the meaning and messages of the text. ■ Stop for your brief, preplanned interactions. This may be a whole-group share, or you may ask students to turn and talk to a partner. ■ Encourage and value all thinking. Occasionally you may want to express some of your own thoughts and/or draw students' attention to key information, illustrations, or text features.	■ Invite an open discussion of the text. Incorporate academic language as appropriate. Guide students toward some of the key understandings and main messages in the lesson. ■ The value of the discussion lies in students' thinking and talking, not in answering questions correctly. Keep teacher talk to a minimum. ■ Write the title and author of the text on a book chart to help students remember the books they have heard and discussed.

FIGURE IRA 7 *Before, during, and after Interactive Read-Aloud*

Writing About Reading

Occasionally, with an especially engaging read-aloud text, you may want to use shared writing or a reader's notebook to write about one aspect of the book. While each lesson provides suggested writing prompts, you will want to use this "assignment" selectively, as it may detract from the enjoyment of hearing and talking about many texts. Text-based talk, rather than writing, is the primary means of thinking in interactive read-aloud.

Rereading and Revisiting a Text

Interactive read-aloud books are intended to be reread and revisited many times, for the same or different purposes. When revisiting a text, you may wish to use a document camera to project the pages so that all students can clearly see the print and art. The more familiar students are with a book, the deeper their understanding of the meaning and the more useful the book becomes as a mentor text. Some books will become favorites of your class. Enjoy and revisit them as often as you consider appropriate.

Fountas & Pinnell Online Resources

The Online Resources site is a repository of resources for interactive read-aloud that includes helpful videos and printable resources, including lessons, graphic organizers, and record keeping forms. Access to this site is included with the purchase of your *Fountas & Pinnell Classroom™* product. To access this site, refer to the instructions on the inside front cover of your *Interactive Read-Aloud Collection Guide.*

Planning Your Time

Allow 10–15 minutes each day for interactive read-aloud.

▶ 1 minute: Introduce the text
▶ 8–10 minutes: Read the text
▶ 3–4 minutes: Discussion after reading
▶ Allow an additional 5–10 minutes for students to engage in additional responses to the text [optional]

Using *The Literacy Continuum*

In conjunction with the lessons, consult pages 56–65 of *The Literacy Continuum* to gain a deeper understanding of the characteristics of texts used in this instructional context, as well as to identify goals for your interactive read-aloud lessons.

Assessment

You can gain important information by observing students as they participate in interactive read-aloud discussions. You may wish to use the questions below to focus your observations or consult pages 56–65 of *The Fountas & Pinnell Literacy Continuum* to identify specific behaviors to observe.

Observing a Student Participating in Interactive Read-Aloud

Does the student:

- ▶ Make appropriate comments spontaneously or when invited during reading?
- ▶ Make comments after reading that indicate an understanding of the book?
- ▶ Summarize the story with all important events and problems or summarize information after hearing the book?
- ▶ Infer or understand the messages or big ideas of the book?
- ▶ Use some of the language of the book?
- ▶ Notice and comment on aspects of the writer's craft?
- ▶ Link the book to other books previously read?
- ▶ Ask questions to deepen understanding of the topic or story?
- ▶ Actively participate in a conversation about the book with other students?
- ▶ Continue a conversation and stay on topic throughout the discussion?
- ▶ Respond to reading through writing that shows an understanding of the book's meaning?

Record Keeping Form

To help you organize and keep track of observations that you make during interactive read-aloud, a downloadable Interactive Read-Aloud Record Keeping Form is available from Online Resources (Figure IRA 8).

FIGURE IRA 8 *Interactive Read-Aloud Record Keeping Form*

Resources

Learn more about Interactive Read-Aloud in the following resources:

Teaching for Comprehending and Fluency, Chapters 3, 5, 15–18

Guided Reading: Responsive Teaching Across the Grades, Chapter 4

The Fountas & Pinnell Literacy Continuum, pages 12–19 and 56–65

On-Demand Mini-Course *Thinking and Talking About Books Across the Day: Creating a Community of Readers* at **fountasandpinnell.com /professionaldevelopment**

Shared and Performance Reading

READING ALOUD FOR THE pleasure of oneself and others is valuable across the grades, including in the intermediate and middle grades. After all, even students who have a well-established reading process still need to expand their abilities, and shared and performance reading can—and should—play continuing roles in that important work.

Through shared and performance reading, intermediate and middle-level readers further develop their competencies in word analysis, vocabulary, fluency, and comprehension as they consider a text in new ways and represent it through the voice. Reading, thinking, and talking as a group allows students to draw support from one another so they can tackle texts that may be beyond their individual ability to process. And, perhaps most important, shared and performance reading reinforce and embody an essential message of the classroom: *we can do this together.*

Additionally, shared and performance reading are highly productive instructional contexts for English language learners. For these students (and for others who have low language skills), shared and performance reading provide:

- Group support so that students can produce the language with others.
- An authentic opportunity to reread texts, use new language structures, and articulate sounds clearly.
- The chance to repeat English language words and sentence patterns.
- The opportunity to practice reading a text to understand its meaning.
- Practice in pronouncing English words.

Support for Shared and Performance Reading

MANY OF THE LESSONS in *Fountas & Pinnell Classroom* include activities for shared and performance reading of texts from the interactive read-aloud, book club, and guided reading collections. Of course, you also can plan your own shared and performance reading experiences. To guide you, we have created two simple lesson templates, which you'll find in the general resources section of Online Resources for the instructional contexts mentioned above. Additionally, we have identified books from the *Fountas & Pinnell Classroom* collections that are particularly well-suited to shared and performance reading. These books are identified by SR throughout this guide, and they also appear in the chart on pages 85–88. Finally, the pages that follow contain useful information about the different contexts for shared and performance reading, processes for using them with students, and suggested behaviors to watch for during and after shared and performance reading activities.

SR

At a Glance

During shared reading, the teacher and students read from the same common text or from individual copies, which may be beyond students' ability to read independently.

- Whole group
- Texts provide experiences with print and promote the development of reading processes
- After the first reading, students take part in multiple, subsequent readings of the text
- Students discuss the text, and the teacher selects teaching points based on student needs

Contexts for Shared and Performance Reading

ALL SHARED READING INVOLVES a group of students reading aloud from a common text, but the specific form—or context—you'll use with your students will depend on their reading proficiency and the level of support they need from you and the group. Below, we describe three contexts for shared and performance reading.

Shared Reading

Shared reading usually refers to students reading from a common enlarged text or from individual copies if these are available. In shared reading, the teacher leads the group, and reading usually is in unison, although there are adaptations such as groups alternating lines or individuals reading some lines.

In shared reading, the emphasis is on enjoying and experiencing a large number of texts together. The teacher actively supports phrasing, fluency, and using the voice to reflect and interpret the meaning of the text. Through shared reading, all students:

- participate in a demonstration of the reading process;
- receive social support in a heterogeneous group of readers;
- build language skills and enhance their vocabulary;
- build knowledge of high-frequency words;
- practice fluent phrased reading;
- build on their understanding of different text types, formats, and structures;
- learn how to use the voice to reflect and interpret the meaning of the text;
- develop understanding of a wide variety of texts;
- develop understanding of text and print features; and
- practice responding to texts critically.

Fountas & Pinnell Classroom System Guide, Grade 4

Choral Reading

Choral reading usually refers to a group of people reading from a common text, which might be enlarged, projected on a screen, or provided as individual copies. Texts for choral reading typically are longer and more complex than those used for shared reading. The emphasis is on more sophisticated vocal interpretations of prose or poetry texts. Some reading is in unison by the whole group or subgroups, and there may be solos or duets. Through choral reading, all students:

- study a text closely to interpret it;
- practice expressive reading;
- become more aware of phrases, ways to stress particular words or phrases, and all elements of fluent reading;
- develop new vocabulary and language structures;
- become aware of complex literary texts;
- show interpretation of a text and how it varies; and
- use the voice as an instrument to create mood and determine meaning.

Readers' Theater

Readers' theater is a fast and engaging way of turning any literary text into a type of play in which readers assume individual or group roles. Readers' theater is similar to traditional play production, but the text is generally not memorized, and costumes and props are rarely used. Usually, individuals read parts, although groups may read some of the roles. The focus is on vocal interpretation, and the "script" is composed from the dialogue and narrative of the original text. Readers' theater scripts can be constructed from all kinds of texts—novels, short stories, poems, speeches, or screenplays—but not from original plays.

Like shared and choral reading, readers' theater allows students to experience a text in another way, one that provides an authentic purpose for oral reading. Readers' theater engages and motivates readers and, like shared and choral reading, is especially effective for English language learners who need opportunities to read and reread the syntax of the language. Through readers' theater, all students:

- use background information from the longer text to interpret oral language provided in the script;
- study characters in order to use the voice to interpret their feelings;
- develop ease with new vocabulary words and language structures by using them in the role of a characters or a narrator;
- practice expressive and meaningful reading;
- pay close attention to phrases and all elements of fluent reading;
- self-assess their own reading performance;
- build self-confidence through reading for an audience;
- build oral expression and speaking skills;
- build a sense of community with others; and
- strengthen their word-analysis skills.

Changes over Time in Shared and Performance Reading

In general, work in shared and performance reading moves from simple to complex. As students reach the upper elementary and middle school grades, they are ready to focus on interpreting mature prose and poetry that reveal complex issues, and they are capable of engaging in a great deal more independent work, as shown in Figure SR 1, below.

Texts for Shared and Performance Reading

ANY TEXT THAT IS age- and grade-appropriate can be used for shared and performance reading. These might be pages from books you've previously read aloud, scripts, poems, plays, speeches, primary source documents, newspaper articles, interviews, or students' own writing about reading.

In selecting and using books and other written texts for shared and performance reading, consider features such as interesting language, rhyme and rhythm, language play, emotional appeal to students, and other aspects of texts that make them a good basis for performance. As with interactive read-aloud, you'll want

SHARED AND PERFORMANCE READING FOR INTERMEDIATE/MIDDLE-LEVEL READERS

TEXTS	GOALS
▪ Scripts for readers' theater ▪ Poems ▪ Enlarged pages of regular-sized texts (articles, novels, short stories, interactive read-aloud books) ▪ Plays ▪ Speeches and historical documents ▪ Charts, or diagrams ▪ Advertisements or commercials ▪ Newspaper articles or interviews	▪ Strengthen word-analysis skills ▪ Expand vocabulary to include literary language ▪ Use all dimensions of fluency (rate, pausing, word stress, intonation, and volume) to interpret a poem or script with the voice ▪ Expand knowledge of nonfiction text features. ▪ Expand knowledge of nonfiction text structure (narrative, expository) ▪ Expand knowledge of underlying text structures (compare/contrast, sequence, problem/solution, and cause/effect) ▪ Notice aspects of the writer's craft (plot structure, character traits and development, narrator, description of setting, dialogue) ▪ Identify arguments and evidence that supports them ▪ Notice how the writer reveals purpose and the significance of a topic ▪ Compare and critique texts ▪ Provide models for writing ▪ Build a sense of community

FIGURE SR 1 *Shared and Performance Reading for intermediate/middle-level readers*

to consider whether the vocabulary in the text is understandable to listeners, but don't be too concerned with word solving. Fourth graders can easily pronounce and appreciate new and unusual words once they are taught their meanings. The important thing is that the texts you select for shared and performance reading be engaging and enjoyable enough for students to want to read them again and again. Also keep in mind that texts for shared and performance reading should be short.

On the pages that follow, you will find suggestions for text types and formats that are particularly well suited to shared and performance reading. Many texts in the categories described below can be found in the public domain and are available for download from the Internet, or you can use books from the *Fountas & Pinnell Classroom Interactive Read-Aloud, Guided Reading, and Book Club Text Collections*. (See page 85 and the chart on pages 85–88.)

Stories

Stories are excellent sources for shared and performance reading. Through authentic oral reading of narratives, students gain greater appreciation for narrative structure. When they read dialogue, they must interpret how the individuals' voices would sound, reflecting traits and feelings. Older students enjoy poetic language that evokes imagery in narratives. And onomatopoetic words are especially delightful when read aloud.

Informational Texts

A wide range of informational texts are appropriate for shared and performance reading. Students will enjoy reading and performing dramatic scenes from biographies or persuasive arguments that incorporate scientific information. Shared writing pieces that you and your students have created together also make good texts for shared reading.

Poems

Students of every age enjoy reading poetry, songs, and chants in chorus, using the voice as an instrument to interpret the meaning. Poems for older students are relatively complex, with memorable language and literary elements such as metaphor and simile. Poems may focus on nature, everyday life, and emotions. They are especially suitable for choral readings. Students can read these in alternating parts, or with "solos." You will find suitable poems to enlarge in the *Fountas & Pinnell Classroom Interactive Read-Aloud* and *Book Club* collections for grade 4 (shown in Figure SR 2 on pages 85–88).

Songs

Songs are simply poems set to music; they are a form of shared reading that many of us regularly do. Even if you read rather than sing them, songs have an inherent rhythm that helps move the reading along. Older students enjoy creating and reading innovations on all kinds of songs and performing them in choral readings, especially those that they are learning to sing in chorus or music class.

Language to Look For

As you select texts for use in readers' theater or choral reading, look for language that:

- Expresses the emotions of characters
- Shows the action and suspense of the plot
- Reflects the writer's message
- Makes the content interesting
- Shows the qualities of the subject of a biographical text
- Reflects the emotion in a memoir

Ready-to-Use Readers' Theater Scripts

Several books in the *Fountas & Pinnell Classroom Guided Reading Collection* contain readers' theater scripts at the end. These scripts are also available in the guided reading section of the Online Resources. Additionally, many readers' theater scripts in the public domain are available for download from the Internet.

Readers' Theater Scripts

Any text that contains a mix of dialogue and narration is suitable for use as a readers' theater script. You can easily create your own scripts or have students work together to create them, following the simple steps listed below. Just remember to keep it simple and enjoyable.

1. *Select an appropriate fiction or nonfiction text.* Look for poems or stories featuring lots of dialogue, intriguing characters, and interesting problems. You can create a script of a complete story or a scene from a longer story. Nonfiction books, articles, and web pages often include dialogue in the form of quotations. Persuasive nonfiction texts can also be good sources for readers' theater scripts.

2. *Select characters and a narrator.* You don't need to include every character—eliminating minor ones keeps it simple. The narrator (more than one if the original text has a lot of narration) introduces the story or nonfiction script and adds important information to move it forward.

3. *Decide which parts to turn into dialogue and narrative.* Eliminate unnecessary text and keep only what makes the script interesting. Consider critical events in the text or action sequences in which the dialogue is short and snappy. Assign the lines to different characters and the narrator, or have students work together to assign the parts.

4. *Decide if you will use props or costumes.* Props and costumes are not necessary and may overcomplicate what should be a quick and easy process. Occasionally, you might have students hold simple objects that represent the characters they play and write the characters' names on sticky notes or labels they can wear on their clothing.

Plays

As students become more proficient, they enjoy taking on the challenge of performing a play. The best way to learn how to read a play is to perform it. You can assign parts and let students read and study them, then read the play orally, just as you do readers' theater. Occasionally, students can memorize the words and perform a short play for an audience.

Many plays that are especially appropriate for students in grades 4–6 are available from the Internet and other sources. But keep in mind that putting on a play can consume a great deal of time and effort, possibly detracting from your overall goal.

Speeches and Documents

History is filled with famous speeches and primary source documents (or parts of them) that are particularly well suited to shared reading and that students will enjoy performing in the classroom. When a student performs a speech or document for others, make sure that it:

- is meaningfully related to ongoing inquiry in a content area;
- has been read, discussed, and understood by the student; and
- is a manageable piece of literature for both speaker and audience.

Students also can prepare and perform their own speeches, giving them opportunities to explore text types like argument and persuasion from the "inside" by creating them.

Enlarged and Projected Pages

Some enlarged texts are published for the purpose of shared and performance reading by elementary and middle school students. Additionally, you can easily enlarge many books from the *Fountas & Pinnell Classroom Text Collections* for use in shared and performance reading. See Figure SR 2 on pages 85–88 for a list of titles from these collections that are particularly well suited to shared and performance reading.

Shared Writing Pieces

Some finished pieces of writing that you constructed as a class through shared writing can be excellent texts to revisit during shared reading. These pieces are especially meaningful to students because they participated in constructing them. Select pieces that contain rhythm, repetition, poetic language, and other features that would make them particularly enjoyable to read. Try to include students' own writing regularly in your shared reading lessons as examples of continuous texts with features that you are noticing and to motivate students in their writing lives.

Fountas & Pinnell Classroom Text Collections

Many of the texts provided in the interactive read-aloud and guided reading text collections within *Fountas & Pinnell Classroom* are particularly useful for shared and performance reading. These texts are indicated by SR in the booklists found throughout this guide. You'll also find them listed in the chart below.

Texts for Shared and Performance Reading from the *Fountas & Pinnell Classroom Collections*			
Title/Author	Genre	Collection	Useful For
The Apothecary's Apprentice Elizabeth Campbell	Fiction/Fantasy	Guided Reading	Readers' Theater
Ban All Cars! Noelle Child	Nonfiction/ Persuasive	Guided Reading	Choral Reading
The Barefoot Book of Earth Poems Compiled by Judith Nicholls	Poetry	Interactive Read-Aloud	Choral Reading/ Shared Reading
Books, Beasts, and Blood: The Mystery of the Teacher's Pet Nikki Loftin	Fiction/ Realistic	Guided Reading	Readers' Theater

FIGURE SR 2 *Texts from other instructional contexts in* Fountas & Pinnell Classroom *can easily be enlarged or projected for use in shared and performance reading.*

Title/Author	Genre	Collection	Useful For
Bored in Space Riley Roam	Fiction/ Science Fiction	Guided Reading	Shared Reading
The Boy Who Lived with Bears: A Native American Tale adapted by Nick Dondero	Fiction/ Folktale	Guided Reading	Readers' Theater
Crown: An Ode to the Fresh Cut Derrick Barnes	Fiction/ Realistic	Interactive Read-Aloud	Shared Reading
Eight Days: Story of Haiti Edwidge Danticat	Fiction/ Realistic	Interactive Read-Aloud	Choral Reading
A Floating School Kim Hanken	Nonfiction/ Expository	Guided Reading	Readers' Theater
Fly Away Patricia MacLaughlin	Fiction/ Poetry	Book Clubs	Shared Reading/ Choral Reading
The Fools of Chelm Retold by Dina McClellan	Fiction/ Folktale	Guided Reading	Reader's Theater
The Great Pie Giveaway Gayle Pearson	Fiction/ Realistic	Guided Reading	Choral Reading
Harmony Island Rebecca Kirshner	Fiction/ Realistic	Guided Reading	Reader's Theater
Imagine Juan Felipe Herrera	Nonfiction/ Memoir	Interactive Read-Aloud	Shared Reading/ Choral Reading
I Wish I Were a Butterfly James Howe	Fiction	Book Clubs	Shared Reading
Laughing All the Way Nathaniel Clinton	Fiction/ Fantasy	Guided Reading	Choral Reading
The Magic Fountain: A Tale from Korea Retold by Kay McKenna	Fiction/ Folktale	Guided Reading	Readers' Theater
Mammalabilia Douglas Florian	Nonfiction/ Poetry	Interactive Read-Aloud	Choral Reading
Mareko the Chicken Brenda Gurr	Fiction/ Realistic	Guided Reading	Shared Reading

	Continued		
Title/Author	**Genre**	**Collection**	**Useful For**
Meet Danitra Brown Nikki Grimes	Fiction/ Poetry	Interactive Read-Aloud	Choral Reading
Molly Mackerel McNo Nadia Higgins	Fiction/ Fantasy	Guided Reading	Choral Reading
Night of the Gargoyles Eve Bunting	Fiction/ Fantasy	Interactive Read-Aloud	Shared Reading
Now You See Me Heller Landecker	Fiction/ Fantasy	Guided Reading	Reader's Theater
The Ogre's Dinner Casie Hermansson	Fiction/ Fantasy	Guided Reading	Reader's Theater
On the Wing David Elliott	Poetry	Interactive Read-Aloud	Choral Reading
Pelorus Jack: The Dolphin That Guided Ships Pamela Dell	Nonfiction/ Narrative	Guided Reading	Reader's Theater
Riley's Letter Donna Gephart	Fiction/ Realistic	Guided Reading	Choral Reading
Safe Haven for Raptors Mary Reid	Nonfiction/ Expository	Guided Reading	Reader's Theater
Shape Me a Rhyme Jane Yolen	Poetry	Interactive Read-Aloud	Choral Reading
Six Dots: The Story of Young Louis Braille Jen Bryant	Nonfiction/ Biography	Interactive Read-Aloud	Readers' Theater
Snook Alone Marilyn Nelson	Fiction/ Fantasy	Interactive Read-Aloud	Shared Reading
The Spy Graham Rodgers	Fiction/ Realistic	Guided Reading	Shared Reading
A Strange Place to Call Home Marilyn Singer	Nonfiction/ Poetry	Book Clubs	Choral Reading
Suiting Up for Space Suzanne Buckingham	Nonfiction/ Expository	Guided Reading	Reader's Theater
Tiny Horses/Big Jobs Susan Buckley	Nonfiction/ Expository	Guided Reading	Shared Reading

	Continued		
Title/Author	**Genre**	**Collection**	**Useful For**
Twelve Kinds of Ice Ellen Bryan Obed	Nonfiction/ Memoir	Interactive Read-Aloud	Shared Reading
The Twits Roald Dahl	Fiction/ Fantasy	Book Clubs	Shared Reading
What Are You Glad About? What Are You Mad About? Judith Viorst	Poetry	Interactive Read-Aloud	Choral Reading
Whirling on the Giant Wheel Kim T. Griswell	Nonfiction/ Biography	Guided Reading	Reader's Theater
The Wolves in the Walls Neil Gaimon	Fiction/ Fantasy	Interactive Read-Aloud	Shared Reading
The World's Biggest Classroom Alicia Fenwick	Nonfiction/ Expository	Guided Reading	Readers' Theater
Young Bike Racers Michael Sandler	Nonfiction/ Expository	Guided Reading	Shared Reading

Putting Shared and Performance Reading into Action

SHARED AND PERFORMANCE READING provide enjoyable experiences for your classroom community and important opportunities for students to "step up together" into more challenging texts while also beginning to notice and acquire the processes they need to read the texts as individuals. As you put this instructional context into action in your classroom, the following practices, materials, and language may be helpful.

Opportunities for Shared and Performance Reading

Look for opportunities and time in your daily schedule to slip in shared and performance reading experiences. You'll find that shared or performance reading provides a good transition between interactive read-aloud and guided reading time in your classroom. It certainly is not necessary or advisable to follow every read-aloud with a shared or performance reading of the text. Occasionally, however, performance reading provides an opportunity for students to dig into the text in a different way.

Several of the grade 4 interactive read-aloud lessons in *Fountas & Pinnell Classroom* contain shared reading and writing activities you might want to try, using books you've already read aloud.

Guided reading time also provides opportunities for shared and performance reading, especially readers' theater. In the general online resources for guided reading, you'll find several readers' theater scripts from the grade 4 guided reading books. Be sure groups have already read and discussed the main text. You may occasionally have individual guided reading groups perform the scripts for the whole class.

The Fountas & Pinnell Classroom Book Clubs Collection also can be a source for shared and performance reading texts. After reading and discussing a book, students will enjoy reading favorite passages aloud together or may decide to perform certain book pages within the group, for other book groups, or for the entire class. Some book club lessons contain suggestions for shared reading and writing activities you can do with students after they finish a book.

Shared and Performance Reading Processes

Intermediate and middle-level readers still benefit from predictable processes and instructional routines. Because your students will engage in shared and performance reading multiple times throughout the year, it's best to establish processes they can anticipate and use each time. The processes described below, and the lesson templates that are available in Online Resources, will help you and your students get started with shared and performance reading.

Shared Reading Process

Shared reading sessions using an enlarged print text typically include the following steps:

1. *Introduce the text:* Provide a brief introduction that arouses readers' interest and may provide some important information that will support their interpretation of the text.

2. *Model the reading of the text:* Model the reading of the entire text before students join in. This is particularly useful with younger students, but even fourth graders may benefit from hearing the whole text first, especially if it is complex.

3. *Read the text together:* You and the students read the whole text, or parts of it, in unison with variations for different purposes. For instance, students can join in only on the dialogue, or they can read in roles. You might also have them read the text in parts, with one group reading one line or page and another group reading the next.

4. *Discuss the text:* Discuss meaning with students, just as you would in guided reading or interactive read-aloud. This discussion can take place at a few useful stopping places or after reading the entire text.

5. *Make teaching points:* Make specific teaching points related to the reading process, revisiting specific pages as needed.

Performance Reading Process

Choral reading and readers' theater sessions typically include the steps described below.

1. Select a text that is appropriate as a foundation for performance reading, or make your own text from a poem or book that students have already read.

Using *The Literacy Continuum*

Pages 136 and 137 will assist you when selecting texts for shared and performance reading. Pages 138–141 identify behaviors and understandings to notice, teach for, and support during shared and performance reading experiences.

(See Figure SR 2 on pages 85–88 for suggested texts from other *Fountas & Pinnell Classroom Collections*.)

2. Give students time to discuss the text and its meaning and messages. They should also talk about characters, if applicable, and examine the language closely.

3. Assign parts yourself or have students work together to assign characters and narrator(s) for readers' theater and stanzas, refrains, or sections for choral reading.

4. Give students a little time to rehearse their parts, then have the group read through the entire text a few times, using their voices to reflect the meaning.

5. It is not necessary for students to perform choral readings or readers' theater scripts for an audience; however, students might want to do so occasionally. If so, keep in mind that costumes and props aren't needed and might take the focus off the interpretive reading of the text, which should remain the primary goal.

After Shared or Performance Reading

Use the following suggestions after shared or performance reading to ensure an effective learning experience for all students.

1. As students gain control of the language and ideas in a shared text, their attention will be freed up to begin to notice more about the craft of print itself. Choose your goals carefully based upon the strengths and needs of the students in your classroom.

2. Become familiar with the grade 4 literacy goals outlined in *The Fountas & Pinnell Literacy Continuum* and *The Fountas & Pinnell Comprehensive Phonics, Spelling, and Word Study Guide*. It is important to use clear, consistent language when teaching students. Don't try to teach too many things in one reading; be selective.

3. You can revisit the text again and again for different purposes.

4. When a text has become very familiar to students, introduce individual copies, if available. Students may read independently, to you, or with a partner. They can glue the text in a poetry anthology or reader's notebook and illustrate it.

5. With a particularly engaging shared reading text, you may choose to respond to the text through shared writing or to have students write a response in a reader's notebook.

Assessment

YOU CAN GAIN IMPORTANT information by observing students as they participate in shared reading. You may use the questions below to focus your observations or use pages 138–141 of *The Fountas & Pinnell Literacy Continuum* to identify specific behaviors and understandings to observe and encourage.

Observing a Student Participating in Shared Reading

Does the student:

❯ Join in on the reading?

❯ Use appropriate stress, intonation, and phrasing while reading?

❯ Notice and use nonfiction text features?

❯ Locate words in the text (e.g., words with particular patterns, structures, and roots)?

❯ Read with expression related to the meaning of the text?

❯ Reflect the relationship between the voice and the meaning of a poem or script?

❯ Talk about the text in a meaningful way and notice details?

❯ Notice how the writer communicates the messages in a story, poem, or the dialogue of a script?

❯ Take on "book language" (the syntax of written language)?

❯ Revisit the text when working independently, and produce an accurate reading?

Resources

LEARN MORE ABOUT SHARED reading in the following resources.

Guided Reading: Responsive Teaching Across the Grades, Second Edition, Chapter 3

Teaching for Comprehension and Fluency, Chapter 21

The Fountas & Pinnell Literacy Continuum, pages 103–109 and 136–141

Guided Reading

GUIDED READING IS A small-group instructional context in which you support each reader's processing of new challenging texts. By bringing together a small group of students who are at a similar point in their reading development and guiding them to process a text that is leveled on a gradient of difficulty, you are able to provide an incremental amount of challenge at each reader's edge of ability. Unlike interactive read-aloud and shared reading, you do not read the text to students. Instead, you provide a carefully planned introduction to the text that enables each student to read (silently) the whole text individually. The text is new to students, so they have the opportunity to apply, to a new context, what they learned as readers in the previous lesson. After reading, you guide a discussion of the meaning and then make a specific teaching point based on your observations of the students as they read and talk about the book. Finally, you engage the students in two or three minutes of active work with words. Extended response in the form of writing is an option that you may sometimes choose.

At a Glance

During guided reading, students read a teacher-selected text in a small group; the teacher provides explicit teaching and support for reading increasingly challenging texts.

▶ Small group
▶ Texts are at students' instructional reading level
▶ Students read the whole text
▶ Teaching is responsive to individual student strengths and needs

FIGURE GR 1 *During a Guided Reading lesson, a teachers listens while one student reads aloud softly.*

Assessing Readers

We suggest you use the *Fountas & Pinnell Benchmark Assessment System* or other text reading assessment for determining the appropriate text level to begin guided reading instruction with the students in your classroom.

Texts for Guided Reading

THE *FOUNTAS & PINNELL CLASSROOM* collection for grade 4 includes 180 original texts that span levels N through V, with lessons that accompany each text. To support your teaching of guided reading, the books are listed on the following pages in a recommended sequence.

Students do not need to read every book at every text level. If your assessments and daily observations of students indicate that they are ready to progress to the next text level, you should provide the challenge they need. The Instructional Level Expectations in Figure GR 2 provide general guidelines for grade-level goals.

Note: Books marked SR provide opportunities for shared or performance reading.

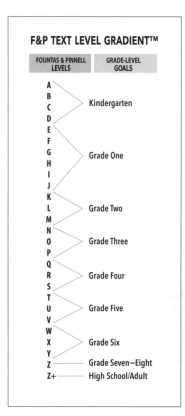

F&P TEXT LEVEL GRADIENT™

FOUNTAS & PINNELL LEVELS	GRADE-LEVEL GOALS
A B C D	Kindergarten
E F G	Grade One
H I J	
K L M	Grade Two
N O P	Grade Three
Q R	Grade Four
S T U	Grade Five
V W X	Grade Six
Y Z	Grade Seven–Eight
Z+	High School/Adult

INSTRUCTIONAL LEVEL EXPECTATIONS FOR READING

	Beginning of Year (Aug.–Sept.)	1st Interval of Year (Nov.–Dec.)	2nd Interval of Year (Feb.–Mar.)	End of Year (May–June)
Grade K		C	D	E
		B	C	D
		A	B	C
				Below C
Grade 1	E	G	I	K
	D	F	H	J
	C	E	G	I
	Below C	Below E	Below G	Below I
Grade 2	K	L	M	N
	J	K	L	M
	C	J	K	L
	Below I	Below J	Below K	Below L
Grade 3	N	O	P	Q
	M	N	O	P
	L	M	N	O
	Below L	Below M	Below N	Below O
Grade 4	Q	R	S	T
	P	Q	R	S
	O	P	Q	R
	Below O	Below P	Below Q	Below R
Grade 5	T	U	V	W
	S	T	U	V
	R	S	T	U
	Below R	Below S	Below T	Below U
Grade 6	W	X	Y	Z
	V	W	X	Y
	U	V	W	X
	Below U	Below V	Below W	Below X
Grades 7–8	Z	Z	Z	Z
	Y	Y	Z	Z
	X	X	Y	Y
	Below X	Below X	Below Y	Below Y

KEY

Exceeds Expectations	
Meets Expectations	
Approaches Expectations: Needs Short-Term Intervention	
Does Not Meet Expectations: Needs Intensive Intervention	

The Instructional Level Expectations for Reading chart is intended to provide general guidelines for grade level goals, which should be adjusted based on school/district requirements and professional teacher judgement.

FIGURE GR 2 *Text Level Gradient™ and Instructional Level Expectations (also downloadable from Online Resources)*

Book Sequence: Level N

For an in-depth description of the characteristics of Level N texts, refer to *The Fountas & Pinnell Literacy Continuum* pages 496–503.

Mastodon Memorial School
Fantasy

My Brother the Dragon
Fiction/ Realistic

Mail Under the Sea
Nonfiction/ Expository

Silly World Records . . . and How to Beat Them
Nonfiction/Expository

The Wacky Ways Some Foods Grow
Nonfiction/ Expository

Book Sequence: Level O

For an in-depth description of the characteristics of Level O texts, refer to *The Fountas & Pinnell Literacy Continuum* pages 504–511.

Trouble
Fiction/ Realistic

Coming Clean
Fiction/ Realistic

The Strange Story of Ketchup
Nonfiction/ Expository

Space Burritos
Nonfiction/ Expository

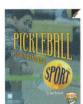

Pickleball: From a Game to a Sport
Nonfiction/ Expository

What Kind of Name Is Pickleball?
Nonfiction/Memoir

The Talking Bird: A Tale from China
Fiction/Folktale

Crow's Secret
Fiction/ Fantasy

Taming Jazz
Fiction/ Realistic

Saving Olive Basset
Fiction/Realistic

Noggin's New Broog
Fiction/ Fantasy

Welcome, Humans: A Visit to the Robot Hotel
Nonfiction/Expository

Bathrooms to Remember
Nonfiction/ Expository

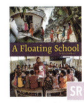

A Floating School
Nonfiction/ Expository

Sinking In: The Truth About Quicksand
Nonfiction/ Expository

Seeds That Fly, Float, and Explode
Nonfiction/Expository

From Garbage to Garden: How to Make Compost
Nonfiction/Procedural

Using *The Literacy Continuum*

The Literacy Continuum is a powerful tool to help you expand your knowledge of the text characteristics and goals for each text level, A–Z. The more familiar you are with these text characteristics, the easier it will be for you to match texts with specific students.

Book Sequence: Level P

For an in-depth description of the characteristics of Level P texts, refer to *The Fountas & Pinnell Literacy Continuum* pages 512–519.

Working in the Clouds: A City Window Washer
Nonfiction/ Narrative

Rapping for Kids: Corey's Story
Nonfiction/ Biography

Big and Bold Art
Nonfiction/ Expository

The First Emoticon
Nonfiction/ Narrative

Roughing It
Fiction/ Realistic

Trouble on the Trail
Fiction/ Realistic

Karma, the Dog Detective
Nonfiction/ Narrative

Crawling with Creatures: Your Body's Friends and Enemies
Nonfiction/Expository

The Great Escape: Animals That Glide
Nonfiction/ Expository

The Sloth: Living with Less
Nonfiction/ Expository

The Great TV Blackout
Fiction/ Realistic

Riley's Letter
Fiction/ Realistic

The Terrible, Terrible Yips
Nonfiction/ Expository

The Spy
Fiction/Realistic

Now You See Me
Fiction/ Fantasy

Book Sequence: Level Q

For an in-depth description of the characteristics of Level Q texts, refer to *The Fountas & Pinnell Literacy Continuum* pages 520–529.

Shh! Wild Animals Sleeping
Nonfiction/ Expository

Vultures: Nature's Cleanup Crew
Nonfiction/ Expository

Beaver Alert!
Nonfiction/ Expository

The Great Pie Giveaway
Fiction/ Realistic

The Gnome War
Fiction/ Fantasy

Dog on the Run
Nonfiction/ Narrative

Using Texts Among Several Classrooms

You may be sharing your texts and the accompanying lessons with other teachers. For ideas and tips on coordinating the use of the guided reading instructional context among several classrooms, see page 110.

Book Sequence: Level Q (continued)

For an in-depth description of the characteristics of Level Q texts, refer to *The Fountas & Pinnell Literacy Continuum* pages 520–529.

Coley's Journey
Nonfiction/Narrative

Tiny Horses, Big Jobs
Nonfiction/Expository

Pelorus Jack: The Dolphin That Guided Ships
Nonfiction/Narrative

Lurking Deep Below: Lake Monsters
Nonfiction/Expository

Pink Lakes and Other Shocking Sights
Nonfiction/Expository

The Iceberg Wrangler
Nonfiction/Narrative

The Case of the Missing Flamingos
Fiction/Realistic (Mystery)

Read Between the Lines
Fiction/Realistic (Mystery)

Blue Ribbons
Fiction/Realistic

Diaper Boy and the Axeman
Fiction/Realistic

Libraries on the Move
Nonfiction/Expository

Banana Blade
Nonfiction/Narrative

Daniel Kish: A Different Way to See
Nonfiction/Biography

Jaylen Arnold: Life with Tourette's
Nonfiction/Narrative

The Monster Chef
Fiction/Fantasy

Trinity's Robot
Fiction/Science Fiction

Jim White's Discovery
Nonfiction/Narrative

Tough Enough
Nonfiction/Memoir

The Fools of Chelm
Fiction/Folktale

Fish for Sillibump: A Noodlehead Tale
Fiction/Folktale

The Seven Brothers: A Noodlehead Tale
Fiction/Folktale

Wiley's Crop
Fiction/Tall Tale

The Field of Gold
Fiction/Folktale

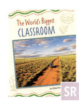

The World's Biggest Classroom
Nonfiction/Expository

Junkyard Art: The Sculptures of Bordalo II
Nonfiction/Biography

Book Sequence: Level R

For an in-depth description of the characteristics of Level R texts, refer to *The Fountas & Pinnell Literacy Continuum* pages 530–539.

Sailing on the Edge
Fiction/Realistic

From Terrifying to Electrifying: Extreme Adventures
Nonfiction/Expository

Catching Air
Nonfiction/Narrative

Really Weird Sports
Nonfiction/Expository

Laughing All the Way
Fiction/Fantasy (Humorous)

The Beast
Fiction/Fantasy

The Dragon of Woolie
Fiction/Fantasy

A Bear Named Winnie
Nonfiction/Narrative

The Boy Who Discovered Snowflakes
Nonfiction/Biography

Looking at Snowflakes
Nonfiction/Expository

Big Bertha's Big Trip
Nonfiction/Narrative

Writing Words in the Sky
Nonfiction/Expository

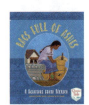

Bags Full of Ashes: A Folktale from Mexico
Fiction/Folktale

The Magic Fountain: A Tale from Korea
Fiction/Folktale

Dream Park: The Straight-A Kid
Fiction/Fantasy

Dream Park: The Soccer Star
Fiction/Fantasy

Dream Park: The Pop Star
Fiction/Fantasy

Dream Park: The Head of the House
Fiction/Fantasy

The Space Rock Hunt
Fiction/Realistic

Gross Fossils: The Secrets of Dinosaur Dung
Hybrid/Expository/Fantasy

Book Sequence: Level R (continued)

For an in-depth description of the characteristics of Level R texts, refer to *The Fountas & Pinnell Literacy Continuum* pages 530–539.

Finding Dinosaur Sue
Nonfiction/
Narrative

They Called Him Mr. Bones
Nonfiction/
Biography

Mareko the Chicken
Fiction/Realistic

Taking the Reins
Fiction/
Historical

Spaghetti Garden
Fiction/
Realistic

Bats in the City
Nonfiction/
Expository

The Real Batman
Nonfiction/
Biography

Emma Gatewood's Long Walk
Nonfiction/
Narrative

Let the Games Begin!
Nonfiction/
Expository

Talking in Crayon
Nonfiction/
Memoir

Book Sequence: Level S

For an in-depth description of the characteristics of Level S texts, refer to *The Fountas & Pinnell Literacy Continuum* pages 540–549.

Watch Out! Animals with Surprising Defenses
Nonfiction/
Expository

Nature's Recycling Team
Nonfiction/
Expository

A Time to Remember
Nonfiction/
Expository

A Village on Stilts
Nonfiction/
Narrative

Growing Up in the Amazon
Nonfiction/
Biography

Book Sequence: Level S (continued)

For an in-depth description of the characteristics of Level S texts, refer to *The Fountas & Pinnell Literacy Continuum* pages 540–549.

The Nenets: Reindeer Herders of Siberia
Nonfiction/ Expository

Althea Gibson, the Tiger of Tennis
Nonfiction/ Biography

A Different Kind of Baseball
Nonfiction/ Expository

Before He Was Babe
Nonfiction/ Biography

Molly Mackerel McNo
Fiction/ Fantasy

The Ogre's Dinner
Fiction/ Fantasy

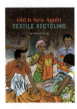

Old Is New Again: Textile Recycling
Hybrid/Expository/ Realistic

Made to Last: Building with Mud
Nonfiction/ Expository

Soap Box Rosie
Fiction/ Historical

Jamal's Prize
Fiction/ Realistic

Harmony Island
Fiction/Realistic

Mirrors on the Mountain
Nonfiction/Narrative

The Truth About Super Strength
Nonfiction/ Expository

Inside the World of Medical Robots
Nonfiction/ Expository

A Fungus Among Us
Fiction/Science Fiction

Trouble at Space Station 6
Fiction/Science Fiction

Once Upon a Time Machine
Fiction/Science Fiction

Drones and Whales: Collecting Snot at Sea
Nonfiction/ Expository

The Great Pacific Garbage Patch
Nonfiction/ Expository

Potato Travels
Nonfiction/ Procedural

Book Sequence: Level S (continued)

For an in-depth description of the characteristics of Level S texts, refer to *The Fountas & Pinnell Literacy Continuum* pages 540–549.

Big Wheel, Big Worries
Nonfiction/
Narrative

Ban All Cars!
Nonfiction/
Persuasive

Wiping Woes: The History of Toilet Paper
Nonfiction/
Narrative

Books, Beasts, and Blood: The Mystery of the Teacher's Pet
Fiction/Realistic
(Humorous)

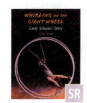

Whirling on the Giant Wheel: Carly Schuna's Story
Nonfiction/
Biography

Wise Folk: A Book of Tales
Fiction/Folktales
(Short Stories)

Book Sequence: Level T

For an in-depth description of the characteristics of Level T texts, refer to *The Fountas & Pinnell Literacy Continuum* pages 550–559.

Emmanuel Yeboah's Incredible Ride
Nonfiction/
Biography

Alone on the Ocean
Nonfiction/
Narrative

DJ Focus
Nonfiction/
Biography

Reach for the Stars: The Story of the Three-Year Swim Club
Nonfiction/
Narrative

Duke Kahanamoku and the Secret History of Surfing
Nonfiction/
Biography

Jason to the Rescue
Nonfiction/
Narrative

Get Cooking
Fiction/
Realistic
(Humorous)

Grandfather's Gamelan
Fiction/Realistic

Meet the Moviemakers
Nonfiction/
Expository

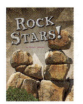

Rock Stars!
Nonfiction/
Expository

Book Sequence: Level T (continued)

For an in-depth description of the characteristics of Level T texts, refer to *The Fountas & Pinnell Literacy Continuum* pages 550–559.

Rockslide
Fiction/
Realistic

Knights on Ice
Fiction/
Realistic

Shorty
Fiction/
Realistic

Stand Tall
Fiction/
Realistic

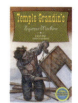

Temple Grandin's Squeeze Machine
Nonfiction/
Biography

Star Power: The Story of Annie Jump Cannon
Nonfiction/Biography

Suiting Up for Space
Nonfiction/
Expository

Mission: Earth
Fiction/Science Fiction

Asha and the Jewel Thief
Fiction/
Realistic
(Mystery)

Fergal's Tale
Fiction/
Historical

Wanted: Flesh-Eating Beetles
Nonfiction/
Expository

Book Sequence: Level U

For an in-depth description of the characteristics of Level U texts, refer to *The Fountas & Pinnell Literacy Continuum* pages 560–569.

Making a Forest
Nonfiction/
Expository

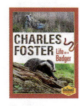

Charles Foster: Life as a Badger
Nonfiction/
Narrative

Stunt Camp
Fiction/
Realistic

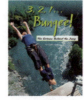

3, 2, 1 . . . Bungee! The Science Behind the Jump
Nonfiction/
Expository

Living on the Edge
Nonfiction/
Expository

Book Sequence: Level U

For an in-depth description of the characteristics of Level U texts, refer to *The Fountas & Pinnell Literacy Continuum* pages 560–569.

The Reluctant Brownie
Fiction/Realistic

Temptation
Fiction/Realistic

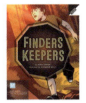

Finders Keepers
Fiction/Realistic

Floodwaters
Fiction/Realistic

The Boy Who Lived with Bears: A Native American Tale
Fiction/Folktale

Magic at the Castle: A Club for Young Magicians
Nonfiction/Biography

The Science of Sleep
Nonfiction/Expository

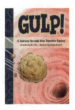

GULP! A Journey Through Your Digestive System
Nonfiction/Expository

Flush!
Nonfiction/Expository

Bored in Space
Fiction/Science Fiction

Miniature Margaret
Fiction/Fantasy

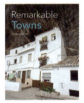

Remarkable Towns
Nonfiction/Expository

Underwater Art
Nonfiction/Narrative

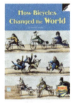

How Bicycles Changed the World
Nonfiction/Expository

Young Bike Racers
Nonfiction/Expository

Rising from the Desert: Building the Burj Khalifa
Nonfiction/Narrative

Durbin's Quest
Fiction/Fairy Tale

Book Sequence: Level V

For an in-depth description of the characteristics of Level V texts, refer to *The Fountas & Pinnell Literacy Continuum* pages 570–581.

The Apothecary's Apprentice
Fiction/Fantasy

Danger Zone
Fiction/Realistic

Taking Cover
Fiction/
Realistic

A Night on Mount Entoto: A Folktale from Africa
Fiction/Folktale

Safe Haven for Raptors
Nonfiction/
Expository

Silent Skies: When the Plane People Came
Nonfiction/
Narrative

The Drowning of Villa Epecuén
Nonfiction/
Narrative

A Laughing Matter
Nonfiction/
Expository

The Treasure of Timbuktu
Nonfiction/
Narrative

Zooming to Zaragon
Fiction/Science Fiction

Marooned on JaSama
Fiction/
Science Fiction

From Heroes to Zeros: Outrageous Sports Cheaters
Nonfiction/
Expository

Reading the Sun
Nonfiction/
Expository

Reading the Wind
Nonfiction/
Expository

Outrageous Outfits: History's Most Extreme Fashions
Nonfiction/
Expository

Optical Illusions: Games for Your Brain
Nonfiction/
Expository

Instructional Design for Guided Reading

FOUNTAS & PINNELL CLASSROOM includes four-page Lesson Folders for each guided reading title. Figure GR 3 A–D provides an overview of the features and instructional support that you can utilize as you plan and conduct a guided reading lesson.

Materials you will need to prepare for and conduct the lesson. Most are included with *Fountas & Pinnell Classroom*, as well as a few common items available at most schools.

You Will Need

- *Drones and Whales: Collecting Snot at Sea*, Level S

Visit **resources.fountasandpinnell.com** to download online resources to support this lesson, including:
- Words: *closet, famous, given, motor, pilot, promise*
- Recording Form

Book	*Drones and Whales: Collecting Snot at Sea*
Level	S
Author	Laura Johnson
Genre	Nonfiction/Expository
Series	The Future Is Here Series

Book Information includes the title, level, author, illustrator, genre, and whether the book is paired with another book or is part of a series.

 ## Goals

Think about the readers and the behaviors and understandings to notice, teach for, and support at Level S in *The Fountas & Pinnell Literacy Continuum*. Select goals that match the needs of your students. The following may be appropriate.

Reading
- Use organizational tools to search for information (table of contents, headings, sidebars).
- Solve multisyllable words by taking them apart using syllables.
- Read with all dimensions of fluency.
- Derive the meanings of new words and expand meanings of known words using context in a sentence (*snot, launched*).

- Understand and acquire content-specific words that require the use of the glossary (*bow, blubber*).
- Understand that the information and ideas in a text are related to each other and notice how the writer presents this.
- Recognize a writer's use of underlying text structures (description, question and answer, problem and solution).

- Infer the writer's message—new technologies make the collecting of scientific data more effective and safer for those involved.

Word Work
- Break apart words with open and closed syllables.

Writing About Reading
- Reflect both prior knowledge and new knowledge from the text.

Goals for the lesson are organized into three categories. Choose or modify goals from each category to match the learning needs of a small group of readers.

Analysis of Book Characteristics *Drones and Whales: Collecting Snot at Sea*, Level S

How The Book Works This series book describes how scientists use drones to safely collect whale snot in order to study and protect whales. The book includes a table of contents, headings, sidebars, photographs, captions, a map, and a glossary. It concludes with an interview.

Genre/Form
- Nonfiction
- Expository
- Series book

Text Structure
- Divided into sections
- Underlying structures (description, narrative, problem and solution, question and answer)
- Embedded interview

Content
- New content that will engage and interest readers and expand knowledge (adventures in science)
- Content that goes beyond students' immediate experience (gathering whale snot)

Themes and Ideas
- Deeper meaning applicable to important human problems (Studying wildlife helps us understand our world, but can be dangerous for scientists and unkind to animals. New technologies are helping to solve this problem.)

Language and Literary Features
- Descriptive language (Mountains tower above the sea along the wild coast of Alaska.)

Sentence Complexity
- Some longer sentences with more than twenty words and many embedded phrases and clauses
- Use of parenthetical material embedded in sentences (This makes it difficult for predators—and scientists—to see the animals.)

Vocabulary
- Many words that appear in the vocabulary of mature language users (hovers, mixture, examine)
- Many words particular to a discipline (drone, blowhole, biologists)

Words
- Many multisyllable words, some technical or scientific (scientists, information, kilometers)

Illustrations
- Variety of layout in illustrations (photographs) and print
- More than one kind of graphic on a page spread

Book and Print Features
- Print placed in sidebars and graphics that provide important information
- Full range of punctuation

Summary of the book and detailed **analysis** of its characteristics

1

FIGURE GR 3 A *An example of a Guided Reading lesson*

Guided Reading — GR

One suggestion for **introducing the text** helps you provide just enough support and information to allow readers to engage successfully with the text, while also building students' vocabulary and content knowledge.

Key Principle of Responsive Teaching

Each lesson provides suggestions for prompting students, but it is *your* observation of what the students can do and need to learn that will guide your minute-by-minute decision making. Observe a student's processing without interruption unless he is in a muddle and/or meaning is lost. After the reading, you may draw the student's attention to parts of the text that he has overlooked or misread.

Students **read the text** in a soft voice while you listen. The suggested prompts may help you interact with students in a responsive manner during their reading.

Supporting English Learners

Support students' understanding of concepts and vocabulary.

- Make sure students understand the labels of text features, such as captions and sidebars, and can find them.
- As needed, help students understand unfamiliar vocabulary, such as *snot, surface, breathe, operated, goo, request, underwater, force, tinker, engineer, disturb, predators,* and *seacoast.*

Prompting Guide, Part 1
Refer to pages 12 and 20 as needed

Supporting English Learners

Help individual students problem solve as needed.

- If a student is unable to pronounce a word and asks for help, demonstrate how to say the word and encourage the student to continue to read. Prompt with *This is how it would sound in English: ___. Say it like I do and continue to read.*

Introducing the Text

Consider the strengths and needs of your readers and the demands of the text as you craft the introduction. The following bulleted items provide an example of one way to introduce the book. The introduction should be interactive and should allow time for students to respond (indicated by ●).

- *This book is titled* Drones and Whales: Collecting Snot at Sea *by Laura Johnson.* Have students read the back cover. *What are you thinking?* ● Ask students to briefly share something they know about drones or whales.

- *Turn to pages 2 and 3 and read the heading and the sidebar.* ● *What is snot?* ● *It looks like the writer wants you to understand the importance of snot in this book.*

- *Look at pages 6 and 7 and read the heading.* ● *What do you think a SnotBot might be?* ● You might mention the word *robot* if students do not make the connection. Have students find the bold words *bow* and *blubber* on page 6. *Words in bold are defined in the glossary on page 16.* If needed, have students quickly find the definitions for *bow* and *blubber* in the glossary.

- Draw students' attention to the photograph and caption on page 6. *The caption gives information about the picture and explains how the bow works. Pay attention to the captions. They will help you understand ideas in the book.*

- *Turn to page 8 and read the first sentence.* ● *Iain Kerr is the scientist who designed the SnotBot. You can use the pronunciation guide in parentheses to help you say his name.*

- *Now, read the first sentence in the fourth paragraph on page 8.* ● *Find the word* launched. ● *The writer includes a clue that helps you understand the meaning of* launched. *What does* launched *mean?* ● *As you read, look for clues like this to help you figure out the meanings of new words.*

- *Turn to pages 12 and 13. The heading says, "Not Just for Whale Snot." I'm thinking that scientists might have other purposes for drones. What do you think?* ● *Be sure to notice the map on page 13 and think about why the writer included it.*

- *Turn to pages 14 and 15—and turn your book!* ● *What happens in an interview?* ● *What do the letters Q and A stand for?* ● Clarify, if needed.

- *Turn back to the beginning and read to find out why biologists use drones to collect whale snot. As you read, think about how new technologies like drones help both scientists and animals.*

Reading the Text

Students will be reading silently, but you may want to sample the oral reading of a particular student or students.

- To help a student solve multisyllable words by taking them apart using syllables, prompt with *Do you see a part you know?* Reinforce with *You noticed a part and it helped you.*

- To support reading with all dimensions of fluency, tell the student to make the reading sound smooth and like talking. *Listen to how my reading sounds.* Demonstrate and then prompt with *Listen to yourself. Did it sound smooth?*

FIGURE GR 3 B *An example of a Guided Reading lesson*

Suggested prompts for **discussing and revisiting the text** to guide students to a deeper understanding

Make Personal Connections As you discuss books and present lessons, you will be able to share information and make connections that reflect your own experiences. Students will enjoy discussions and benefit from lessons even more when you add your own personal knowledge.

Discussing and Revisiting the Text

Engage all group members in sharing their responses to the book. Encourage them to listen and respond to each other's thinking during the discussion.

- Invite students to share their thinking about *Drones and Whales: Collecting Snot at Sea*.
- To encourage discussion, you may want to select from the following questions/prompts or refer to *Prompting Guide, Part 2*:
  - *Let's talk about what you learned from reading this book.* Share something you learned when you first read the book and invite students to do the same.
  - *This book is mainly about how new tools are changing the way scientists collect research data about wildlife. But it also gives information about older methods of data collection. Talk about why the writer chose to describe those older methods, too.*
  - *Did you find the interview interesting? Go to pages 14 and 15 and talk about some of the answers. Is there anything else you would ask Dr. Kerr?*
  - Read the inside back cover to students. *Why do you think the writer includes this information?*
  - *Let's look at the table of contents and talk about how the writer has organized the information in this book. The writer grouped similar types of information in each section. Choose one and talk with a partner about what you found in that section.*
  - *Is this book nonfiction? The genre of this book is expository nonfiction. What does the writer want you to know about scientists and their research?*
- Continue the discussion, guiding students toward the key understandings and the main messages of the text. Some key understandings students may express:

Prompting Guide, Part 2
Refer to pages 35, 36, and 39 as needed

Supporting English Learners
Support students' discussion of the text.
- Provide oral sentence frames for students (e.g., *From this book, I learned that ___. New tools can be better than the old tools because ___. I do/do not think the interview is interesting because ___.*).

Drones and Whales: Collecting Snot at Sea Level S

Thinking *Within* the Text
- Scientists have developed a drone called the SnotBot to safely study whales.
- Scientists gather snot from whales to learn more about how whales get sick and if they are stressed.
- Scientists also use drones to study other hard-to-reach animals, such as leopard seals.
- Dr. Iain Kerr, a biologist, got the idea for the SnotBot while on a family boat trip.

Thinking *Beyond* the Text
- Scientists do not want to harm the animals they study, and they do not want to be injured themselves.
- Technology allows scientists greater access to wildlife.
- As technology improves, so will scientists' abilities to conduct research.
- Sometimes, unexpected events inspire great ideas, such as the SnotBot.

Thinking *About* the Text
- The writer uses a variety of organizational tools to present information, including a table of contents, headings, sidebars, and a glossary.
- There are many highly descriptive passages that make the book interesting.
- Photographs, captions, and a map support ideas in the text.
- The book is expository nonfiction. It presents information about a topic.

MESSAGES New technologies make the collecting of scientific data more effective and safer for both animals and researchers. People invent machines to help with work that they want or need to do.

Key understandings from the text guide discussion and offer opportunities to reinforce and revisit new vocabulary and concepts as well as deepen understanding of the text.

Teaching Point

Select a teaching point that will be most helpful to your group of readers. If it's appropriate, use the suggestion below, which supports thinking about the text.

Analyzing: Text Structure

- *Writers organize and present information in many different ways. Often, one book will have several different kinds of organization, or structure.*
- *In this book, the writer presents information mainly through description. You'll find an example in the first paragraph on page 2. Reread the paragraph.* ● *What details does the writer include to help you picture the scene?*
- *Now, reread the sidebar on page 3.* ● *Notice the sidebar's title.* ● *How is this information organized?* ● *This is a question-and-answer structure.*
- Have students look more closely at pages 6 and 8. Then, invite them to talk about how this information is organized (problem and solution).

Prompting Guide, Part 1
Refer to page 12 as needed

Prompting Guide, Part 2
Refer to page 39 as needed

Messages help you guide students to an understanding of the book's big ideas or themes.

Possible **teaching points** are provided, which you can tailor, as appropriate, based on your observations of students' reading and their talk about the text.

3

FIGURE GR 3 C *An example of a Guided Reading lesson*

Suggestions for modifying or scaffolding instruction to **support English learners** in processing the text and benefiting from the teaching

Word Work provides hands-on activities that help students develop flexible word-solving skills and automaticity in decoding and processing text.

Supporting English Learners
Support students' word work.

- Say each word slowly so students can hear the syllables and vowel sounds.
- Pair students who know more English with English learners to say the words, divide them into syllables, and group them.
- Make sure students understand the meaning of each word used in Word Work.

Word Work

Help the readers become more flexible with open and closed syllables.

Break Apart Words with Open and Closed Syllables

- On the whiteboard, write the words *manage* and *travel* in one column and *ocean* and *mucus* in a second column. Use any word students may not understand in a sentence.

- Say and tap each word with me. ● As they tap, draw a slash to show where each word is divided [man/age, trav/el, o/cean, mu/cus].

- What do you notice about both words in the first column? ● *The first syllable in each word ends with a consonant and the vowel sound is short. This is called a closed syllable. The word is broken after the consonant.*

- What do you notice about both words in the second column? ● *The first syllable in each word ends with a vowel and the vowel sound is long. This is called an open syllable. The word is broken after the vowel.*

- If time permits, give partners the following set of words: *closet, famous, given, motor, pilot, promise.* Have partners take turns reading a word, tapping the parts, and drawing a slash to divide the word into syllables. Then, have them sort the words into two groups, words with closed syllables and words with open syllables.

Optional **writing about reading** suggestions include shared or independent writing activities. Rather than requiring writing after every book, encourage students to record their thinking in a reader's notebook when a specific text evokes a lot of interest and conversation.

Supporting English Learners
Support students' language development through independent writing.

- Make sure students understand the concept of drones.
- Provide oral sentence frames for students to discuss (e.g., *I knew that whales ___, but I didn't know that whales ___. I learned ___.*).
- Have partners use the oral sentence frames to write details in each chart column.

 ## Writing About Reading (Optional)

If you choose to have the students write about what they have read, the following is an option.

Independent Writing: Two-Column Chart

- Have students discuss what they knew about drones and whales before reading the book. Then, invite them to talk about new information they learned.

- Help students reflect on prior knowledge and new knowledge by creating a chart in the *Reader's Notebook.* Direct them to set up a two-column chart with the headings *What I Knew* and *What I Learned.* Have them complete the chart with information about drones and whales. Students may want to revisit the book to check details.

- When students finish, have them reread their writing to make sure it clearly states their ideas.

What I Knew	What I Learned
Drones are operated by remote control.	Drones can collect whale snot.
Drones have cameras.	Drones are used to study animals all over the world, even in Antarctica.
Whales swim to the surface to breathe air.	Stress can make whales sick and even kill them.
Whales blow water and air out of a blowhole.	Different kinds of whales have spouts that are different shapes.

Specific guidance for **observing behaviors and understandings** as you assess students' learning

For a detailed description of coding, scoring, and analyzing reading records, see *Guided Reading: Responsive Teaching Across the Grades,* Chapter 11.

Prompting Guide, Part 1
Refer to page 12 as needed

GR0828

Assessment

Refer to the goals stated on page 1 of this lesson guide and make notes of behavioral evidence, demonstrating that these goals were achieved.

- Refer to Level S in *The Fountas & Pinnell Literacy Continuum* and note the behaviors and understandings the readers control or need to control. Make notes about what the readers learned how to do and what they need to learn how to do next.

- Use the Recording Form to take a reading record and assess an individual's processing on yesterday's new book. You may want to select a student before or after the lesson, or at some other point in the day, to code the record. After coding the reading, select an immediate teaching point that will be helpful to the particular reader.

4

FIGURE GR 3 D *An example of a Guided Reading lesson*

Putting Guided Reading into Action

GUIDED READING IS A highly effective form of small-group instruction. Students gain confidence and problem-solving experience by reading a text that is neither too easy, nor too hard. As you put this instructional context into action in your classroom, the following practices, tools, and language may be helpful.

Forming Groups for Guided Reading

Guided reading groups are formed from a detailed analysis of what individual students in your class know and can do as readers. We recommend that you use reading records in the *Fountas & Pinnell Benchmark Assessment System* or another text-level-assessment tool to observe, record, and analyze the specific reading behaviors students are using as they read and to determine the level at which to start teaching.

You will form approximately four guided reading groups for your classroom. Review the text level assessments you have completed, and form groups of students who have similar reading behaviors and are reading instructionally at about the same level.

Based on the reading behaviors you have observed and noted in your assessments, identify some teaching goals for each guided reading group. Consult *The Fountas & Pinnell Literacy Continuum* guided reading section for specific teaching goals. Your goals will change as you observe the learning that takes place in the students. You may also consult the *Fountas & Pinnell Prompting Guide* for specific language to teach, prompt for, and reinforce with students.

Example schedule for meeting with four guided reading groups each day

Monday	Tuesday	Wednesday	Thursday	Friday
Group A	Group D	Group C	Group B	Group A
Group B	Group A	Group D	Group C	Group B
Group C	Group B	Group A	Group D	Group C
Group D	Group C	Group B	Group A	Group D

You may not have time to meet with each guided reading group every day. We recommend that you meet every day with the groups of students who are experiencing the most difficulty in learning to process text. You can rotate the other groups so that you meet with them every other day. You may wish to create a weekly schedule for yourself.

Example schedule for meeting with three out of four guided reading groups each day

Monday	Tuesday	Wednesday	Thursday	Friday
Group A	Group C	Group D	Group A	Group B
Group B	Group A	Group B	Group C	Group A
Group C	Group D	Group A	Group B	Group D

Fountas & Pinnell Online Resources

The Online Resources site is a repository of resources for guided reading that includes:

▶ helpful videos
▶ printable resources, such as lessons, recording forms, and word cards
▶ other resources referenced in the "You Will Need" section of each lesson

Access to this site is included with the purchase of your *Fountas & Pinnell Classroom*™ product. To access this site, refer to the instructions on the inside front cover of your *Guided Reading Collection Guide.*

Steps in the Guided Reading Process

1. Know your readers and form groups.

2. Select and analyze a text to use with each group.

3. Introduce the text to the group.

4. Students read the text.

5. Students discuss the text.

6. Make one or two teaching points that students can apply not only to this text but to other texts they read.

7. Students engage in a short Word Work activity.

8. Extend understanding through writing (optional).

9. Reflect on the lesson, and plan the following lesson.

Sharing Guided Reading Texts Among Several Classrooms

You may be sharing the guided reading texts with a team of fellow teachers. If so, consider the following tips and ideas for coordinating the use of the texts and accompanying lessons.

▶ Meet before the school year begins to create a plan for sharing the books and lessons.

▶ Store books in an area that is easily accessible to all teachers who are sharing them. You may wish to create a book room for your school (Figure GR 4). A book room houses a wide range of leveled books from Levels A through Z that you share with your team. Books and accompanying lessons are stored together in bags and organized in bins by level.

▶ You may wish to create a simple check-out system for keeping track of which classroom is using which titles.

For detailed advice on how to create and use a school bookroom, see *Guided Reading: Responsive Teaching Across the Grades* or *Leveled Books, K–8: Matching Texts to Readers for Effective Teaching.*

FIGURE GR 4 *A school book room*

Readers' Theater

To help students develop fluency with increasingly complex texts, some titles include a Readers' Theater script. You may wish to have students practice reading from the script several times in their small group and then "perform" their reading for the whole class. These short, enjoyable performances allow students to

▶ develop ease and familiarity with new vocabulary and language structures,

▶ practice reading expressively for an authentic purpose, and

▶ self-assess their own reading performance.

For more information on using readers' theater scripts from the Fountas & Pinnell Guided Reading Collection, please see page 91 in the Shared and Performance Reading section of the *Fountas & Pinnell Classroom™ System Guide.*

Assessment

ONCE YOU BEGIN GUIDED reading groups with students in your classroom, we recommend administering a reading record (also called a running record) for each student at least once or twice a month. A Recording Form for each guided reading book in *Fountas & Pinnell Classroom* can be downloaded from Online Resources. Figure GR 5 A–C provides an overview of the features and support that you can utilize as you administer the reading record.

After each guided reading lesson, we recommend selecting one student and administering a reading record of the **text read on the previous day.** Students who are gaining control of literacy concepts at a slower pace will need more frequent monitoring through the use of more frequent records, possibly as often as once a week. This ongoing data will help you monitor students' progress as well as inform your instruction.

The **text of a guided reading book** is reprinted, page by page, or excerpted on the form so that you can accurately code a student's reading behaviors. Remember that your goal is to observe without intervening.

The columns allow you to efficiently record the **sources of information** that influence a student's error (E) or that are used by the student in making a self-correction (SC). For detailed information on recording and analyzing meaning (M), structure (S), and visual information (V) used by a student while reading, see *Guided Reading: Responsive Teaching Across the Grades*, Chapter 11.

FOUNTAS & PINNELL CLASSROOM, GUIDED READING · *Drones and Whales: Collecting Snot at Sea* · LEVEL S · NONFICTION

Student _____   Grade _____ Date _____

Teacher _____   School _____

Recording Form

Part One: Oral Reading

Summary of Scores:	
Accuracy	_____
Self-correction	_____
Fluency	_____
Comprehension	_____

Excerpt is taken from pages 2 through 4, paragraph 1.
Place the book in front of the student. Read the introduction provided and invite the student to read the excerpt to you.
Introduction: Read this part of the book about scientists' use of drones to study whale snot.

Sources of Information Used

Page	Start Time ____ min. ____ sec.		E	SC	E			SC		
		Drones and Whales: Collecting Snot at Sea Level S, RW: 246			M	S	V	M	S	V
2	SNOT, WHALES, AND DRONES Mountains tower above the sea along the wild coast of Alaska. Today the surface of the sea is smooth—until an 80-ton (73-metric- ton) whale suddenly bursts out of the water. As soon as the whale appears, a small flying robot, called a **drone**, speeds toward it. The drone **hovers**, or hangs in the air, about 12 feet (3.7 meters) above an opening called a **blowhole** on the top of the whale's head. The drone waits for the whale to breathe through its blowhole. Each time the									
		Subtotal								

Fountas & Pinnell Classroom, Guided Reading   1

FIGURE GR 5 A *An example of a guided reading Recording Form*

The **accuracy rate** chart is specific to the guided reading book and helps you quickly determine the percent of total words that a student read correctly. The accuracy rate, along with the comprehension information, can help you group readers effectively.

In determining the number of self-corrections, you may wish to use the Fountas & Pinnell Calculator/Stopwatch. This valuable tool also automates the calculation of accuracy rate and doubles as a stopwatch to calculate reading rate, or words per minute (WPM). Keep in mind that speed may vary according to the reader's purpose and the features of the text.

When the student finishes reading orally, you may wish to use the rubric to assign a **fluency score.** This information will be useful in selecting emphases for teaching.

FOUNTAS & PINNELL CLASSROOM, GUIDED READING · *Drones and Whales: Collecting Snot at Sea* · LEVEL S · NONFICTION

Accuracy Rate	Errors	14 or more	12–13	9–11	7–8	4–6	2–3	0–1
	%	below 95%	95%	96%	97%	98%	99%	100%

Self-Corrections _____

Fluency Score   0   1   2   3

Fluency Scoring Key

0   Reads primarily word-by-word with occasional but infrequent or inappropriate phrasing; no smooth or expressive interpretation, irregular pausing, and no attention to author's meaning or punctuation; no stress or inappropriate stress, and slow rate.

1   Reads primarily in two-word phrases with some three- and four-word groups and some word-by-word reading; almost no smooth, expressive interpretation or pausing guided by author's meaning and punctuation; almost no stress or inappropriate stress, with slow rate most of the time.

2   Reads primarily in three- or four-word phrase groups; some smooth, expressive interpretation and pausing guided by author's meaning and punctuation; mostly appropriate stress and rate with some slowdowns.

3   Reads primarily in larger, meaningful phrases or word groups; mostly smooth, expressive interpretation and pausing guided by author's meaning and punctuation; appropriate stress and rate with only a few slowdowns.

Reading Rate *(optional)*

End Time   ____ min. ____ sec.

Start Time   ____ min. ____ sec.

Total Time   ____ min. ____ sec.

Total Seconds _____

(14,760) ÷ Total Seconds = Words Per Minute (WPM)

_____ WPM

FIGURE GR 5 B *An example of a guided reading Recording Form*

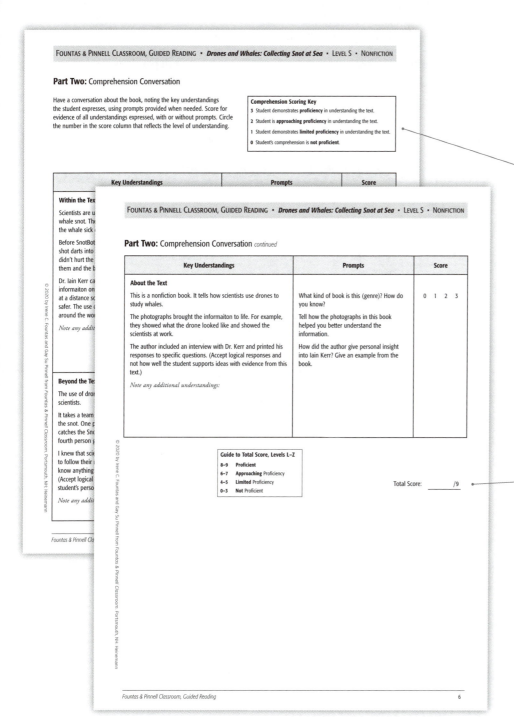

FOUNTAS & PINNELL CLASSROOM, GUIDED READING • *Drones and Whales: Collecting Snot at Sea* • LEVEL S • NONFICTION

Part Two: Comprehension Conversation

Have a conversation about the book, noting the key understandings the student expresses, using prompts provided when needed. Score for evidence of all understandings expressed, with or without prompts. Circle the number in the score column that reflects the level of understanding.

Comprehension Scoring Key

3 Student demonstrates **proficiency** in understanding the text.

2 Student is **approaching proficiency** in understanding the text.

1 Student demonstrates **limited proficiency** in understanding the text.

0 Student's comprehension is **not proficient**.

Key Understandings	Prompts	Score

Within the Tex...

Scientists are u...
whale snot. Th...
the whale sick ...

Before SnotBot...
shot darts into...
didn't hurt the...
them and the b...

Dr. Iain Kerr ca...
informaiton on...
at a distance so...
safer. The use o...
around the wor...

Note any additi...

Beyond the Te...

The use of dro...
scientists.

It takes a team ...
the snot. One p...
catches the Sno...
fourth person g...

I knew that scie...
to follow their ...
know anything ...
(Accept logical ...
student's perso...

Note any addi...

Fountas & Pinnell Cla...

© 2020 by Irene C. Fountas and Gay Su Pinnell from Fountas & Pinnell Classroom, Portsmouth, NH: Heinemann

---

FOUNTAS & PINNELL CLASSROOM, GUIDED READING • *Drones and Whales: Collecting Snot at Sea* • LEVEL S • NONFICTION

Part Two: Comprehension Conversation *continued*

Key Understandings	Prompts	Score
About the Text This is a nonfiction book. It tells how scientists use drones to study whales. The photographs brought the informaiton to life. For example, they showed what the drone looked like and showed the scientists at work. The author included an interview with Dr. Kerr and printed his responses to specific questions. (Accept logical responses and not how well the student supports ideas with evidence from this text.) *Note any additional understandings:*	What kind of book is this (genre)? How do you know? Tell how the photographs in this book helped you better understand the information. How did the author give personal insight into Iain Kerr? Give an example from the book.	0 1 2 3

Guide to Total Score, Levels L–Z

8–9	**Proficient**
6–7	**Approaching** Proficiency
4–5	**Limited** Proficiency
0–3	**Not** Proficient

Total Score: _____ /9

© 2020 by Irene C. Fountas and Gay Su Pinnell from Fountas & Pinnell Classroom, Portsmouth, NH: Heinemann

Fountas & Pinnell Classroom, Guided Reading   6

FIGURE GR 5 C *An example of a guided reading Recording Form*

Once the student has completed the oral reading, have a **brief conversation** with the student about the book. You will be noticing evidence of understanding within, beyond, and about the text.

Once you have calculated a total score for comprehension, record all of the scores in the Summary of Scores box on page 1 of the Recording Form. See the information on the next page to determine a recommended placement level.

Determining Recommended Placement Level

One goal of a reading record is to determine a student's independent, instructional, and hard reading levels. Figure GR 6 helps you analyze a student's accuracy rate and comprehension score to identify a level. Most of the time, the instructional level is the same as the recommended placement level, but when you analyze a student's reading behaviors, you may draw a different conclusion.

Finding the Three Levels, L–Z

Benchmark Criteria for Levels L–Z	Comprehension			
Accuracy	Proficient 8–9	Approaching Proficiency 6–7	Limited Proficiency 4–5	Not Proficient 0–3
98–100%	Independent	Independent	Instructional	Hard
95–97%	Instructional	Instructional	Hard	Hard
Below 95%	Hard	Hard	Hard	Hard

FIGURE GR 6 *Finding the Three Levels, L–Z*

Record Keeping Form

To help you organize and keep track of observations that you make during guided reading, a downloadable Guided Reading Record Keeping Form is available in Online Resources (Figure GR 7).

FIGURE GR 7 *Guided Reading Record Keeping Form*

Resources

LEARN MORE ABOUT GUIDED reading in the following resources:

Guided Reading: Responsive Teaching Across the Grades, Chapters 5, 6, 8, 13, 14 and Section 4

Teaching for Comprehending and Fluency, Chapters 2–5, 12, 24–26

The Fountas & Pinnell Literacy Continuum, pages 496–570

On-Demand Mini-Courses at **fountasandpinnell.com/professionaldevelopment**:

> ▶ *The F&P Text Level Gradient™: Using Fountas & Pinnell Resources to Match Books to Readers*
> ▶ *Introducing Texts Effectively in Guided Reading Lessons*

Digital Assessment Tools

Updated to support the *Fountas & Pinnell Classroom* Guided Reading instructional context, these tools will be helpful as you record and analyze student learning data:

▶ The Fountas & Pinnell Online Data Management System (ODMS) is a web-based, password-protected tool that provides robust support for teachers and administrators in monitoring progress over time.

▶ The *Fountas & Pinnell Reading Record iPad® App,* available through the Apple iTunes store, provides all recording forms digitally, saves individual records as PDFs, times the conference, calculates oral reading fluency, and syncs data to ODMS.

▶ The *Fountas & Pinnell Reading Record iPad® App* is also available as an institutional purchase. For details, visit **www.fountasandpinnell.com/apps/**

Independent Reading

THE READERS IN YOUR classroom need extensive opportunities to engage in choice, independent reading. This context offers students the chance to read, enjoy, and talk about self-selected texts. During independent reading, students have full control of the reading process, although you support them by offering a rich, well-organized collection of books through which they can browse and select titles that appeal to them and you confer with them regularly on an individual basis.

Your classroom collection offers engaging texts of varying genres and levels of complexity so that all students will be able to find a book they can and want to read. A key factor in independent reading is choice. Students do not select books by level for independent reading but, rather, according to their personal interests.

Independent reading is an instructional context that is nested within an instructional framework of minilessons, conferring, and sharing. Students are given opportunities throughout the day to share their thinking about books with other students through discussion and writing about reading. During independent reading, students also practice applying to their own reading what they have learned through minilessons. You are encouraged to have brief conferences with students as they are reading. Through an individual conference, you can observe students' understanding of the text as well as support their thinking and help them extend their understandings.

FIGURE IR 1 *A fourth grader reads a self-selected text independently.*

At a Glance

During independent reading, students read books of their choosing. Minilessons, brief conferences, and opportunities to share ideas support students' learning.

- Individual teaching
- Texts are generally at a student's independent reading level; may include revisiting texts that have been read aloud
- Students share their thinking through discussion and writing
- Teaching occurs in brief conferences that support students' thinking
- Listen briefly to students' oral reading as needed and prompt for strategic actions.

Get to Know Students' Reading Interests

During the first weeks of school, you may wish to conduct reading interviews to learn about students' reading attitudes, habits, and interests. Their responses will help you guide students to titles they'll be interested in reading, as well as gauge which reading experiences are appropriate for the whole class and which are more appropriate for a small group or an individual. Find reading interview forms at: **resources .fountasandpinnell.com**

Texts for Independent Reading

The *Fountas & Pinnell Classroom* collection for independent reading includes 200 texts that can be used to begin or expand your classroom library. Each book has been carefully selected to ensure that the collection is appropriate and engaging for fourth graders and represents a diverse range of experiences, topics, perspectives, and cultures. We suggest augmenting your library with *Fountas & Pinnell Select Collections* and other high-quality books such as Caldecott and Newbery Medal and Honor books. For more suggestions on building your library, see page 135.

Supporting Student Choice

Students need to choose the books they want to read. Without genuine choice, students will not experience the full role and authentic pleasure of a reader. At the same time, the ability to choose suitable, rewarding, comprehensible books is not something that you can expect all students to know automatically. You can teach them how to make good choices through book talks, minilessons, and conferences.

- A **book talk** is a brief introduction—a teaser of sorts—to a book. It can pique readers' interest and make them curious to take a closer look at the book. The conferring card for each book in the Independent Reading collection begins with a book talk, which you can tailor to appeal to your class.

- Short **minilessons** on the topic of choosing "just-right" books for independent reading can be valuable for your whole class at the beginning of the year. These minilessons, which are provided for you in *The Reading Minilessons Book,* can help students learn and apply techniques for choosing books, such as reading a little of a book at the beginning and in the middle and then asking themselves, *Am I interested in the topic or the kind of story? Did I understand it? Can I read it smoothly?*

- As students learn to choose books, you can engage individuals in short **conferences**. These brief conversations, between a young reader and an expert reader, help you expand a student's thinking about what makes a "good" book for her and allows you to support the student in learning how to find just such a book among a library of titles.

Independent Reading Collection (alphabetical by title)

Title		Author	Genre
	21st Century: Mysteries of Deep Space	Paris, Stephanie	Nonfiction
	Abby Takes a Stand	McKissack, Patricia C.	Fiction
	Abel's Island	Steig, William	Fiction
	Able to Play: Overcoming Physical Challenges	Stout, Glenn	Nonfiction

Title	Author	Genre
Ada Lovelace and Computer Algorithms	Labrecque, Ellen	Nonfiction
The All-Star Joker	Kelly, David A.	Fiction
Alone in the Arctic: Can Science Save Your Life?	Bailey, Gerry	Nonfiction
Amaterasu: Return of the Sun	Storrie, Paul D.	Fiction
Amazing Women	Jenner, Caryn	Nonfiction
Amazon Rainforest	Rice, William B.	Nonfiction
Amusement Parks: Perimeter and Area	Irving, Dianne	Nonfiction
Anansi and the Box of Stories	Krensky, Steven	Fiction
Ancient China: 305 BC	Slepian, Curtis	Nonfiction
Andy Russell, NOT Wanted by the Police	Adler, David A.	Fiction
Animal Architects	Bradley, Timothy J.	Nonfiction
Animals Helping with Healing	Squire, Ann O.	Nonfiction
Animals Nobody Loves	Simon, Seymour	Nonfiction
Anyone But Me	Krulik, Nancy	Fiction
Are Crop Circles Real?	Lassieur, Allison	Nonfiction

Title	Author	Genre
Around the World	Phelan, Matt	Fiction
The Astro Outlaw	Kelly, David A.	Fiction
Astronomers Through Time	Greathouse, Lisa E.	Nonfiction
At Home in a Coral Reef	Spilsbury, Louise and Richard	Nonfiction
Attack of the Bullfrogs	Shea, Therese	Nonfiction
Bad Kitty School Daze	Bruel, Nick	Fiction
Batcat and the Seven Squirrels	Walters, Eric	Fiction
Beachcombing: Exploring the Seashore	Arnosky, Jim	Nonfiction
Becoming Invisible: From Camouflage to Cloaks	Mooney, Carla	Nonfiction
Before It Wriggles Away	Wong, Janet S.	Nonfiction
Behind the Canvas: An Artist's Life	Apodaca, Blanca, and Serwich, Michael	Nonfiction
Being Teddy Roosevelt	Mills, Claudia	Fiction
Beowulf: Monster Slayer	Storrie, Paul D.	Fiction
The BFG	Dahl, Roald	Fiction
Big Fantastic Earth	Green, Jen	Nonfiction

Title	Author	Genre
Bizarre Animals	Bradley, Timothy	Nonfiction
Blackberries in the Dark	Jukes, Mavis	Fiction
Blazing Courage	Milner Halls, Kelly	Fiction
The Blue Hill Meadows	Rylant, Cynthia	Fiction
The Boy of a Thousand Faces	Selznick, Brian	Fiction
Boys Against Girls	Naylor, Phyllis Reynolds	Fiction
Bug Builders	Bradley, Timothy	Nonfiction
Building an Igloo	Steltzer, Ulli	Nonfiction
Buildings in Disguise	Arbogast, Joan Marie	Nonfiction
Bunnicula Meets Edgar Allan Crow	Howe, James	Fiction
Button Down	Ylvisaker, Anne	Fiction
Button Hill	Bradford, Michael	Fiction
Capybaras After Dark	Niver, Heather M. Moore	Nonfiction
Cat and Mouse in a Haunted House	Stilton, Geronimo	Fiction
Charlie Bumpers vs. The Perfect Little Turkey	Harley, Bill	Fiction

Title	Author	Genre
China: Land of the Emperor's Great Wall	Osborne, Mary Pope	Nonfiction
Chocolate Fever	Smith, Robert Kimmel	Fiction
Clara Barton: Angel of the Battlefield	Hollingsworth, Tamara	Nonfiction
Cliques, Phonies, & Other Baloney	Romain, Trevor	Nonfiction
Could We Survive on Other Planets?	Wood, Alix	Nonfiction
Coyotes	Gagne, Tammy	Nonfiction
The Curtain Went Up, My Pants Fell Down	Winkler, Henry, and Oliver, Lin	Fiction
Dancing Bees and Other Amazing Communicators	Lindeen, Mary	Nonfiction
A Day at Work with a Chemist	Gaddi, Rosalie	Nonfiction
A Day at Work with a Geologist	Letts, Amelia	Nonfiction
Detecting Floods	Ventura, Marne	Nonfiction
Detecting Hurricanes	Bell, Samantha S.	Nonfiction
Detecting Tornadoes	Ventura, Marne	Nonfiction
Dewey the Library Cat: A True Story	Myron, Vicki, and Witter, Bret	Nonfiction
Dirt Bikes	Lanier, Wendy Hinote	Nonfiction

Title	Author	Genre
Discovering New Planets	Jemison, Dr. Mae, and Rau, Dana Meachen	Nonfiction
Dolphins and Sharks	Osborne, Mary Pope, and Boyce, Natalie Pope	Nonfiction
Don't Know Much About the Solar System	Davis, Kenneth C.	Nonfiction
Dragon Rider	Funke, Cornelia	Fiction
Drita: My Homegirl	Lombard, Jenny	Fiction
Dude, Where's My Spaceship?	Greenburg, Dan	Fiction
Dumpling Days	Lin, Grace	Fiction
Earthquake in the Early Morning	Pope Osborne, Mary	Fiction
Edmund Hillary Reaches the Top of Everest	Yomtov, Nel	Nonfiction
Election Madness	English, Karen	Fiction
Elephant Orphans	Hibbert, Clare	Nonfiction
Engineering: Feats & Failures	Paris, Stephanie	Nonfiction
Ereth's Birthday	Avi	Fiction
Everything for a Dog	Martin, Ann M.	Fiction
The Extraordinary Education of Nicholas Benedict	Stewart, Trenton Lee	Fiction

Title	Author	Genre
Fame and Glory in Freedom, Georgia	O'Connor, Barbara	Fiction
Families Through Time	Dustman, Jeanne	Nonfiction
Fearless! Stunt People	Cohn, Jessica	Nonfiction
Fishers: Then and Now	Zamosky, Lisa	Nonfiction
Footprints on the Moon	Siy, Alexandra	Nonfiction
Fractions = Trouble	Mills, Claudia	Fiction
Framed	Korman, Gordon	Fiction
From Russia with Lunch	Hale, Bruce	Fiction
Full Court Pressure	Gunderson, Jessica	Fiction
Ghosts	Osborne, Mary Pope, and Boyce, Natalie Pope	Nonfiction
Gloria's Way	Cameron, Ann	Fiction
Going Home: The Mystery of Animal Migration	Berkes, Marianne	Nonfiction
A Grain of Rice	Pittman, Helena Clare	Fiction
Great White Sharks	Markle, Sandra	Nonfiction
Hand to Heart: Improving Communities	Cohn, Jessica	Nonfiction

Title	Author	Genre
Hansel and Gretel and the Haunted Hut	Blevins, Wiley	Fiction
Hellen Keller: A New Vision	Hollingsworth, Tamara Leigh	Nonfiction
How Can We Reduce Household Waste?	Pratt, Mary K.	Nonfiction
How Coyote Stole the Summer: A Native American Folktale	Krensky, Steven	Fiction
How Snakes and Other Animals Taste the Air	Rajczak, Kristen	Nonfiction
Human Environmental Impact: How We Affect Earth	Sawyer, Ava	Nonfiction
The Hundred Dresses	Estes, Eleanor	Fiction
Hunter Moran Digs Deep	Giff, Patricia Reilly	Fiction
I Survived the Japanese Tsunami, 2011	Tarshis, Lauren	Fiction
I Wonder Why Stars Twinkle and Other Questions about Space	Stott, Carole	Nonfiction
I'm Out of My Body...Please Leave a Message	Greenburg, Dan	Fiction
The Ice Dove and Other Stories	de Anda, Diane	Fiction
Incredible Bugs	Farndon, John	Nonfiction
Island of the Aunts	Ibbotson, Eva	Fiction
It's Disgusting and We Ate It!: True Food Facts from Around the World and Throughout History	Solheinm, James	Nonfiction

Title	Author	Genre
Jack Adrift: Fourth Grade Without a Clue	Gantos, Jack	Fiction
Jack and the Bloody Beanstalk	Blevins, Wiley	Fiction
Kindred Souls	MacLachlan, Patricia	Fiction
Let's Talk About Race	Lester, Julius	Nonfiction
Life and Non-Life in an Ecosystem	Rice, William B.	Nonfiction
The Life Cycle of a Butterfly	Kalman, Bobbie	Nonfiction
Little Dead Riding Hood	Blevins, Wiley	Fiction
Look Inside: Your Skeleton and Muscles	Williams, Ben	Nonfiction
Look Out for the Fitzgerald-Trouts	Spalding, Esta	Fiction
Love, Amalia	Ada, Alma Flor	Fiction
The Magic Half	Barrows, Annie	Fiction
The Magic Pomegranate	Schram, Peninnah	Fiction
The Magic Thief: Found	Prineas, Sarah	Fiction
The Malted Falcon	Hale, Bruce	Fiction
Markets Around the World	Petersen, Casey Null	Nonfiction

Title	Author	Genre
May B.	Rose, Caroline Starr	Fiction
The Miraculous Journey of Edward Tulane	DiCamillo, Kate	Fiction
The Missing Marlin	Kelly, David A.	Fiction
Mistakes Were Made	Pastis, Stephan	Fiction
Money Through History	McManus, Lori	Nonfiction
The Most Endangered Animals in the World	Gagne, Tammy	Nonfiction
Mr. Chickee's Funny Money	Curtis, Christopher Paul	Fiction
Murder, My Tweet	Hale, Bruce	Fiction
My Life as a Book	Tashjian, Janet	Fiction
My Son, the Time Traveler	Greenburg, Dan	Fiction
Mystery of the Missing Luck	Pearce, Jacqueline	Fiction
Natural Disasters: Violent Weather	Parker, Steve, and West, David	Nonfiction
Never Trust a Cat Who Wears Earrings	Greenburg, Dan	Fiction
Niagra Falls, or Does It?	Winkler, Henry, and Oliver, Lin	Fiction
Night of the Living Worms	Coverly, Dave	Fiction

Title	Author	Genre
Now Look What You've Done	Pastis, Stephan	Fiction
Off to Class: Incredible and Unusual Schools Around the World	Hughes, Susan	Nonfiction
Oh, Rats! The Story of Rats and People	Marrin, Albert	Nonfiction
Out to Lunch	Krulik, Nancy	Fiction
Pecos Bill: Colossal Cowboy	Tulien, Sean	Fiction
Pigling: A Cinderella Story	Jolley, Dan	Fiction
Pleasing the Ghost	Creech, Sharon	Fiction
Poppy and Rye	Avi	Fiction
The Prairie Adventure of Sarah and Annie, Blizzard Survivors	Figley, Marty Rhodes	Fiction
Revenge of the Dragon Lady	McMullan, Kate	Fiction
Robin Hood: A Graphic Novel	Shephard, Aaron, and Watson, Anne	Fiction
Sadako and the Thousand Paper Cranes	Coerr, Eleanor	Fiction
Savvy	Law, Ingrid	Fiction
The Science Behind Wonders of Earth: Cave Crystals, Balancing Rocks, and Snow Donuts	Leavitt, Amie Jane	Nonfiction

Title	Author	Genre
Scumble	Law, Ingrid	Fiction
The Shadow Door	Bannister	Fiction
Shouldn't You Be in School?	Snicket, Lemony	Fiction
Shredderman: Attack of the Tagger	Van Draanen, Wendelin	Fiction
Shredderman: Secret Identity	Van Draanen, Wendelin	Fiction
Sideways Stories from Wayside School	Sachar, Louis	Fiction
A Smart Girl's Guide: Friendship Troubles	Criswell, Patti Kelley	Nonfiction
Snicker of Magic	Lloyd, Natalie	Fiction
Star Scouts	Lawrence, Mike	Fiction
Still Firetalking	Polacco, Patricia	Nonfiction
Surprise Island	Warner, Gertrude Chandler	Fiction
Switch	Law, Ingrid	Fiction
The Tale of Despereaux	DiCamillo, Kate	Fiction
A Taste of Blackberries	Buchanan Smith, Doris	Fiction

Title	Author	Genre
A Thief in the Village and Other Stories of Jamaica	Berry, James	Fiction
The Thing About Georgie	Graff, Lisa	Fiction
Three Good Deeds	Vande Velde, Vivian	Fiction
Thunder Creek Ranch	Spreen Bates, Sonya	Fiction
Tiny Creatures	Bradley, Timothy	Nonfiction
Titanic: *Collision Course*	Korman, Gordon	Fiction
Titanic: *S.O.S.*	Korman, Gordon	Fiction
Titanic: *Unsinkable*	Korman, Gordon	Fiction
Tools and Treasures of the Ancient Maya	Doeden, Matt	Nonfiction
The Truth of Me	MacLachlan, Patricia	Fiction
Upside-Down Magic	Mlynowski, Sarah, Myracle, Lauren, and Jenkins, Emily	Fiction
The Volcano Goddess Will See You Now	Greenburg, Dan	Fiction
Waiting for Normal	Connor, Leslie	Fiction
Water Habitats	Kalman, Bobbie	Nonfiction

Title	Author	Genre
Wayside School Is Falling Down	Sachar, Louis	Fiction
We Meet Again	Pastis, Stephan	Fiction
Wedding Drama	English, Karen	Fiction
A Wedding for Wiglaf?	McMullan, Kate	Fiction
"When Did You See Her Last?"	Snicket, Lemony	Fiction
"Who Could That Be at This Hour?"	Snicket, Lemony	Fiction
Who Was Ferdinand Magellan?	Kramer, Sydelle	Nonfiction
Who Was Jackie Robinson?	Herman, Gail	Nonfiction
Who Was Marie Curie?	Stine, Megan	Nonfiction
A Whole New Ballgame	Bildner, Phil	Fiction
The Willoughbys	Lowry, Lois	Fiction
The Witches	Dahl, Roald	Fiction
The Wolves of Willoughby Chase	Aiken, Joan	Fiction
The Year of the Baby	Cheng, Andrea	Fiction

Title	Author	Genre
The Year of the Book	Cheng, Andrea	Fiction
The Year of the Fortune Cookie	Cheng, Andrea	Fiction
The Yellow House Mystery	Warner, Gertrude Chandler	Fiction
Your Life as an Explorer on a Viking Ship	Troupe, Thomas Kingsley	Nonfiction
Zita the Spacegirl: Far from Home	Hatke, Ben	Fiction

FIGURE IR 2 *A student reflects on a book in preparation for writing about her reading.*

Conferring with Students

Conferring Cards

Fountas & Pinnell Classroom includes a Conferring Card for each independent reading book. Figure IR 3 A–B provides an overview of the features and instructional support that you can utilize as you confer with students during or after their independent reading.

Messages help you encourage students to articulate and reinforce the universal or "big ideas" of the text.

IR Independent Reading
Conferring Card

Fountas & Pinnell LITERACY™
FOUNTAS & PINNELL CLASSROOM

Title	*Capybaras After Dark* (Animals of the Night)
Grade	4
Author	Heather M. Moore Niver
Photographers	Various
Genre	Nonfiction/Expository
Message(s)	Learning about wild animals helps you understand the natural world. There is a huge variety of animal life in the world.

Book Talk provides a brief introduction—a teaser of sorts—to the book. You may wish to spend a few minutes at the beginning of each group meeting introducing several titles that you think would be of interest to some of your students. If books are part of a series, you may want to gather all the titles in the series and do one book talk, as the books will be similar in style and/or have the same characters. Book talks remind students of the wide variety of books available to them in your classroom library, encouraging them to browse and explore.

Book Talk

Can you imagine a guinea pig the size of a big dog? Capybaras, cousins to guinea pigs, are the largest rodents in the world. They are most active at night, spend a lot of time in the water, and hang around in herds, making all kinds of sounds. Check out this book in the Animals of the Night series to learn all about these amazing animals.

Summary

Capybaras are semiaquatic, nocturnal rodents living in Central and South America. Related to guinea pigs and chinchillas, capybaras are the largest rodents in the world. Adult capybaras are about two feet tall at the shoulder and between three and four feet long—about the size of a large dog. Capybaras live in herds and are very social animals. Although herds will often live near each other, their grazing areas are separate, defended territories. They are herbivores, eating only plants, such as grasses, melons, and grains. Capybaras are vocal, making a variety of sounds, including barks, chirps, and whistles, to communicate with each other and to protect their members from danger, such as an attack by predators. Young capybaras—able to run, swim, and dive within hours of birth—are cared for by any nursing female in the herd. The author includes some tips about how to stay safe if face-to-face with a capybara. The book begins with a glossary and a table of contents and ends with a list of further resources and an index.

You may not have read, or read recently, the books that students choose for independent reading. The **summary** provides a quick refresher of the book's plot or content so that you can have meaningful conversations with students about their reading.

Focus on Book and Print Features

Unlike most nonfiction books, the glossary in this book comes before the table of contents. With the student, review the words defined in the glossary. What do these words lead the student to expect from this book? Invite the student to describe how placing the glossary up front changes her experience with this book, as compared to other nonfiction books.

You may wish to **focus on a key characteristic** of the text as you discuss the book with a reader.

FIGURE IR 3 A *An example of a Conferring Card*

The back of the Conferring Card contains **prompts** that you can use to guide your conversation with a reader and to support the student's thinking. You may want to begin by simply asking *What are you thinking about this book?* and then use the prompts on the card if and when they fit into your conversation. The amount of time you spend with an individual reader varies. A conference may be as brief as 1–2 minutes, or you may find that a longer interaction would be beneficial.

Make Personal Connections As you discuss books and present lessons, you will often be able to share information and make connections that reflect your own experiences. Students will enjoy discussions and benefit from lessons even more when you add your own personal knowledge.

Occasionally you may want to encourage students to expand their thinking about the book through writing or drawing. Choose or modify a **Writing About Reading** prompt that would best support and extend a student's understanding of the text.

When students discover a book they like, **point them to similar books** in your classroom or school library to encourage more independent reading.

Teaching in the Moment From your conversation with the reader, determine one or two points that you can teach on the spot. One explicit point tailored to an individual student can contribute profoundly to the student's success as a reader. You might also want to reinforce the concept or principle you taught in the day's reading minilesson. Do this in a conversational way. You are relating to the student as another reader, making specific teaching points, summarizing what you have taught, and making notes that will guide your next instructional encounter.

Conferring Prompts

Have a brief conversation to check in on the student's enjoyment and understanding of the book, and to answer any questions. You may want to select from the following prompts depending on where the student is in reading the book. Sample and support the student's oral reading and discuss writing in the *Reader's Notebook* if appropriate.

Book Choice and Engagement

■ What led you to choose this book? Share some of your reasons.

■ Did you know about capybaras before reading this book? Are you interested in wild animals? What is another animal you'd like to read about?

Thinking *Within* the Text

■ The author says that capybaras are *nocturnal, semiaquatic,* and *herbivores.* What does each of these words tell you about capybaras?

■ Baby capybaras are called *pups.* What have you learned about capybara pups in this book?

Thinking *Beyond* the Text

■ Think about the capybara's habitat. What features does a capybara need in the place where it lives?

■ How do the photographs make you feel about capybaras? What do they help you learn about these animals? Let's look at a couple and talk about what they show.

Thinking *About* the Text

■ How has author Heather M. Moore Niver organized the information in this book? Why do you think she made that choice?

■ Author Heather M. Moore Niver has included a Fun Fact on many pages of the book. Turn to one that you found interesting and talk about what you learned and how this fact is connected to the rest of the information on the page.

Writing About Reading Prompts

You may want to select from these prompts to engage the student in sharing responses to the book through drawing or writing in the *Reader's Notebook.*

Thinking *Within* the Text

■ Using information from the text and the photographs, draw a picture of a capybara. Label some of this animal's important physical features.

Thinking *Beyond* the Text

■ All the female capybaras help to care for and feed the pups in their group. Write some sentences to tell what you think about this. How does it help capybaras survive as a species?

Thinking *About* the Text

■ Write about what you found most interesting about capybaras. How did Heather M. Moore Niver make this information interesting to you? Use some examples of her way of writing in your work.

The student might also enjoy these books about wild animals found in the Independent Reading Collection.

FIGURE IR 3 B *An example of a Conferring Card*

Genre-Based Conferring Cards

Students will want to read a wide range of books during independent reading. To support your conversations with readers about any book, General and Genre-Based Conferring Cards are provided with *Fountas & Pinnell Classroom.* Figure IR 4 A–B provides an overview of the card for fiction texts.

IR Independent Reading
Conferring Card: Fiction Texts
Grade 4

Fountas & Pinnell LITERACY™
FOUNTAS & PINNELL CLASSROOM

Conferring About Fiction Texts

At the fourth-grade level, fiction texts have more complex plots and multiple story problems, multiple plots, and chapters connected to a single plot. Readers may also encounter collections of short stories related to an overarching theme. Themes begin to reflect important human challenges and social issues, including identity, self-esteem, popularity, sportsmanship, the transition to adolescence, social justice and social awareness, and the environment. Fictional texts may be realistic fiction, with believable characters and narratives that occur within the parameters of the real world, or fantasy fiction, including folktales, animal tales, fairy tales, fables, and tall tales, as well as more complex modern fantasy, including science fiction. Students may also encounter special types of fiction, like adventure stories and mysteries, as well as different forms, including series books chapter books, and graphic texts.

Some general prompts to use during a brief reading conference are suggested below. You can select from these prompts when conferring about any fiction text. Selection will depend on how much of the book has been read. When conferring with students about a fictional text, you might discuss genre, author, literary elements, big ideas, illustrations, author or illustrator's craft, and text structure. The goal is to check in on the student's enjoyment and understanding of the book and to answer any questions.

For additional prompts, see *Prompting Guide, Part 2, Prompting Guide for Fiction,* and *Prompting Guide App* for iPhone® and iPad®.

Thinking Within The Text

- Who are the important characters in this story?
- Where does this story take place? How important is the place to the story?
- What is the problem in the story?
- Tell about something that one of the characters does to solve the problem in the story.
- What are the most important parts of the story?

Thinking Beyond the Text

- How would you describe a character you like or care most about? Why do you like that character?
- What do you think will happen in this story? What makes you think that?
- How does the story end? Were you able to guess how it would end?
- Did you like the ending? Why or why not?
- What did you think about when you were reading this story?
- Do the characters or the things that happen to the characters remind you of anything in your own life?
- Is there a message or big idea in the book? What do you think it is?

Conferring Cards are provided for the following **genres:** fiction, nonfiction, folktales, fantasy, historical fiction, and biography. A Conferring Card with general prompts can be used with any book.

The purpose of your conference is to move the student forward as a reader. Choose or modify prompts to help the reader think more deeply **within, beyond, and about the text.**

FIGURE IR 4 A *Grade 4 Conferring Card for fiction texts*

As students gain experience in talking about texts, they acquire the technical, **academic language** to discuss various genres with precision and depth.

Thinking About the Text

- Were you interested in the story right from the beginning? What did the author do to make you interested?
- What are some words the author uses that are interesting or fun?
- How does the story make you feel? What makes you feel that way?
- What do you learn from or enjoy about the illustrations?

Developing a Shared Language for Talking About Texts

If students talk about texts every day, they build a shared language that gradually grows more complex. This kind of vocabulary is called *academic language*. Acquiring language to talk about books is a cumulative process. Below are some terms related to fiction texts that students in fourth grade can begin to understand and use.

General Language	Beginning	Genre
▪ Author	▪ Ending	▪ Fiction
▪ Illustrator	▪ Message or lesson	▪ Realistic fiction
▪ Title	▪ Dialogue	▪ Historical fiction
Organizational Tools	**Text Design**	▪ Fantasy
▪ Table of contents	▪ Front cover	▪ Folktale
▪ Chapter	▪ Back cover	▪ Fairy tale
▪ Chapter title	▪ Book jacket	▪ Fable
▪ Section	▪ Title page	▪ Tall tale
Literary Elements	▪ Endpapers	**Types or Forms**
▪ Character	**Text Resources**	▪ Adventure story
▪ Main character	▪ Dedication	▪ Mystery story
▪ Character change	▪ Acknowledgments	▪ Series book
▪ Setting	▪ Author's note	▪ Chapter book
▪ Time and place	▪ Illustrator's note	▪ Graphic novel
▪ Events	**Graphics**	
▪ Problem	▪ Illustration	
▪ Solution	▪ Drawing	

IR5671

FIGURE IR 4 B *Grade 4 Conferring Card for fiction texts*

Putting Independent Reading into Action

WHEN STUDENTS HAVE A choice in the books they read and have easy access to a high-quality collection from which to choose, they're likely to flourish as readers. As you put this instructional context into action in your classroom, the following practices, tools, and language may be helpful.

Classroom Library

During independent reading, students may choose a book from your classroom library, including books from the Independent Reading collection, or revisit books read during interactive read-aloud, shared reading, or guided reading. Students may also wish to read a book in preparation for an upcoming book club. Students' personal poetry books and books that other students have written are also resources.

You may find it helpful for students to use personal book bags. A clear, one-gallon, plastic bag with a child's name on it works well. Students can keep books that they are currently reading in their personal bags to enjoy both in class and at home.

- **Independent Reading:** For your convenience, a list of titles in Online Resources includes the level of each book in the Independent Reading collection. This information is for your use in suggesting books.
- **Guided Reading:** You may wish to include books that students have previously read or new books that are at their independent level.
- **Shared Reading:** You can add small versions of the enlarged texts students have read together, if available.
- **Interactive Read-Aloud:** Many of the books that you read aloud will also be suitable choices for students to read.

Getting Started with a Readers' Workshop

The workshop structure puts a strong instructional frame around independent reading and provides regular opportunities for students to share their thinking. The workshop moves from a whole-class meeting to individual reading and small-group work, back to a whole-class meeting.

- The **initial whole-class meeting** can include book talks and minilessons.
- During **individual reading and small-group work,** students read independently and write in the *Reader's Notebook,* while you conduct guided reading groups, facilitate book clubs, and hold individual conferences.
- In the **final whole-class meeting,** students share and reflect on the learning that took place during the workshop.

Building Your Library

The texts included with *Fountas & Pinnell Classroom*™ are a wonderful starting point for the independent reading library in your classroom. You may wish to supplement your library with titles from the following collections and book lists:

- *LLI Choice Library* (Gold)

- American Library Association Awards, including the Caldecott, Newbery, Sibert, Coretta Scott King, and Pura Belpre Awards, at **ala.org**
- Orbis Pictus Award for Outstanding Nonfiction for Children at **ncte.org**
- We Need Diverse Books at **weneeddiversebooks.org**
- The Brown Bookshelf at **thebrownbookshelf.com**
- School Library Journal at **slj.com**
- The Horn Book at **hbook.com**

For a more complete list of websites, please see the Online Resources.

Using *The Literacy Continuum*

Pages 56–65 of *The Literacy Continuum* can help you identify behaviors and understandings to notice and support as you confer with individual readers.

Fountas & Pinnell Online Resources

The Online Resources site is a repository of resources for independent reading that includes helpful videos and printable resources, such as Conferring Cards, bookmarks with prompts, and labels. Access to this site is included with the purchase of your *Fountas & Pinnell Classroom*™ product. To access this site, refer to the instructions on the inside front cover of this guide.

Instructional Actions

Implementing independent reading in your classroom as an *instructional context* goes beyond simply providing a rich, well-organized collection of books, as important and essential as that is. As the teacher, you serve as a fellow, but expert, independent reader. In this capacity, you:

▸ Introduce new books through **book talks** as you add them to your classroom library collection. Your brief introduction might include talking about the title, author, illustrator, and genre; providing a brief "teaser" of the plot or interesting facts; showing one or two particularly engaging pictures; and ensuring that readers know where they will be able to find (and return) the book within the collection. The students in your class may also learn to share a book talk with the class on books they have read and would recommend to their peers.

▸ Listen to individual students read a portion of a book orally. Circulate around the room and sit beside a student you select for a conference. (Avoid "lean over" conferences.) You can ask a student to begin reading aloud from whatever point she is currently at in the book. A brief **oral reading** of a text selected by a student allows you to observe a student's control of several strategic actions, including monitoring and self-correcting, searching for and using information, solving words, and maintaining fluency.

▸ Confer individually with students about the books they are reading (Figure IR 5). The goal of **conferring with students** is to listen to their expression of thinking about the book and to promote further thinking. *To confer* means to have a genuine conversation with the reader about how the reading is going. The conference enables you to understand how each student is progressing and provide powerful, customized instruction that will help the individual student refine and extend his reading competencies.

FIGURE IR 5 *Teacher conferring with student during independent reading*

Writing About Reading (optional)

Writing about reading is a tool for reflection and a way to share and explain one's personal reactions to, questions about, and interpretations of texts. The writing students do about their reading is not a test of what they know but another modality in which to collect their thinking about the books they have read.

You learn a great deal from students who provide a personal response, without prompting. Additionally, suggested writing prompts can be found on each Conferring Card, and bookmarks with these prompts are available in Online Resources. Students do **not** have to write a response to a prompt, but writing once a week about the books they are reading independently can be beneficial.

Reader's Notebook

Students can use the *Fountas & Pinnell Reader's Notebook: Grades 2–4* to write about their reading (Figure IR 6). If you do not have the *Reader's Notebook*, you can use spiral-bound notebooks or composition books or make your own notebooks by stapling blank pages together. You may wish to write a message to students to prompt deeper thinking about a book. A simple comment or question is enough. You may also have students respond to the book they are reading.

You may want to teach students how to keep track of the books they have read during independent reading. You can show them how to record their reading in the *Reader's Notebook*. You can always add a title on the page when conferring with a student. If you don't have the *Reader's Notebook*, you may wish to use the Independent Reading Tracking Sheet found in Online Resources by printing copies for each student.

Using *The Literacy Continuum*

In addition to the prompts found on the Conferring Cards, you are encouraged to use pages 191–197 of *The Literacy Continuum* to identify behaviors and understandings to notice, teach for, and support as students write about their reading.

Fountas & Pinnell Reader's Notebook: Grades 2–4

FIGURE IR 6 *A student shares her thinking in the Reader's Notebook.*

Instructional Contexts: Independent Reading

Assessment

YOU CAN GAIN IMPORTANT information by observing students as they read and discuss books. As you discuss a book with a particular student, write your observations and teaching points in a notebook or on a note card dedicated to that student. These notes will document student growth over time and assist you in noticing patterns among multiple readers that can inform your choice of appropriate reading minilessons for whole-class instruction.

Observing a Student During Independent Reading

Does the student:

▶ Summarize the story, covering essential parts?

▶ Use some language appropriate to the book when retelling?

▶ Demonstrate sustained attention by reading the entire book?

▶ Notice words in the text that have particular patterns, structures, or parts?

▶ Demonstrate ability to talk about and write about the book?

Record Keeping Form

To help you organize and keep track of observations that you make during independent reading, a downloadable Independent Reading Record Keeping Form is available in Online Resources (Figure IR 7).

FIGURE IR 7 *Independent Reading Record Keeping Form*

Resources

LEARN MORE ABOUT INDEPENDENT reading, conferring with students, and writing about reading in the following resources:

Guided Reading: Responsive Teaching Across the Grades, pages 533–535 and 538–539

The Fountas & Pinnell Literacy Continuum, pages 161–167 and 191–197

Fountas & Pinnell Prompting Guide: Part 2 for Comprehension

Fountas & Pinnell Genre Prompting Guide for Fiction

Fountas & Pinnell Genre Prompting Guide for Nonfiction, Poetry, and Test Taking

Teaching for Comprehending and Fluency, pages 329–352, 442–443, 457–459, and 509. Also see accompanying DVD for models of exemplary book talks and individual reading conferences.

Book Clubs

Book clubs, also called literature circles or literature discussion groups, bring a small group of students together to talk about a book they have each chosen from the set the teacher has presented. They have read or listened to the selection so they can talk about their thinking. These enjoyable community experiences deepen readers' appreciation for a common text, extend their thinking as they process and interpret the perspectives and opinions of their peers, expand their ability to express their ideas orally, and provide an authentic context for applying the norms for listening and speaking and for using academic language. At times, a student may choose a text that is beyond his competencies and ability to process independently; in these instances, the student may listen to an audio recording of the text, or an adult may read the text to the student. The amount of support you provide for the discussion will vary. At first, you will be providing a higher level of support, but as students gradually take over the discussion, your support will lessen. The nature of your support will change as well, as students require less help with the process of having a book discussion and more with understanding the content, messages, and themes of the books they've read. We caution that your presence is essential to lift the thinking and occasionally to bring it into focus even when you are observing more than talking.

At a Glance

During book clubs, students discuss a book that they have all read or listened to.

- Small group teaching
- Students choose a book from a limited selection of titles
- Texts may be at or beyond students' independent reading level
- Students meet to talk about the text and share their thinking
- Instructional focus is on constructing meaning through language and print

Building Coherence

The Reading Minilessons Book, Grade 4 includes the umbrella "Getting Started with Book Clubs." Depending on your students' needs and experience, you may wish to teach several minilessons to support the first book clubs of the year.

FIGURE BC 1 *Fourth graders share their ideas in a book club.*

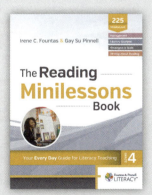

Using Texts Among Several Classrooms

You may be sharing your texts and the accompanying Discussion Cards with other teachers. For ideas and tips on coordinating the use of the book clubs instructional context among several classrooms, see page 152.

Texts for Book Clubs

THE *FOUNTAS & PINNELL CLASSROOM* Book Clubs collection includes 48 titles organized into 12 text sets, allowing you to conduct book clubs once or twice per month throughout the school year. The four books in each text set at grade 4 are connected by genre, theme, topic, author, or illustrator. The text sets for grade four include a mix of picture and chapter books with appropriately sophisticated themes. Some books are longer than students may be used to reading and some genres will be unfamiliar. Allow three weeks to get ready for the first book club, and use some of that time for groups to choose a book.

The themes of the text sets are connected to the themes of the text sets in the Interactive Read-Aloud collection. The text sets are listed below in a recommended sequence, by months of the school year, that aligns to the sequence of the corresponding Interactive Read-Aloud text sets. It is important that students first encounter a theme through interactive read-aloud before participating in the thematically related book club. However, once you have introduced the Interactive Read-Aloud text set, you may present the Book Club text set at any time, based on your students' interests and needs. The books also relate to titles in other instructional contexts, allowing students to make connections among texts throughout *Fountas & Pinnell Classroom*.

Note: Books marked SR provide opportunities for shared or performance reading.

Months 1–2

TEXT SET Friendship		**IRA** Corresponding Text Set Friendship

Essential Question *What does it mean to be a good friend?*

Title		Author	Genre
	A Boy Called Bat	Arnold, Elana K.	Fiction
	Click	Miller, Kayla	Fiction
	The Midnight War of Mateo Martinez	Yardi, Robin	Fiction
	The Mystery of Meerkat Hill	Smith, Alexander McCall	Fiction

TEXT SET Empathy and Helping Others

 IRA **Corresponding Text Set**
Empathy

Essential Question *Why is it important to try to understand the feelings of others?*

Title		Author	Genre
	Fly Away	MacLachlan, Patricia	Fiction
	Hoop Hustle	Maddox, Jake	Fiction
	New Shoes	Meyer, Susan Lynn	Fiction
	Uncle Willie and the Soup Kitchen	DiSalvo-Ryan, DyAnne	Fiction

TEXT SET Memoir

 IRA **Corresponding Text Set**
Genre Study: Memoir

Essential Question *Why is it important for people to write about significant memories in the form of memoir?*

Title		Author	Genre
	Fatty Legs: A True Story	Jordan-Fenton, Christy, and Margaret Pokiak-Fenton	Nonfiction
	Knucklehead: Tall Tales and Almost-True Stories of Growing Up Scieszka	Scieszka, Jon	Nonfiction
	Sisters	Telgemeier, Raina	Nonfiction
	Leon's Story	Tillage, Leon Walter	Nonfiction

TEXT SET Ed Young

 Corresponding Text Set
Illustrator Study:
Floyd Cooper

Essential Question *How does an illustrator use art to interest readers?*

Title	Author	Genre
The Emperor and the Kite	Yolen, Jane	Fiction
I Wish I Were a Butterfly	Howe, James	Fiction
Sadako	Coerr, Eleanor	Fiction
A Strange Place to Call Home	Singer, Marilyn	Nonfiction

TEXT SET Biography

IRA **Corresponding Text Set**
Biography: Artist

Essential Question *What is the writer's reason for writing?*

Title	Author	Genre
The Boy Who Invented TV	Krull, Kathleen	Nonfiction
Hank Aaron, Brave in Every Way	Golenbock, Peter	Nonfiction
In Her Hands: The Story of Sculptor Augusta Savage	Schroeder, Alan	Nonfiction
Uncommon Traveler: Mary Kingsley in Africa	Brown, Don	Nonfiction

Months 3–4 (continued)

TEXT SET Patricia Polacco

> **IRA** **Corresponding Text Set**
> Author/Illustrator Study:
> Douglas Florian

Essential Question *How does an author/illustrator make decisions to interest the reader?*

Title		Author	Genre
	Chicken Sunday	Polacco, Patricia	Fiction
	The Graves Family	Polacco, Patricia	Fiction
	Mrs. Mack	Polacco, Patricia	Nonfiction
	Mr. Lincoln's Way	Polacco, Patricia	Fiction

Months 5–6

TEXT SET Historical Fiction

> **IRA** **Corresponding Text Set**
> Genre Study:
> Historical Fiction

Essential Question *What makes a book historical fiction?*

Title		Author	Genre
	Freedom Summer	Wiles, Deborah	Fiction
	I Survived the Destruction of Pompeii, AD 79	Tarshis, Lauren	Fiction
	Sylvia & Aki	Conkling, Winifred	Fiction
	Train to Somewhere	Bunting, Eve	Fiction

TEXT SET Biography: Perseverance	IRA Corresponding Text Set Perseverance

Essential Question *Why is it important to practice perseverance?*

Title	Author	Genre
America's Champion Swimmer: Gertrude Ederle	Adler, David A.	Nonfiction
Keep On! The Story of Matthew Henson, Co-Discoverer of the North Pole	Hopkinson, Deborah	Nonfiction
Louis Sockalexis: Native American Baseball Pioneer	Wise, Bill	Nonfiction
Wilma Unlimited	Krull, Kathleen	Nonfiction

Months 7–8

TEXT SET Taking Action	IRA Corresponding Text Set Taking Action, Making Change

Essential Question *Why is it important to take action when you see that something is wrong?*

Title	Author	Genre
Eight Dolphins of Katrina: A True Tale of Survival	Coleman, Janet Wyman	Nonfiction
Elephant Rescue: True-Life Stories	Leaman, Louisa	Nonfiction
Mission: Wolf Rescue	Jazynka, Kitson	Nonfiction
Rhino Rescue!	Meeker, Clare	Nonfiction

TEXT SET The Idea of Home

 Corresponding Text Set
The Idea of Home

Essential Question *Why is it important to have a place that feels like home?*

Title	Author	Genre
As Long as the Rivers Flow	Loyie, Larry	Hybrid
Dancing Home	Ada, Alma Flor, and Gabriel M. Zubizarreta	Fiction
Sweet Clara and the Freedom Quilt	Hopkinson, Deborah	Fiction
When Jessie Came Across the Sea	Hest, Amy	Fiction

Months 9–10

TEXT SET Fantasy

 Corresponding Text Set
Genre Study: Fantasy

Essential Question *What makes fantasy fun to read?*

Title	Author	Genre
Bless This Mouse	Lowry, Lois	Fiction
The Magic Finger	Dahl, Roald	Fiction
Rowan of Rin	Rodda, Emily	Fiction
The Twits	Dahl, Roald	Fiction

Months 9–10 *(continued)*

 Corresponding Text Set
Genre Study: Fairy Tales

TEXT SET Fairy Tales

Essential Question *Why are fairy tales important to people?*

Title		Author	Genre
	The Flint Heart	Paterson, Katherine, and John	Fiction
	The King's Equal	Paterson, Katherine	Fiction
	Princess Furball	Huck, Charlotte	Fiction
	The Tale of the Mandarin Ducks	Paterson, Katherine	Fiction

Instructional Design for Book Clubs

Inquiry Overview Cards

Fountas & Pinnell Classroom includes an Inquiry Overview Card for each text set. The Inquiry Overview Card gives general information about the theme of the set and provides opportunities for students to explore the essential questions and big ideas discussed in *Interactive Read-Aloud,* as well as projects for further investigation. See Figure BC 2 A–B for an overview.

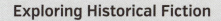

Exploring Historical Fiction

Freedom Summer   **Sylvia & Aki**   **I Survived the Destruction of Pompeii, AD 79**   **Train to Somewhere**

About This Text Set

Historical fiction books depict the way people lived in the past and focus on the problems and issues of life in a particular historic time period. With historical fiction, the time and setting are important to the story, and often have a significant impact on the characters and themes. The books in this text set will help students make connections to historical figures from the past, gain knowledge of historical events, and view the present from a different perspective.

You might wish to refer to the following additional books and the Inquiry Overview Card for the corresponding text set in Interactive Read-Aloud.

 The Other Side   *Step Right Up*   *Tea with Milk*   *These Hands*   *The Dam*

Thinking About Books

While reading the books in this text set, help students make connections to their own experiences, and facilitate ways of learning and finding out more about historical fiction.

- What information do the photographs and illustrations give?
- How does this book help you understand more about a topic?
- How does the author use imagery that is specific to the time period?
- What are some of the historical details that shape the plot?

Essential Question and Big Ideas

Engage students by keeping this essential question and these big ideas in mind as you read and talk about the texts in this set. Be sure to use language appropriate for the grade level. This question can also be explored through a variety of inquiry projects, including the suggested projects on the next page.

The author uses facts and true historical events to write a fictional story. → **What makes a book Historical Fiction?** → The characters are often made up or are portrayals of real people from that time period.

The book is set in the past.

Book Clubs

Exploring Historical Fiction Grade 4

An **overview** of the text set explains how the books in the set are connected and suggests titles from other sets or instructional contexts that you may want to include.

By **thinking about the books** in the text set, students expand their ability to notice patterns, discuss similarities and differences, make connections to their own lives, and synthesize evidence from several sources.

An **essential question** helps students think about underlying themes and big ideas and make connections among ideas presented in the books they are hearing and discussing.

FIGURE BC 2 A *An example of an Inquiry Overview Card*

Projects for Exploration are designed to help students bring together what they have learned and explore a topic in more depth. Based on your schedule and your students' interests, you can decide which project(s) you would like to do and at what point during the text set you would like students to complete the project. Some projects are best completed at the end of a text set, while other projects can be engaged in as you read through a text set.

Asking open-ended questions about the big ideas addressed by the texts can help students identify lines of inquiry they might like to research and explore.

Exploring Historical Fiction Grade 4

Book Clubs

BC

Learning Through Exploration and Investigation

Asking Questions

Think about the essential question and big ideas on the previous page in order to formulate some questions that will help guide students in identifying projects for further exploration of the essential question.

| How do authors research a topic that they want to write about? | What parts of Historical Fiction are often true? | How do authors write historical fiction books in a way that is believable or seems real? |

Suggested Projects for Exploration

The following are suggested projects for students to further explore the questions and big ideas related to the books in this text set. If students work in groups, you will need to meet with each group to support their investigation.

Dissect a Historical Fiction Book

Historical Fiction books, though a type of fiction, are filled with true information. Talk briefly about how authors use both facts and fiction to write and illustrate Historical Fiction books. After discussion, invite students to reread a Historical Fiction book of their choosing. During rereading, students should be searching for, and taking notes on, all of the different information that the author (most likely) researched in order to present accurate historical information. Students may find that the illustrations also needed research performed to portray accurate setting. Once students finish dissecting books, invite them to perform research on a historical event or topic of their choosing. They can research by using the Internet, nonfiction books, published articles, or news videos. Students should then choose how to present their findings while including both their research and a fictional storyline. They might wish to write their own Historical Fiction story, create a journal or diary from that time period, write letters from a historical person's perspective, or use another medium that showcases their findings. Remind students to weave the historical facts with a storyline, and to do this in a way that is believable but is still a work of historical fiction.

Book Discussion

Invite students to discuss the events that occurred in the Historical Fiction book they have been reading together. As they discuss the book, encourage students to talk about what they might have done differently if they were a character in the book. Would they solve the problem in another way? Would they take more initiative? What actions might they have taken to achieve another result? Is there a part of the book that they don't find believable? Invite students to bring forth their own ideas and opinions and explain their thinking.

Character Study

Use shared writing to make a list of the historical fiction books that students have read in class or at home. Choose one that most of the children are familiar with and reread the story aloud. On chart paper, record information about who the characters are, what the setting is, and what the problem, solution, and ending of the story are. Ask students whether they think the characters are real or imagined. Explain that parts of the story are made up by the author, even though they seem like they could be real. Ask students to brainstorm in groups to come up with their own character, setting, problem, and solution that could be used in a historical fiction book. Invite students to share their ideas with the class.

BC7231

FIGURE BC 2 B *An example of an Inquiry Overview Card*

Discussion Cards

Fountas & Pinnell Classroom includes a Discussion Card for each *Book Club* title. Figure BC 3 A–B provides an overview of the features and instructional support that you can utilize as you support groups of readers during their discussion.

 Book Clubs    Fountas & Pinnell **LITERACY**™
FOUNTAS & PINNELL CLASSROOM

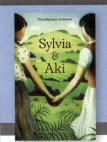

Title	*Sylvia & Aki*
Grade	4
Author	Winifred Conkling
Genre	Fiction/Historical
Text Set 7	Historical Fiction

Book Talk

When Aki and her family are sent to a desert camp during World War II just because they are Japanese, Sylvia and her family move into their house. But life is hard for this Mexican family, too. Read Sylvia & Aki *to find out what happens to both families.*

Summary

Based on real events and people, this novel alternates between Sylvia's story and Aki's. When Aki's family is sent to a Japanese internment camp, Sylvia's family leases their farm. When Sylvia and her brothers are not allowed to register at the same school Aki attends, Sylvia's father sues the schools over the policy. Meanwhile Aki's family deals with the harsh conditions at the camp. The stories come together when Sylvia writes Aki and then visits her. Ultimately, *Mendez vs. Westminster School District* led to the desegregation of California schools.

Messages and Themes

▨ For a society to be fair or just, all people must be treated fairly or justly.
▨ It takes courage to persist against tremendous odds.
▨ It is important to fight discrimination wherever it exists.
▨ Friendships with people from other cultures and backgrounds enrich us.

 Continuum Connection

Goals

Refer to *The Fountas & Pinnell Literacy Continuum* for Grade 4 and choose appropriate goals. Consider these:

Listening and Speaking

▨ Monitor your participation and learn how to encourage others to participate
▨ Compare and contrast people, places, and events

Building Deep Understanding

▨ Understand the differences and similarities between the two girls' experiences

▨ Infer that the fences stand for unjust forms of segregation that affect Aki and Sylvia
▨ Understand the time of the setting and why a lawsuit against the school was needed

Extend the Discussion

▨ Write to explain the significance of the girls exchanging dolls at the end of the book

Book Talk provides a brief introduction–a teaser of sorts–to the book. When introducing new text sets, you may wish to give a brief introduction to each book to spark students' interest and help readers decide which text they would like to read.

You may not have read, or read recently, the books that students choose for book clubs. The **summary** can provide a quick refresher of the book's plot or information so that you can have meaningful conversations with students about what they have read.

A description of the book's **messages and themes** helps you encourage students to articulate and reinforce the universal or "big ideas" of the text.

Teaching goals for the book align to *The Fountas & Pinnell Literacy Continuum.* Choose or modify goals that match the learning needs of your students and will lead them forward in their ability to process and talk about texts.

FIGURE BC 3 A *An example of a Book Club Discussion Card*

Suggested prompts help you guide groups as they **discuss the text**. Use the initial questions and follow-up prompts to promote higher-level thinking by opening up new topics for discussion and lines of thought for consideration. Each prompt is open-ended to encourage students to share varying interpretations of stories and develop content knowledge from informational texts rather than simply offering right-or-wrong responses. For some longer books, we suggest a stopping point midway through so you can allow the discussion to carry over to a second session.

Book clubs offer a wonderful opportunity for students to take responsibility for their own learning and support the learning of fellow readers. Encourage groups to **summarize and evaluate** their discussion and brainstorm how future book clubs can be improved.

Occasionally you may want to encourage students to expand their thinking about the book through **writing** in a reader's notebook or other response activities.

Prepare for the Discussion

Tell students that you will meet to discuss the book. *To prepare for our book club, read or listen to the book. You may want to use sticky notes to mark pages that you want to talk about.*

Discuss the Book

▸ Invite students to talk about the book. Remind them to take the group to places in the book they have marked and want to talk about.

▸ Facilitate the discussion by guiding students to think about the big ideas in the text. Additional suggestions to guide the discussion are provided below.

Facilitating the Discussion	Suggested Prompts
The author switches from Sylvia's story to Aki's story and then back again. Is this a good way to tell the story?	▸ Why or why not? Say more about your thinking. ▸ Does anyone see it another way?
Talk about the different fences in the book. Why do you think the author keeps describing them? What big idea is she getting at?	▸ Can you say more about that? ▸ Did anyone else think that?
Talk about Sylvia's sense of connection to Aki and how it grows over time.	▸ Can you say more about why Sylvia feels that way? ▸ Who can add to that?
Sylvia and her brothers can go to Westminster School if their father will drop the case. What do you think of his decision?	▸ Do you agree or disagree with their father's decision? ▸ How do you think the author feels about it?
What do you learn from the proverbs at the beginning of the chapters? Why do you think the author includes them?	▸ Can you give a specific example? ▸ What do you think the author wants you to take with you from this book?

Evaluate the Discussion

Refer to the goals. Invite students to self-evaluate how well they listened to one another, as well as their participation and contribution to helping one another build understanding of the book.

Extend the Discussion: Further Response

The girls exchange dolls at the end of the book. Why do you think they do that? Write your ideas, including details from the story.

BC5678

FIGURE BC 3 B *An example of a Book Club Discussion Card*

Putting Book Clubs into Action

BOOK CLUBS PROVIDE AN authentic opportunity for students to apply many of the literacy behaviors and understandings that they have learned through other instructional contexts: thinking within, beyond, and about a text; listening and understanding; interacting socially; engaging in extended discussions; and more. As they bring together much of their learning in this one context, students find themselves in control. The experience of exchanging ideas with their peers and co-constructing richer understandings of texts is genuinely rewarding. As you put this instructional context into action in your classroom, the following practices, tools, and language may be helpful. In addition, *The Reading Minilessons Book, Grade 4*, contains a variety of minilessons designed to help students get started with book clubs and learn conversational moves to use when discussing books with the group.

Forming Book Club Groups

Introduce each of the four books from the set to students, through a book talk. You can assign each book a number. Have students write on a sheet of paper their names and the numbers of the top three books they would like to read, in rank order (i.e., 1 for first choice, 2 for second choice, and 3 for third choice). Form heterogeneous groups using student preferences. Not every student will necessarily get his or her top choice because you do not want too many students in any given group. You can, however, hold another round of book clubs for a particular text set if certain titles are very popular.

Before, During, and After Reading

Book clubs require some planning and preparation. Use the following suggestions and practices in Figure BC 4 to make the most of this community experience.

Fountas & Pinnell Online Resources

The Online Resources site is a repository of resources for book clubs that includes narrated videos showing book clubs in action, as well as printable resources, such as discussion cards. Access to this site is included with the purchase of your *Fountas & Pinnell Classroom™* product. To access this site, refer to the instructions on the inside front cover of your *Book Clubs Collection Guide*.

Before Reading	During Reading	After Reading
Introduce the four titles from the text set to the whole class. Your introductions are an engaging invitation to read the books. Each student identifies the two or three books from the set that he would most like to read. You then form book club groups based on students' preferences.	Each student has a copy of the book to read. Students can use stick-on notes to mark places in the books that they find interesting or notable to later refer to during the discussion. Many students will be able to read the text independently, as the books at fourth grade were carefully chosen. However, some students may need to hear an oral version of the text. This could be facilitated by an audio recording or reading the text aloud to the students.	When all students in a group have finished reading or listening to the book, bring them together for a discussion. Students sit in a circle on the floor or in chairs (but without a table between them). At grade four and above, you still may need to direct the discussion, especially early in the year, but your goal over time will be for students to initiate the talk, respond to others in the group, and add to each other's ideas. You may occasionally want students to write about their reading in a reader's notebook or engage in other response activities. This allows students an opportunity to expand their thinking about books read during book clubs. After you have completed a book club, collect the books and store as a set.

FIGURE BC 4 *Before, during, and after book clubs*

Frequency and Length

Consider holding book clubs once a month. In fourth grade, a book club could meet for 20–30 minutes.

Characteristics and Benefits

During book clubs, each student has a copy of the text. As a group, students

- sit in a circle on the floor or in chairs (but without a table between them) to discuss the text,
- take turns and give their opinion,
- listen to others and ask questions,
- all turn to the page that is being discussed,
- support their thinking by showing information in the book,
- discuss the pictures, and
- talk about how the book club went.

Sharing Book Club Texts Among Several Classrooms

You may be sharing the book club texts with a team of fellow teachers. If so, consider the following tips and ideas for coordinating the use of the texts and accompanying Inquiry Overview Cards and Discussion Cards.

- Meet before the school year begins to create a plan for sharing the text sets and cards. Remember to plan to present the thematically related Interactive Read-Aloud text set before the corresponding Book Club text set.
- Store books in an area that is easily accessible to all teachers who are sharing them.
- You may wish to create a simple check-out system for keeping track of which classroom is using which titles.
- Consider bringing together students from multiple classrooms who have read the same book for a discussion.

Assessment

YOU CAN GAIN IMPORTANT information by observing students as they participate in book clubs and literature discussions. You may wish to use the questions below to focus your observations or consult pages 56–65 of *The Fountas & Pinnell Literacy Continuum* to identify specific behaviors to observe.

Observing a Student Participating in Book Clubs

Does the student:

- Respond to the meaning of the text?
- Make comments that indicate an understanding of the book?
- Summarize important information from the book?
- Discuss aspects of the book such as structure, language, or writer's craft?
- Use some of the language of the book?
- Listen to other students' comments, and follow along in their own book?
- Build upon the thoughts of others?
- Ask others for clarification when needed?
- Sustain a discussion for a period of time?

Resources

LEARN MORE ABOUT Book Clubs in the following resources:

Teaching for Comprehending and Fluency, Chapters 3, 5, 18–20

The Fountas & Pinnell Literacy Continuum, Chapters "Interactive Read-Aloud and Literature Discussion" and "Oral and Visual Communication"

On-Demand Mini-Course *Thinking and Talking About Books Across the Day: Creating a Community of Readers* at **fountasandpinnell.com /professionaldevelopment**

Reading Minilessons

A WHOLE-GROUP INSTRUCTIONAL CONTEXT, Reading Minilessons are concise, explicit, inquiry-based lessons about a principle that students can apply to their own independent reading. Often, interactive read-aloud books that students have already heard serve as mentor texts from which they generalize the understanding. To help students develop deep knowledge and broad application of principles, reading minilessons in *Fountas & Pinnell Classroom* are grouped under "umbrella" concepts. As lessons build on each other, the anchor charts, or visual representations of the principles, that you create will be a useful reference tool as students learn new routines, encounter new texts, and write about their reading in a reader's notebook.

Instructional Design for Reading Minilessons

THE GRADE 4 SYSTEM of *Fountas & Pinnell Classroom* includes a book of 225 minilessons that are organized into four types:

- *Management Minilessons:* These lessons cover routines that are essential to the smooth functioning of the other instructional contexts. Most of your minilessons at the beginning of the school year will focus on management.

- *Literary Analysis:* These lessons build students' awareness of the characteristics of various genres and of the elements of fiction and nonfiction texts. The books that you read during interactive read-aloud and shared reading can serve as mentor texts when applying the principles of literary analysis.

- *Strategies and Skills Minilessons:* While most of your teaching related to processing texts will take place in guided reading, these general lessons can reinforce broad principles that every reader in your class may need to be reminded of from time to time.

- *Writing About Reading:* Throughout the year, students will respond to what they read in a reader's notebook. These lessons introduce the reader's notebook and help students use this important tool for independent literacy learning.

Each type of reading minilesson is further organized into umbrellas. An *umbrella* is the broad category in which there are several lessons that contribute to the understanding. Presenting several lessons within one umbrella helps students develop a deeper understanding of concepts and their applications. A complete list of umbrellas appears on the next page (Figure RML 1).

At a Glance

During reading minilessons, the teacher presents specific, explicit instruction to help students become independent readers for life.

- Whole group teaching
- 5–10 minutes
- Four types: Management; Literary Analysis; Strategies and Skills; and Writing About Reading
- Previously read books serve as mentor texts and as examples for generalizing the principle
- Students practice and apply the principle during independent reading

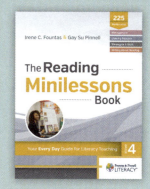

	UMBRELLAS
Management	■ Being a Respectful Member of the Classroom Community ■ Getting Started with Independent Reading
Literary Analysis	■ Living a Reading Life ■ Studying Authors and Their Process ■ Getting Started with Book Clubs ■ Learning Conversational Moves in Book Club ■ Reading Graphic Texts ■ Understanding Fiction and Nonfiction Genres ■ Studying Poetry ■ Exploring Different Kinds of Poetry ■ Thinking About the Author's Purpose and Message ■ Thinking About Themes ■ Reading Like a Writer: Analyzing Writer's Craft ■ Studying Illustrators and Analyzing Illustrators' Craft ■ Noticing Book and Print Features ■ Studying Memoir ■ Exploring Persuasive Texts ■ Studying Biography ■ Noticing How Nonfiction Authors Choose to Organize Information ■ Reading Informational Text Like a Scientist ■ Learning Information from Illustrations/Graphics ■ Using Text Features to Gain Information ■ Understanding Realistic Fiction ■ Studying Fantasy ■ Studying Fairy Tales ■ Studying Historical Fiction ■ Thinking About Setting in Fiction Books ■ Understanding Plot ■ Understanding Characters' Feelings, Motivations, and Intentions ■ Understanding a Character's Traits and Development ■ Analyzing Writer's Craft in Fiction Books
Strategies and Skills	■ Solving Multisyllable Words ■ Using Context to Understand Vocabulary ■ Understanding Connectives ■ Maintaining Fluency ■ Summarizing ■ Reading in Digital Environments ■ Monitoring Comprehension with Digital Texts
Writing About Reading	■ Introducing a reader's notebook ■ Using a reader's notebook ■ Writing Letters to Share Thinking About Books ■ Using Graphic Organizers to Share Thinking About Books ■ Introducing Different Genres and Forms for Responding to Reading

FIGURE RML 1 *Umbrellas*

Umbrellas

Each umbrella is introduced by a page that offers an overview of that umbrella. Figure RML 2 is an example of a Literary Analysis umbrella.

Studying Biography | **Umbrella 14**

Minilessons in This Umbrella

RML1	Biographies are alike in many ways.
RML2	The definition of biography is what is always true about it.
RML3	Biographers choose their subjects for a variety of reasons.
RML4	Biographers decide when to start and stop telling the story of the subject's life.
RML5	Biographers include details about the society and culture of the time in which the subject lived.
RML6	Biographers usually include the people who influenced the subject's life.
RML7	Biographers choose to include facts that reveal something important about the subject's personality traits and motivations.
RML8	Sometimes biographers include some imagined scenes but base them on facts.
RML9	Sometimes biographers include quotes by the subject.
RML10	Think about how the subject's accomplishments have influenced life today.

Biography: Artists

Genre Study: Biography

Before Teaching Umbrella 14 Minilessons

During a genre study (pp. 39–41), students learn what to expect when reading the genre, expand comprehension skills, notice distinguishing characteristics, and develop tools to navigate a variety of texts. Before beginning this genre study, students must read many biographies.

Select books that are clear examples of biography, such as the following books from the *Fountas & Pinnell Classroom*™ *Interactive Read-Aloud Collection.*

Biography: Artists

Action Jackson by Jan Greenberg and Sandra Jordan

The East-West House by Christy Hale

Radiant Child: The Story of Young Artist Jean-Michel Basquiat by Javaka Steptoe

Mary Cassatt: Extraordinary Impressionist Painter by Barbara Herkert

Me, Frida by Amy Novesky

Genre Study: Biography (Individuals Making a Difference)

Six Dots: A Story of Young Louis Braille by Jen Bryant

The Secret Kingdom by Barb Rosenstock

Farmer Will Allen and the Growing Table by Jacqueline Briggs Martin

Fly High! The Story of Bessie Coleman by Louise Borden and Mary Kay Kroeger

As you read aloud and enjoy these texts together, help students

- notice things that are *always* and *often* true about biographies, and
- understand the choices a biographer makes when writing a biography.

Section 2: Literary Analysis

Umbrella 14: Studying Biography ■ 293

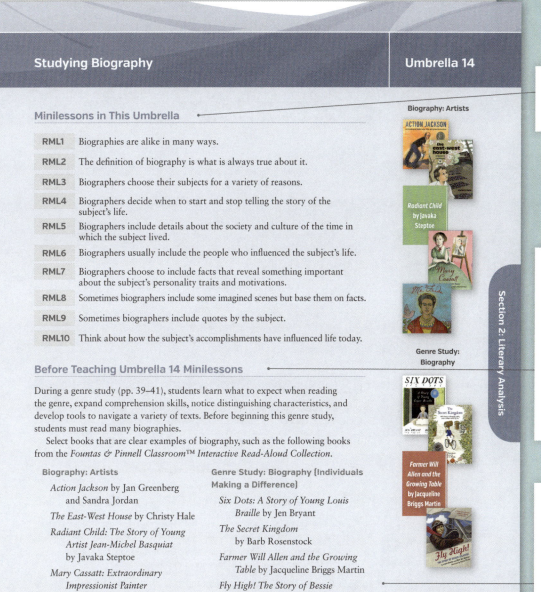

A **list of minilessons** organized under this umbrella

Often certain classroom or learning conditions need to be met to make a series of minilessons effective. The suggested activities in **Before Teaching Minilessons** help you prepare to present the minilessons under this umbrella.

You may wish to use the **suggested mentor texts** as examples in the minilessons in this umbrella, or you may choose to use books from your classroom library that have similar characteristics.

FIGURE RML 2 *An example of the opening page of an umbrella*

Minilessons

Figure RML 3 A–B is the fifth minilesson in the umbrella.

The **goal** of the minilesson is clearly identified, as is the **rationale,** to help you understand why this particular minilesson may be important for the students in your classroom.

Materials you will need to prepare for and present the lesson. Most are included with *Fountas & Pinnell Classroom,* as well as a few common items available at most schools.

Academic language and **important vocabulary** that students will need to understand in order to access the learning in the minilesson

Suggested language to use when **teaching the minilesson principle**

The **Reading Minilesson Principle** is a brief statement that describes the understanding that students will need to learn and apply.

Specific behaviors and understandings to observe as you **assess students' learning** after presenting the minilesson

---

RML 5
LA.U14.RML5

Studying Biography

Reading Minilesson Principle
Biographers include details about the society and culture of the time in which the subject lived.

Goal
Understand why biographers include details about the society and culture of the time in which the subject lived.

Rationale
When students learn to think about the details that a biographer chooses to include about the time period, they learn to consider how culture and society affected the subject and prompted the subject's accomplishments.

Assess Learning
Observe students when they talk about the time period in a biography and notice if there is evidence of new learning based on the goal of this minilesson.

▶ Are students talking about the significance of the details about the time period that the biographer chooses to include?

▶ Do they use the terms *biography, biographer, subject, time period, society,* and *culture*?

You Will Need

▶ several familiar biographies that have details about the time in which the subject lived, such as the following:

  • *The Secret Kingdom* by Barb Rosenstock and *Fly High* by Louise Borden and Mary Kay Kroeger, from Text Set: Genre Study: Biography (Individuals Making a Difference)

  • *Mary Cassatt,* by Barbara Herkert, from Text Set: Biography: Artists

▶ chart paper and markers

▶ basket of biographies

▶ sticky notes

Academic Language / Important Vocabulary

▶ biography

▶ biographer

▶ subject

▶ time period

▶ society

▶ culture

Continuum Connection

▶ Understand that biographies are often set in the past (p. 62)

▶ Notice how the writer reveals the setting in a biographical or historical text (p. 64)

Minilesson

To help students think about the minilesson principle, help them notice the effect of the time period's society and culture on the subject. Here is an example.

▶ Begin to build students' awareness of how the time period influenced the subject of a biography.

> How does the biographer let you know when Nek Chand lived?

> What do you know about that time period?

> Why do you think the author includes information about Nek's time period?

▶ As students offer suggestions, record their thinking on chart paper. Make a column for the title and subject, the time period, and the significance of the time period.

> Now think about the biography about Bessie Coleman. Think about the facts that the author includes about the time period.

▶ Show the illustrations on pages 18 and 21 of *Fly High.* Read the first three lines of text on page 23 and the author's note.

> What information do the illustrations and words give you about the time period in which Bessie lived?

> Why is it important that you know about the society and culture at that time to understand Bessie Coleman's accomplishments?

▶ Record students' responses.

302 ■ *The Reading Minilessons Book, Grade 4*

FIGURE RML 3 A *An example of a Reading Minilesson*

As you **summarize** the minilesson principle, guide students to **apply** what they have learned to their independent reading.

Suggestions for students to **apply the new thinking** from the minilesson, usually with a partner

RML5
LA.U14.RML5

Lessons include a sample **anchor chart** that you may wish to use as a model as you create your own.

Have a Try

Invite the students to talk with a partner about the significance of time-period details in a biography.

▸ Read and show pages 1–2 and the author's note of *Mary Cassatt.*

> Think about the details that the author includes about the time Mary Cassatt lived. Turn and talk about why these details are important in a book about Mary Cassatt's life.

▸ After time for discussion, ask students to share. Add to the chart.

Summarize and Apply

Summarize the learning and remind students to think about the facts about time period in biographies.

> Today you talked about why a biographer includes facts about the time period in a biography.

▸ Add the principle to the chart.

> If you are not already reading a biography, choose one from the basket, As you read, think about facts that the biographer included and why they are important. Mark any pages with sticky notes that give a clue. Bring the book when we meet so you can share.

Share

Following independent reading time, gather students in small groups. Make sure at least one person in each group read a biography.

> If you read a biography today, share with your group the reasons you think the author included facts about the time period and why those facts are important.

Extend the Lesson (Optional)

After assessing students' understanding, you might decide to extend the learning.

▸ **Writing About Reading** Suggest that students write in a reader's notebook about what might have happened if the subject of a biography lived in a different time period. For example, would Nek Chand have built his garden if he lived fifty years earlier or later? Would Louise Borden and Mary Kay Kroeger write about Bessie Coleman if Bessie became a pilot today?

Biographers include details about the society and culture of the time in which the subject lived.

Title and Subject	Time Period	Why is it important that the author included facts about when the subject lived?
Nek Chand	1947 and after	• In 1947, Pakistan and India were divided, so Nek had to leave his home. • His memories of home inspired him to make the rock garden.
Bessie Coleman	early 1900s	• Women and African Americans did not fly planes in those days. • Bessie was the first African American to get a pilot's license.
Mary Cassatt	1860s	• Women did not become artists at that time. • Mary had to work very hard to become an artist because it was not considered proper for women.

Section 2: Literary Analysis

Suggestions for students to **share** their learning and how they applied the principle during independent reading

Optional suggestions for **extending the learning** of the minilesson over time or in other contexts

Umbrella 14: Studying Biography ■ 303

FIGURE RML 3 B *An example of a Reading Minilesson*

Putting Reading Minilessons into Action

THE MINILESSONS IN *Fountas & Pinnell Classroom*™ can be used in the recommended order, or you may pick and choose lessons as you observe a need within your classroom. As you select the emphasis for your teaching from the menu of minilessons under a particular umbrella, think about what the students in your classroom can already do, almost do, and not yet do. Omit any minilesson for which you have evidence that the students have already mastered the principle and can act on it independently.

As the name implies, minilessons are brief. Each one will take approximately 5–10 minutes to deliver during a whole-group time. The type of minilesson you are teaching will determine *when* during the day you teach it. Minilessons are most powerful when taught in response to an authentic need that you observe in most readers in your classroom. Present a minilesson as soon as possible after identifying a need.

You can gain important information by observing students as they apply and share their learning of a minilesson principle. Write down your observations, and then follow up with individuals or small groups who need more intensive support in learning a particular principle.

Building Coherence

The minilessons in *The Reading Minilessons Book, Grade 4* use texts from the *Interactive Read-Aloud* collection as the basis for instruction and modeling. You may wish to introduce certain texts based on upcoming minilessons that you plan to present.

Fountas & Pinnell Online Resources

The Online Resources site is a repository of resources for minilessons that includes narrated videos showing minilessons in action, as well as printable resources referenced in the minilessons. Access to this site is included with the purchase of your *Fountas & Pinnell Classroom*™ product. To access this site, refer to the instructions on the inside front cover of *The Reading Minilessons Book, Grade 4.*

FIGURE RML 4 *A teacher constructing an anchor chart during a reading minilesson*

Assessment

AFTER THE COMPLETION OF each umbrella, take time to assess student learning.

| Umbrella 14 | Studying Biography |

Assessment

After you have taught the minilessons in this umbrella, observe students as they talk and write about biographies across instructional contexts: interactive read-aloud, independent reading, guided reading, and book club. Use *The Literacy Continuum* (Fountas and Pinnell 2017) to guide the observation of students' reading and writing behaviors.

▶ What evidence do you have of new understandings related to biographies?

- Can students articulate the ways biographies are alike and create a definition of biography?
- Are they talking about the reasons a biographer chooses a subject to write about?
- Can they discuss the influence of people and the time period on a subject?
- Are they talking about the decisions an author makes in writing a biography (e.g., which facts to include, whether to use quotes, where to begin and end the story)?
- Can they identify the ways that a subject's accomplishments have influenced life today?
- Do they use vocabulary such as *biography, biographer, subject, decisions,* and *authentic*?

▶ In what other ways, beyond the scope of this umbrella, are students demonstrating an understanding of genre?

- Are students reading historical fiction or types of nonfiction?

Use your observations to determine the next umbrella you will teach. You may also consult Minilessons Across the Year (pp. 59–61) for guidance.

> Use the **guiding questions** on the last page of each umbrella to determine strengths and next steps for your students.

> Your analysis can help you determine what minilesson to reteach, if needed, and what **umbrella to teach next.**

Read and Revise

After completing the steps in the genre study process, help students read and revise their definition of the genre based on their new understandings.

▶ **Before:** A biography is the story of a person's life written by someone else.

▶ **After:** A biography is the story of all or part of a real person's life written by someone else. The subject of the biography can be someone who is living or dead.

Reader's Notebook

When this umbrella is complete, provide a copy of the minilesson principles (see resources.fountasandpinnell.com) for students to glue in the reader's notebook (in the Minilessons section if using *Reader's Notebook: Intermediate* [Fountas and Pinnell 2011]), so they can refer to the information as needed.

314 ■ *The Reading Minilessons Book, Grade 4*

FIGURE RML 5 *An example of an umbrella assessment*

Resources

LEARN MORE ABOUT READING minilessons in the following resources:

Guided Reading: Responsive Teaching Across the Grades

Teaching for Comprehending and Fluency, Chapters 13, 14, 16, 22, 23

FIGURE RML 6 *Interactive read-aloud books that students have already heard often serve as mentor texts from which they can generalize a minilesson principle.*

Word Study Lessons

IN AN ALPHABETIC LANGUAGE such as English, *phonics* describes the relationships between the sounds of language and its graphic symbols, i.e., the letters. When younger children learn these relationships, they are able to "decode" print more efficiently. For example, they see the letter *a* at the beginning of a word and know that this symbol often stands for the sound /a/, the sound at the beginning of the words *astronaut, ask, apple,* and many others. Older students learn to use letter/ sound information as they break down words into syllables to solve them. They derive word meanings through recognizing base words, prefixes, and suffixes; and they expand word knowledge through the study of Latin and Greek word roots. In any coherent system of literacy learning, such as *Fountas & Pinnell Classroom,* phonics, spelling, and word study are not the end goal. Instead, these important understandings contribute to students' competence and ease in reading and writing continuous text.

At a Glance

During word study lessons, the teacher provides short, explicit instruction to help students learn about and efficiently use more complex letter/sound relationships, word parts, root words and base words, prefixes and suffixes, and word history.

- Whole-class lessons and individual application
- 10 minutes of teaching the lesson; 10–15 minutes of application
- Six areas of learning, ranging from Letter-Sound Relationships to Word-Solving Actions
- Texts within *Fountas & Pinnell Classroom* serve as mentor texts and as examples for generalizing and applying a concept

FIGURE PWS 1 *Fourth grade teacher conducts a whole-class word study lesson.*

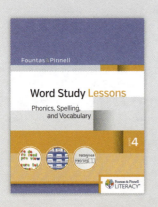

How Can Word Study Be Taught Effectively?

STUDENTS LEARN ABOUT WORDS best as part of a wide range of engaging literacy experiences accompanied by clear teaching. The majority of time in the classroom is devoted to reading and writing continuous text. Students learn to solve words "on the run" while reading for meaning and writing to communicate. As teachers work alongside readers and writers, they demonstrate effective behaviors, draw attention to important information, and prompt students to use their knowledge.

When considering effective word study instruction, two issues often arise:

▶ Should instruction be *explicit* or *implicit*, that is, embedded in the processes of reading and writing?

▶ Should we teach students directly or allow them to discover or generalize essential concepts for themselves?

A cohesive literacy system, such as *Fountas & Pinnell Classroom*, answers these questions in the affirmative, with a "both/and" (instead of an "either/or") approach.

Students learn much more than we teach them; they often astound us with the creativity of their insights. One goal of our teaching is to help students become active examiners and analyzers of print. We want them always to be searching for connections and patterns, to form categories of knowledge, and to have a store of examples to which they can refer.

In the tug-of-war between direct teaching and discovery, going to extremes can be dangerous. Leaving everything to discovery will almost surely mean that many students will not attend to or acquire the understanding they need. Yet assuming that students learn only through direct teaching may lead us to neglect the power of the learning brain, that is, the excitement that makes learning real. And, we want to be sure that what students learn in explicit lessons is applied and expanded in reading and writing continuous text.

We believe that well-planned and organized explicit teaching of language principles is critical but that effective lessons must also contain an element of inquiry. You may decide to show some clear examples first and invite students to notice patterns, make connections and generalizations, and discover a principle for themselves. Or, you may decide to show the principle first and then generate examples that will make it clear, always leaving room for students to notice more about sounds, letters, and words. In these lessons, the principle is stated in simple language appropriate for use in the classroom. Students are also encouraged to categorize words, notice features of words, and search for examples.

The combination of discovery and direct teaching makes learning efficient and memorable; teaching prompts discovery.

Nine Areas of Learning

FOUNTAS & PINNELL CLASSROOM includes 105 word study lessons for grade 4, most of which are generative, thus providing many more. The concepts upon which the lessons are based are organized into six of the nine areas of learning (Figure PWS 2). As you begin to select lessons from each area that address the particular needs of the students in your classroom, you may find it helpful to consult *The Fountas & Pinnell Comprehensive Phonics, Spelling, and Word Study Guide* to review the continuum of concepts within each area.

Nine Areas of Learning for Phonics, Spelling, and Word Study

Early Literacy Concepts	Early literacy concepts include **foundational understandings** such as knowing how to read from left to right and voice-to-print matching.
Phonological Awareness	A key to becoming literate is the ability to **hear the sounds** in words. A general response to the sounds of language is called *phonological awareness*. *Phonemic awareness* involves recognizing individual sounds in words, and eventually, being able to identify, isolate, and manipulate them.
Letter Knowledge	*Letter knowledge* refers to knowing how letters look, how to distinguish them from one another, how to detect them within continuous text, and how to use them in words. The ability to **identify letters** is an essential prerequisite to associating those letters with sounds.
Letter-Sound Relationships	The sounds of oral language are related in both simple and complex ways to the twenty-six letters of the alphabet. Learning the **connections between letters and sounds** is basic to understanding print.
Spelling Patterns	Efficient word solvers look for and find patterns in the way words are constructed. Knowing **spelling patterns and word parts** helps students notice and use larger parts of words in both solving words (decoding) and writing words (encoding).
High-Frequency Words	A core of high-frequency words is a valuable resource as students build their reading and writing processing systems. Recognizing high-frequency words **quickly and automatically** frees attention for understanding as well as for solving other new words.
Word Meaning/ Vocabulary	For comprehension and coherence, students need to know the **meaning of words** in the texts they read and write. It is important for them to constantly expand their listening, speaking, reading, and writing vocabularies and to develop more complex understandings of words.
Word Structure	Words are built according to **rules.** Looking at the structure of words will help students learn how words are related to each other and how they can be changed. Readers who can break down words and notice variations of word parts can apply word-solving strategies efficiently.
Word-Solving Actions	While word solving is related to all of the previous eight areas of learning, this category focuses on the **strategic moves** that readers and writers make when they use "in-the-head" actions while reading and writing continuous text. They acquire information across the other eight areas and simultaneously put it into action in reading and writing contexts.

Taught at Grade 4

FIGURE PWS 2 *Nine areas of learning for phonics, spelling, and word study*

Instructional Design for Word Study

Fountas & Pinnell Classroom includes one or more four-page lessons for numerous grade 4 concepts within six of the nine areas of learning. The word study lessons are designed so that, as you use them, you will always consider the particular students you teach. You will decide which lessons to use and whether or not to modify them to meet the needs of your particular students.

Certainly, you will note the connections you can make to your own students' discoveries and learning about sounds, letters, words, and word parts across the instructional contexts of *Fountas & Pinnell Classroom* (Figure PWS 3). Although the lessons are presented in a standard format, each one is inherently different because of the conversations you will have with the students you teach. Your students will offer their own examples and make their own connections, and you will enrich their learning as you acknowledge and extend their thinking.

A total of 105 lessons across the six areas of learning is included in *Fountas & Pinnell Word Study Lessons: Phonics, Spelling, and Vocabulary, Grade 4*. Most lessons are generative. You can use them to create more lessons (using the *Phonics, Spelling and Word Study Continuum* or the *Fountas & Pinnell Comprehensive Phonics, Spelling, and Word Study Guide*) that will develop the understanding your students need to experience over time. Within each area, the lessons are numbered for ease of reference, but the numbering does not imply an unalterable sequence. If you are new to teaching or have not taught word study before, you may want to consult the Master Lesson Chart: Suggested Sequence for Word Study Lessons. The sequence includes brief suggestions for repeating or extending learning for each lesson. As you implement these lessons, you will not only learn more about students' development of word-solving strategies but you will also gain invaluable insight into our English linguistic system. Ultimately, you can feel confident in building your own sequence of explicit lessons that moves your students systematically toward a flexible and powerful range of strategies.

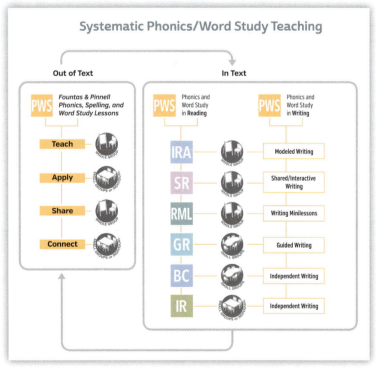

FIGURE PWS 3 *Systematic Phonics/Word Study teaching*

The grade 4 lesson shown in figure PWS 4 A–D provides an overview of the features and instructional support that you will find in grade 4 lessons.

What do your students already know, and what do they need to learn next? As you **consider your students**, your insights will guide your choice of lessons and help you tailor instruction to students' specific learning needs.

Each **lesson title** reflects the content of the lesson using precise language taken from *The Fountas & Pinnell Comprehensive Phonics, Spelling, and Word Study Guide.*

All materials needed for the Teach and Apply sections of the lesson are listed. Lesson-specific materials provided are as reproducibles in Online Resources. If students are working individually, as partners, or in simultaneous small groups, you will need additional copies.

Understand the Concept of Latin Roots, and Recognize Their Use in Determining the Meanings of Some English Words

WORD MEANING/VOCABULARY 22

EARLY MIDDLE **LATE**

Plan

▶ Consider Your Students

Use this lesson to introduce the concept of Latin roots. Many students may find the concept unfamiliar and challenging at first. Explain that an understanding of this concept will help students solve increasingly complex words in various areas of study, such as science and history. You may find it helpful to teach this lesson over several days, focusing on a single word root each day. You may wish to modify the lesson to teach word roots that students are currently encountering in their reading or in content-area instruction. You can create new sorts and word cards using blank templates and Gamemaker in Online Resources. You may also wish to use this lesson in conjunction with lessons on prefixes and suffixes [WMV 11, WMV 12, and WS 22–34], as word roots are attached to affixes to form complete words that can stand alone.

▶ Working with English Language Learners

The concept that many English words are made up of more than one meaning-bearing part is essential for English language learners to understand. To illustrate this concept, you may find it helpful to have students put together and break apart word cards containing word roots and affixes. Emphasize that word roots do not stand alone. Gaining control of the precise meanings of word roots may be challenging for English language learners, because the meanings of word roots may seem abstract in isolation or unconnected to the meanings of the English words in which they appear. Students will likely need to experience word roots in a variety of rich contexts over a period of time in order to gain control of meanings.

YOU WILL NEED

Ready Resources
▶ Word Roots from Latin List

Online Resources
▶ **WMV 22** Task Sheet
▶ **WMV 22** Three-Way Sorts
▶ **WMV 22** Word Cards

Other Materials
▶ chart paper
▶ word study notebooks

Generative Lesson ✓
A generative lesson has a simple structure that you can use to present similar content or concepts. Use this lesson structure and the list of word roots from Latin in *Ready Resources* to teach a variety of word roots that come from Latin.

Generative lessons provide a recurring structure you can use with similar items within a knowledge set. As students acquire knowledge, they build systems for similar concepts that help them generalize a principle and accelerate their learning.

Typically it takes several years for students to learn English as a second language and to learn to read, write, and think consistently in their new language. As you adjust the lesson to teach differently for **English language learners**, your instruction becomes clearer and more explicit in ways that help all your students.

EXPLAIN THE PRINCIPLE

A root is a word part from another language. Roots can be found in most English words.

A word root may contain hints about the meaning of an English word.

Many English words come from Latin. They have Latin roots.

We help you **understand the language principle** underlying each lesson so you can teach with clarity and a well-defined purpose.

UNDERSTAND THE PRINCIPLE

A word root is a word part, usually from another language, that carries the essential meaning of the word but that cannot stand alone. Many English words contain word roots that come from Latin, such as *aqua,* meaning "water," as in *aquarium; cap,* meaning "take or contain," as in *capture; mem,* meaning "having in mind," as in *memorial;* and *rupt,* meaning "break," as in *interrupt.* Understanding how Latin roots contribute to the meanings of English words helps students make connections among words, solve more complex words, and expand their vocabularies with greater efficiency.

Comprehensive Phonics, Spelling, and Word Study Guide
Refer to: page **49**, row **27**

Concise, clear language "rings inside students' heads." Avoid jargon and technical labels; use a common language to **explain a principle** that enables you to reach your readers and writers simply and easily. Sometimes you will show students examples and invite them to think of the principle; other times, you will state the principle, give a few examples, and invite the students to add examples.

Word Meaning/Vocabulary: Understand the Concept of Latin Roots, and Recognize Their Use in Determining the Meanings of Some English Words

87

FIGURE PWS 4 A *An example of a Word Study lesson*

Refer to *The Fountas & Pinnell Comprehensive Phonics, Spelling, and Word Study Guide* to see how the **principle** aligns to other related concepts.

Easy-to-use **organizational headers** (referenced to the Nine Areas of Learning Across the Year as well as the Master Lesson Chart) provide the area of learning, the lesson number within the area, and the approximate time of year to teach the lesson. Use this information to find and select appropriate lessons for your students.

Each Teach activity is specific and explicit and can be used with a larger group of students.

In many lessons, a gray dot ● indicates an opportunity to pause for students' responses.

We repeat the **principle** in language suitable for students so you can refer to it during your teaching.

The **teaching** in each lesson is presented step-by-step, suggesting effective language you might use. Sometimes, the lesson is oral only, without written examples. Make frequent use of chart paper on an easel or a pocket chart to hold words. Occasionally, you may write the principle on the chart before the lesson and generate examples with students during the lesson. Most often, students work first with examples and derive the principle.

---

22 WORD MEANING/VOCABULARY

EARLY MIDDLE **LATE**

ACTIVITY: LATIN ROOTS

INSTRUCTIONAL PROCEDURE

EXPLORE WORD MEANINGS

See page 32 for detailed descriptions of Instructional Procedures.

EXPLAIN THE PRINCIPLE

A root is a word part from another language. Roots can be found in most English words.

A word root may contain hints about the meaning of an English word.

Many English words come from Latin. They have Latin roots.

Comprehensive Phonics, Spelling, and Word Study Guide

Refer to: page 49, row 27

88

Latin Roots

mot "move"	vis "see"	fin "end or boundary"
motor motion promote	vision invisible revise	confine define final

---

Teach

1. Write the following words on chart paper: *motor, motion, promote.* Have students read the words with you. *What do you notice about all of the words?* ● Allow time for students to observe that each word contains the letters *mot.* Underline the word root *mot* in each word.

2. *What do the words mean?* ● As needed, support students in defining the words: *motor,* "an engine that makes a machine go"; *motion,* "movement"; *promote,* "move up in rank or importance." You may wish to have students use each word in a sentence.

3. *What do you notice about the meanings of the words?* ● *The meaning of each word is related to movement.* Introduce the principle. *The word part* mot *is a word root from Latin. It means "move."* Write *mot, "move"* as a heading.

4. Repeat the process for the word root *vis* (meaning "see") using the words *vision* ("sense of sight"), *invisible* ("not able to be seen"), and *revise* ("look at again and improve").

5. Repeat the process for the word root *fin* (meaning "end or boundary") using the words *confine* ("keep within limits"), *define* ("settle the boundary of"), and *final* ("at the end").

6. Guide students to summarize their observations. *What are you noticing about word meanings?* ● Build on students' comments to summarize the learning and explain the principle. *A root is a word part from another language. Many English words have Latin roots, such as* mot, vis, *or* fin. *The word root may contain hints about the meaning of the word.*

7. Tell students that they are going to say and sort words by word roots. After they complete the sort, students read each group of words to a partner. Partners then choose one word from each group to research.

Fountas & Pinnell Word Study Lessons, Grade 4

FIGURE PWS 4 B *An example of a Word Study lesson*

Modify the steps for implementing the lesson to fit your own group of students. Much will depend on your students' experience and their familiarity with specific routines.

In each Apply section we show **an example** of the product or process in which students will engage as they practice and apply what they've learned.

Each Apply activity is based on a **specific activity** that is sometimes the same as—but sometimes different from—the Teach activity.

Students work independently (individually, with partners, in small groups) to **apply and practice** what they've learned in the lesson.

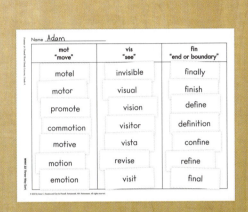

Each Teach activity and each Apply activity is built around one of ten **instructional procedures** to develop students' knowledge of words and how they work.

WORD MEANING/VOCABULARY 22

EARLY MIDDLE **LATE**

ACTIVITY: WORD SORT

INSTRUCTIONAL PROCEDURE
SAY AND SORT

See page 32 for detailed descriptions of Instructional Procedures.

WORD SORT
- say words
- sort words
- read words
- research words

The lesson routines are identified in concise words on tags that remind students of what to do. Post **action tags** where everyone can refer to them as they work. Tags help your students become independent learners.

Apply

- Remind students to read the words they have sorted to a partner. Encourage partners to think about and discuss the meanings of the words as they relate to the word roots. The connection between the word roots and the meanings of some English words may not be obvious. Invite students to discover connections through their research. Students may need to use dictionaries in the classroom, in the school library, and online as they conduct their research.

- Encourage partners to record their findings in their word study notebooks. Students may wish to define the words, use the words in example sentences, list closely related words, and describe how the meanings connect to the Latin roots (e.g., *An em<u>oti</u>on is a feeling that <u>moves</u> me in some way.*)

Share

- Invite partners to share the results of their research. Take time to enjoy rich discussions about the connections that students make between Latin roots and the meanings of English words. You may wish to have partners share over the course of several days.

- Review the principle, and remind students to notice and use word roots to determine the meanings of some words when they read.

Assess

- Give students a Latin root, and explain its meaning. Display three or four words containing the word root. Ask students to explain the meanings of the words as they relate to the word root.

- As you observe students reading, notice how efficiently they recognize and solve words that have word roots they have learned.

- You may wish to use Word Meaning/Vocabulary Assessment C.

Word Meaning/Vocabulary: Understand the Concept of Latin Roots, and Recognize Their Use in Determining the Meanings of Some English Words

89

Use the guidelines to reinforce the principles and help students **share** their learning. In many lessons, we suggest behaviors to notice and support.

FIGURE PWS 4 C *An example of a Word Study lesson*

Assess the impact of the lesson and application in ways that are informal and integral to the work students are doing. For some lessons, we suggest using the more formal and systematic procedures in Online Resources to help you determine students' needs for further lessons.

Connect learning across an effective and coherent design for responsive literacy teaching through interactive read-aloud, shared reading, shared writing, and independent writing. Your observations across learning contexts will help you think of specific connections you can bring to your students' attention; add your own notes to enhance the lesson.

22 WORD MEANING/VOCABULARY

EARLY MIDDLE **LATE**

Connect Learning Across Contexts

Guided Reading During word work, write a few words containing Latin roots on a whiteboard. Read the words with students, and have them identify the word roots. Guide students to use the word roots to determine the meanings of the words.

Independent Reading In a conference, ask a reader to point out one or two words containing word roots in the book that she has been reading. Briefly discuss how the word roots provide hints about the meanings of the words.

Shared Writing As you construct pieces of writing, point out words with Latin roots that students have learned. Encourage students to talk about how the word roots convey the essential meanings of the words.

Independent Writing During conferences, draw a writer's attention to his use of words with Latin roots. You may find opportunities to discuss how writers can build upon the meaning of a word root within surrounding sentences: e.g., *Your description of the plane landing in the storm is thrilling. You state that the visibility is zero. Then you follow up with this detail: "The pilots couldn't see beyond the nose of the plane." That detail helps me picture how bad the storm is. It also gives readers information about the meaning of the word* visibility.

If students need more experience, you can **repeat the lesson format** using these suggestions for variations, different examples, or more challenging activities.

Extend Learning

■ Repeat the Teach activity to include the word roots *mov* (meaning "move," as in *movie, move, movement*) and *vid* (meaning "see," as in *evidence, provide, video*) on the chart.

■ Invite students to study additional words containing the Latin roots *mot, vis,* and *fin.* Use the opportunity to identify and discuss words that have the same letters but that do not originate from Latin: e.g., the word *finger* contains the letters *fin* and would seem to be connected in meaning to the Latin root ("end of the hand"), but it originates from Old English. You may wish to consult the list of Latin roots in *Ready Resources.*

90   *Fountas & Pinnell Word Study Lessons, Grade 4*

FIGURE PWS 4 D *An example of a Word Study lesson*

Putting Word Study Lessons into Action

THE WORD STUDY LESSONS in *Fountas & Pinnell Classroom* may be used with whole groups, individuals, partners, and small groups. As you put this instructional context into action, the following practices, tools, and language may be helpful.

Mentor Texts

Many of the texts in *Fountas & Pinnell Classroom* can serve as mentor texts for the principles in the phonics, spelling, and word study lessons. Use these texts to draw students' attention to the spelling patterns, syllables, word parts, such as base words, root words, affixes, and other print elements that you're teaching. Texts that you create with students during shared writing also provide excellent opportunities to notice and apply principles.

Planning Your Lessons

Each lesson follows a simple structure: Teach, Apply, and Share (Figure PWS 5). As you plan a lesson, consider how to customize each part to most effectively support individual learners in your classroom.

Importance of Word Play

A general goal in presenting *any* lesson is to arouse students' curiosity about words–seeking patterns, noticing similarities, taking words apart and reassembling them, thinking about various parts of words and what they mean, accessing the origins of words, and more. When students perceive word study as *word play,* an important instructional goal has been achieved.

Structure for Word Study Lessons

Teach the Word Study Lesson	You provide a concise lesson based on one clear principle that the students in your class need to learn.	▪ You will often begin by asking students to look closely at some examples of words that exemplify the principle. ▪ Students then discover and construct the principle. ▪ You state the principle in precise, easily understood language. ▪ Students generate more examples, with your guidance. ▪ You then explain the application activity.
Apply	Students engage in an active, "hands-on" application activity independently, with a partner, or in a small group.	▪ The application is based on instructional routines and activities that students have been taught and that they know well. ▪ Students might make words, sort words, write, or engage in other active exploration that offers opportunities for them to make their own discoveries.
Share	Students meet with you for a brief discussion at the end of the activity.	▪ Students can share what they discovered through application. ▪ You reinforce the principle by connecting to students' discoveries, incorporating the same clear language that you used during the lesson.

FIGURE PWS 5 *Structure for Word Study lessons*

Assessment

MUCH OF YOUR ASSESSMENT of students' learning in the area of phonics, spelling, and word study will be observational. Each lesson offers suggestions for informally assessing the impact of the lesson and application activity, e.g., noticing how individual students are responding during the lesson or quickly engaging a student in a learning game that uses the same materials the student is working with during the application. Several quick but more formal assessment procedures (some individual and some group-administered) are available for each area of study, along with record keeping forms. See the Assessment Guide in Online Resources. More formal and systematic assessments can be beneficial in pinpointing a student's specific edge of understanding so that you can customize a lesson for one-on-one or small group use.

Observing a Student Using Phonics, Spelling, and Word Study Principles

Does the student:

▸ Successfully apply principles in reading and writing?
▸ Take words apart by syllables to solve them?
▸ Connect words by prefix, suffix, base, and root?
▸ Recognize Greek and Latin word roots, and use them to uncover the meaning of words?
▸ Use understandings of phonics and core of words to monitor reading?
▸ Use understandings of spelling patterns within multisyllable words to monitor for conventional spelling?
▸ Continue to acquire a repertoire of known words?
▸ Recognize and use figurative language, including similes, metaphors, and idioms?
▸ Recognize connotative meaning of words?
▸ Use cognates to understand words?

Resources

LEARN MORE ABOUT PHONICS, spelling, and word study lessons in the following resources:

The Fountas & Pinnell Comprehensive Phonics, Spelling, and Word Study Guide

The Fountas & Pinnell Literacy Continuum, pages 378–382

Guided Reading: Responsive Teaching Across the Grades, Chapter 17

Word Matters: Teaching Phonics and Spelling in the Reading/Writing Classroom

Assessment and Record Keeping

THE OBSERVATION AND ASSESSMENT of students' learning are essential parts of the teaching process. As you observe and work with students during literacy instruction and activities, you can gather important information that helps you:

▶ Understand the strengths and needs of individual students

▶ Determine your next teaching moves and make instructional decisions

▶ Monitor students' growing control of literacy behaviors and understandings

▶ Report students' progress to parents and administrators

If assessment is seen as "separate" from instruction, it will always be superfluous, ineffective, even a dreaded and annoying interruption. Yet without effective assessment, instruction will be mere guesswork. *Assessment allows you to see the results of your teaching* and make valid judgments about what students have learned to do as readers and writers, what they need to learn to do next, and what teaching moves will support them. In short, assessment makes evidence-based, student-centered, responsive teaching possible.

For these reasons, assessment is an integral part of each instructional context in *Fountas & Pinnell Classroom*. Through systematic observations and accurate record-keeping, you will have a continuous flow of reliable information about students' progress as literacy learners. The decisions you make based on the data will be the heartbeat of your responsive teaching.

Positive Outcomes of Assessment

▶ Determine what each student can do, both independently and with teacher support.

▶ Inform your teaching decisions on an ongoing basis.

▶ Document each student's progress over time.

▶ Monitor progress over a given period: weekly, biweekly, monthly, or quarterly.

▶ Check on the results (effectiveness) of your teaching.

▶ Obtain information for reporting progress to families and administrators.

FIGURE 7–1 *A reading record provides a teacher with immediate feedback on the effectiveness of her teaching.*

Contexts for Observing Students

As a teacher, you are always observing students. As you observe, you gather information about whether students are behaving appropriately, finishing their work, or performing tasks accurately. When noticing the precise behaviors that relate to literacy learning, observations need to be focused and intentional in order to make effective teaching decisions that benefit the learners in your classroom.

Four contexts (Figure 7–3) are highly productive for observing and gathering information about literacy learning: oral reading, student talk, writing about reading, and phonics, spelling, and word study. When observing oral reading, you are documenting what you see and hear as a student processes a text. When you observe a student's talk, you are listening for what the student has to say about her reading. A student's writing about reading represents his thinking around a particular text. When you observe a student participating in phonics, spelling, and word work activities, you are noticing what the student knows about the phonetic rules of English and how words work. All four of these contexts provide you with a window into a student's thinking. The closer and more often you observe, the better you will understand what a student knows and can do as a reader.

FIGURE 7–2 *Using a reading record to observe a student's processing of a text*

CONTEXTS FOR OBSERVATION

Context	Behaviors and Understandings to Observe	Recommended Observation Tool(s)	When to Conduct Observations
Oral Reading	■ Significant behaviors such as pauses, repetitions, errors, and self-corrections ■ Fluency ■ Accurate reading	■ Reading Record ■ Independent Reading Record Keeping Form	**During:** ▪ Guided Reading ▪ Independent Reading
Talk About Reading	■ Understanding of the "big ideas" of the text ■ Ability to summarize ■ Ability to infer ■ Ability to synthesize new information ■ Ability to notice aspects of the writer's craft ■ Ability to think critically about a text	Observational notes	**During:** ▪ Interactive Read-Aloud ▪ Shared Reading ▪ Guided Reading ▪ Independent Reading ▪ Book Clubs
Writing About Reading	■ Ability to articulate understandings through writing/drawing ■ Ability to summarize ■ Ability to infer ■ Ability to synthesize new information ■ Ability to notice aspects of the writer's craft ■ Ability to think critically about a text	■ *Reader's Notebook* entries ■ Writing samples	**During:** ▪ Guided Reading Independent Literacy Activities **After:** ▪ Interactive Read-Aloud ▪ Shared Reading ▪ Book Clubs
Observe Phonics and Word Study While Reading and Writing	■ Understanding of spelling patterns ■ Knowledge of high-frequency words ■ Understanding of word meaning/vocabulary ■ Understanding of word structures ■ Knowledge of word-solving actions	■ Observational notes ■ BAS Optional Assessments	**During:** ▪ Word Study ▪ Shared Reading ▪ Guided Reading ▪ Independent Reading

FIGURE 7–3 *Contexts for observation*

Because you must take into account what students already know in order to teach at the edge of what they are capable of doing, responsive teaching relies on assessment. The four contexts for observation on the previous page form a first step in a seamless cycle (Figure 7–4) from assessment to teaching that helps you teach responsively to each individual student in your classroom.

ASSESSMENT TO TEACHING CYCLE

Step One	Step Two	Step Three	Step Four
Observe students' reading, writing, and language behaviors.	Use observational evidence to make inferences about what students know and can do.	Prioritize the behaviors and understandings that you want to notice, teach for, and support.	Teach for change and growth in strategic actions.
Oral Reading: What you see and hear as a reader processes a text **Talk About Reading:** What you hear as students talk about their reading **Writing About Reading**: What you notice about students' ideas in their written thinking about a text **Observe Word Study While Reading and Writing:** What you observe about students' knowledge of words as they read and write	As students read orally, you will observe evidence of their using the following strategic actions: ▪ Searching for and Using Information ▪ Monitoring and Self-Correcting ▪ Solving Words ▪ Maintaining Fluency ▪ Adjusting As students talk and write, you will observe evidence of their using the following strategic actions: ▪ Summarizing ▪ Predicting ▪ Making Connections ▪ Synthesizing ▪ Inferring ▪ Analyzing ▪ Critiquing	Think about your observations of your students' reading behaviors and compare them to the behaviors and understandings listed in *The Fountas & Pinnell Literacy Continuum*. Prioritize a few emphases for subsequent teaching. 	Once you have chosen your teaching emphases, demonstrate, prompt for, and reinforce the behaviors and understandings you have identified.

FIGURE 7–4 *Assessment to teaching cycle*

TWO ESSENTIAL KINDS OF ASSESSMENT

Interval Assessment	Continuous Assessment
■ *Benchmark Assessment System* (BAS) to determine text levels for instruction and to chart progress 2–3 times per year. ■ BAS Optional Assessments to pinpoint specific learning needs: Antonyms, Compound Words, Concept Words, Consonant Blends, Grade 4 Word Features Test, Phonograms, Prefixes, Reading High-Frequency Words, Suffixes, Syllables in Longer Words, Synonyms, Vocabulary in Context, Vowel Clusters.	■ A reading record to code, analyze, and score a student's reading of a text. Administer the reading record at regular intervals. You take the record on the previous day's new text, which has been read once by the student with your teaching support during a guided reading lesson. A Recording Form for each guided reading book is provided in Online Resources.

FIGURE 7–5 *Two Essential Kinds of Assessment*

Using Standardized Assessment

Many school districts require that all students be assessed using a standardized system so that student progress can be documented and achievement patterns analyzed over time. In Figure 7–5, we recommend two types of standardized assessment that are essential for effective teaching: interval and continuous assessment.

Ongoing Observational Notes

When you take observational notes on the students in your class throughout the day and across the course of the year, you can identify individual strengths and needs as well as document change in students' learning over time. We recommend that you use the forms provided in Online Resources or create a flip chart such as the example in Figure 7–6 to record observations of individual students throughout the day.

FIGURE 7–6 *Flip chart for observational notes*

Observing Students in Instructional Contexts

Each instructional context in *Fountas & Pinnell Classroom* is an opportunity to observe and record evidence of specific learning behaviors and understandings. The questions and ideas below can provide a framework for your observations and record keeping throughout the school day. You may also wish to refer to *The Fountas & Pinnell Literacy Continuum* to determine specific behaviors to notice and observe.

IRA Observing a Student Participating in Interactive Read-Aloud

Does the student:

- Make appropriate comments spontaneously or when invited during reading?
- Make comments after reading that indicate an understanding of the book?
- Summarize the story with all important events and problems, or summarize information after hearing the book?
- Infer or understand the messages or big ideas of the book?
- Use some of the language of the book?
- Notice and comment on aspects of the writer's craft?
- Link the book to other books previously read?
- Ask questions to deepen understanding of the topic or story?
- Actively participate in a conversation about the book with other students?
- Continue a conversation and stay on topic throughout the discussion?
- Respond to reading through writing that shows an understanding of the book's meaning?

SR Observing a Student Participating in Shared Reading

Does the student:

- Join in on the reading?
- Use appropriate stress, intonation, and phrasing while reading?
- Notice and use nonfiction text features?
- Locate words in the text (e.g., words with particular patterns, structures and roots)?
- Read with expression related to the meaning of the text?
- Reflect the relationship between the voice and the meaning of a poem or script?
- Talk about the text in a meaningful way and notice details?
- Notice how the writer communicates the messages in a story, poem, or the dialogue of a script?
- Take on "book language" (the syntax of written language)?
- Revisit the text when working independently and produce an accurate reading?

GR Observing a Student During Guided Reading: Using Reading Records

Once you begin guided reading groups with the students in your classroom, we recommend administering a reading record for each student at least once or twice a month. A Recording Form for each guided reading book is provided in Online Resources. You may find it helpful to take a weekly reading record with students who are experiencing the most challenge.

IR Observing a Student During Independent Reading

You can learn a great deal about students' literacy understandings by observing their behavior as they engage with books individually or with a partner. Does the student:

▶ Summarize the story, covering essential parts?

▶ Use some language appropriate to the book when retelling?

▶ Demonstrate sustained attention by reading the entire book?

▶ Notice some words in a text that have particular patterns, structures, or parts?

▶ Demonstrate ability to talk about and write about the book?

BC Observing a Student Participating in Book Clubs

Does the student:

▶ Respond to the meaning of the text?

▶ Make comments that indicate an understanding of the book?

▶ Summarize important information from the book?

▶ Discuss aspects of the book such as structure, language, or writer's craft?

▶ Use some of the language of the book?

▶ Listen to other students' comments, and follow along in their own book?

▶ Build upon the thoughts of others?

▶ Ask others for clarification when needed?

▶ Sustain a discussion for a period of time?

RML Observing Students Following a Reading Minilesson

You can gain important information by observing students as they apply and share their learning of a minilesson principle. Write down your observations, and then follow up with individuals or small groups who need more intensive support in learning a particular principle.

PWS Observing a Student Using Word Study Principles

Does the student:

- ⏵ Successfully apply principles in reading and writing?

- ⏵ Take words apart by syllables to solve them?

- ⏵ Connect words by prefix, suffix, base, and root?

- ⏵ Recognize Greek and Latin word roots, and use them to uncover the meaning of words?

- ⏵ Use understandings of phonics and core of words to monitor reading?

- ⏵ Use understandings of spelling patterns within multisyllable words to monitor for conventional spelling?

- ⏵ Continue to acquire a repertoire of known words?

- ⏵ Recognize and use figurative language, including similes, metaphors, and idioms?

- ⏵ Recognize connotative meaning of words?

- ⏵ Use cognates to understand words?

Linking Assessment to Individual Lessons

The lessons supporting *Interactive Read-Aloud, Shared Reading, and Guided Reading* each include an assessment of the lesson goal(s). Assessments include observation, student writing, reading records, and use of *The Fountas & Pinnell Literacy Continuum* to observe specific behaviors. Lesson assessments will help you evaluate the learning of the students in your class and the need for further instruction or learning opportunities.

Record Keeping Forms

To help you organize and keep track of observations that you make during interactive read-aloud, guided reading, and independent reading, downloadable Record Keeping Forms are available in Online Resources (Figure 7–7).

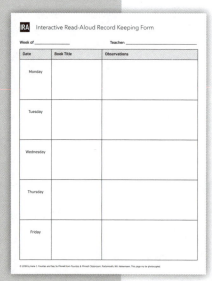

FIGURE 7–7 *Record Keeping Forms for Interactive Read-Aloud, Guided Reading, and Independent Reading*

Fountas & Pinnell Classroom System Guide, Grade 4

Assessments Across the Year for Grade 4

As you select assessments appropriate for your fourth graders and begin to plan your assessment schedule, you may find it helpful to develop a calendar, such as the one below (Figure 7–8), that identifies assessments you will use at the beginning of the year, at midyear, and at the end of the school year. As you refine the calendar to meet your specific district or school assessment goals, keep in mind the importance of doing enough assessment to inform your instruction without over-assessing. The data derived from each assessment should be directly linked to your instruction or be used to demonstrate progress over time.

ASSESSMENT CALENDAR

Beginning of School Year	Midyear	End of School Year
■ Text Reading Level	■ Text Reading Level	■ Text Reading level
■ Writing Sample	■ Writing Sample	■ Writing Sample
■ Vocabulary	■ Vocabulary	■ Vocabulary

Individual lesson assessments and observation notes are **ongoing throughout the school year.**

FIGURE 7–8 *Assessment Calendar*

Learn More

For further information about observation, assessment, and record-keeping, see *Guided Reading: Responsive Teaching Across the Grades,* Section Two, Chapters 8–11.

Cohesive Assessment

The *Fountas & Pinnell Benchmark Assessment System* assesses each of the areas listed in Figure 7–8.

Professional Learning Calendar

COLLABORATION WITH COLLEAGUES IS an extremely valuable form of professional learning. Through regular and planned professional development opportunities, you and your fellow teachers can further develop your craft, strengthen your instructional decision making, and confidently deliver high-impact literacy instruction that enhances the learning experience of each student.

Consider gathering together as a group of fourth-grade teachers, or as an intermediate team, each month to focus on professional learning and development. Before school begins, create a calendar scheduling when you can meet without interfering with staff meetings and other school commitments. You may wish to use the following calendar of suggested activities as a framework for your time together, or you may use it as a menu from which to build your own mix of learning emphases. It is important to have an agenda for each meeting, as it will help you focus on appropriate goals and get the most out of your time together. At the end of each session, review the agenda and learning goals for the following month so that everyone will be prepared for the next session.

Fountas & Pinnell Professional Learning Resources

As you plan your professional learning for the year, take advantage of the following resources from Fountas & Pinnell Literacy.

- Join the Fountas & Pinnell Literacy Community at **fountasandpinnell.com**
- Explore the website's many resources, including a blog, discussion board, webinar videos, study guides, and more
- Follow **@FountasPinnell** on Twitter and **@FountasandPinnell** on Facebook
- Join the Fountas & Pinnell Literacy™ Learning Group on Facebook
- Add any of the Additional Resources on page 21 to your professional library
- Register for an On-Demand Mini-Course at fountasandpinnell.com/professionaldevelopment

FIGURE 8–1 *A professional learning community gathers after school.*

GOAL Create an organized classroom to optimize learning

Meet with a small group of colleagues to assess your classroom as a setting for a community of learners. If possible, meet before the first day of school. If not, meet as soon as you can in the school year. If teachers are coming from different schools, choose one building that has the most classrooms to view and discuss.

Ask the following questions:

- Do you see order, cleanliness, bright color, and a welcoming environment?
- Is there a clearly designated meeting area for the whole group that is attractive, comfortable, and functional?
- Are there well-defined areas for small-group and independent work?
- Is the classroom library inviting and well-organized so books are easy to find and return?
- Does each student have an organized way of keeping personal items and supplies?
- How does the environment reflect students' homes, languages, and cultures?
- Are there areas to display and value student work?
- Are furniture and dividers arranged so that you can have a full view of the classroom?

Chances are you will find many positive aspects, but be diligent about finding areas for improvement. You can have a good environment and still find ways to make it more efficient or responsive to students. Work as a group to identify some short- and long-term goals for each member of the group.

Suggested Resources

Guided Reading: Responsive Teaching Across the Grades, Chapters 21 and 22

MONTH 2

GOAL Create a schedule to optimize literacy learning

Bring several copies of your class schedule to share with your colleagues. Use this list of questions to assess how well your schedule is working for the students in your class. Your schedule should reflect your values.

▶ How much time in the day is spent on literacy activities? Is it enough?

▶ How much time is spent at morning meeting?

▶ How much time is spent playing outdoors and/or in organized athletic activities?

▶ How much time do students spend reading continuous text?

▶ How much time do students spend writing their own compositions or in response to reading?

▶ How much time is spent on transitioning between academic activities and non-academic activities?

▶ How much time do you have every day to meet with guided reading groups? Is it enough? How do you balance the groups?

▶ What are the other students doing while you are meeting with guided reading groups?

▶ Is there time for inquiry?

▶ What would you like more time for? Why?

▶ How could you adjust your schedule to make more time for your priorities and to better reflect your values?

Enlist suggestions from your colleagues for ways to adjust your schedule based on your responses to the questions above. Make sure to give each teacher in the group time to evaluate his or her schedule and share what's working and what could be revised.

Suggested Resources

Guided Reading: Responsive Teaching Across the Grades, Chapters 21 and 22

GOAL Use guided reading groups to support literacy learning

Meet with a group of grade-level colleagues to support each other around your work with guided reading groups. Have each teacher bring the assessment data they collected to form their current guided reading groups. This data might include:

- Text-level benchmark assessment
- Reading high-frequency words
- Writing samples
- Other assessments

Work with a partner to review the assessment data and the students in one particular guided reading group. How are the students the same? How do they differ? What are the strengths of the group? What needs have been identified from the assessment data? What goals will you prioritize for your teaching with this group? Refer to *The Fountas & Pinnell Literacy Continuum* to help you identify goals for each of your guided reading groups.

As a group, discuss how you schedule your guided reading groups. Do you meet with the guided reading group(s) that is experiencing the most difficulty taking on literacy every day? How do you schedule your groups over the course of a week?

Suggested Resources

Guided Reading: Responsive Teaching Across the Grades, Chapter 10, pages 239–246, and Chapter 11

The Fountas & Pinnell Literacy Continuum

MONTH **4**

GOAL Optimize independent literacy work

Meet with a group of colleagues. Discuss the independent literacy work that your students engage in while you are meeting with guided reading groups and/or conferring with individual students. Discuss the following questions with your colleagues.

▶ Are the students engaged and motivated?

▶ Do the students have some choice in what they do?

▶ Are the students able to sustain their attention for longer periods of time?

Discuss as a group how you could strengthen the independent work that the students in your classroom are engaged in.

Suggested Resources

Guided Reading: Responsive Teaching Across the Grades, Chapter 23

The Fountas & Pinnell Literacy Continuum

MONTH 5

GOAL Use Interactive Read-Aloud as an engaging and powerful teaching tool

Meet with a group of colleagues and bring a book that you might want to add to a text set in your Interactive Read-Aloud collection—not one that has been provided for you with *Fountas & Pinnell Classroom.* With a partner, use pages 56–57 in *The Fountas & Pinnell Literacy Continuum,* and compare the characteristics of the text you chose with the characteristics listed for choosing interactive read-aloud books for fourth grade.

- ❯ What did you notice?
- ❯ What would you want your students to learn from listening to and discussing this book?
- ❯ Talk about how this exercise will help you in selecting and introducing books to read to the students in your class.

If the book you brought is not familiar to others, first read or summarize the book to the group. Then share what you learned from using *The Fountas & Pinnell Literacy Continuum.*

As a second activity, select one text set from the *Fountas & Pinnell Classroom* Interactive Read-Aloud collection. (You can also choose a text set that you have assembled.) Discuss the connections among texts in the set, and share plans for fostering thinking across texts. Ask for a volunteer to use the text set and report back to the group.

Suggested Resources

Guided Reading: Responsive Teaching Across the Grades, pages 283–284

Teaching for Comprehending and Fluency

The Fountas & Pinnell Literacy Continuum

MONTH 6

GOAL Use reading records to inform your teaching decisions

Bring the reading records of three students reading the same text from one of your guided reading groups and a copy of the book. Working with a partner, refer to Selecting Goals in *The Fountas & Pinnell Literacy Continuum* for guided reading at that text level. Discuss the following questions:

▶ What behaviors and understandings do the students demonstrate at that text level?

▶ What teaching is needed to assure success at that level?

Now review the goals for guided reading at the *next* text level. Discuss these questions:

▶ What do students need to know how to do to successfully read texts at the next level?

▶ What will you expect to do in the next lessons to enable students to lift their reading toward the next level?

Share your thinking with the whole group.

Suggested Resources

Guided Reading: Responsive Teaching Across the Grades, Chapter 9

The Fountas & Pinnell Literacy Continuum

Bring the reader's notebooks of two very different readers/writers to a meeting of your grade-level colleagues. Using pages 191–197 in *The Fountas & Pinnell Literacy Continuum,* work with a partner to identify the types of writing these two students have used in their entries and the behaviors and understandings their writing demonstrates. Think about some goals you would like to teach and support for each student. Share your observations with the group.

Suggested Resources

Guided Reading: Responsive Teaching Across the Grades, pages 557–565

The Fountas & Pinnell Literacy Continuum

MONTH **8**

GOAL Use observation to inform teaching decisions

Choose an instructional context on which you would like to focus. Bring your observational notes on three to five students that you recorded during that instructional context over the past few weeks. With a small group of colleagues, review and reflect on your observations and the way in which you recorded them. Discuss the following questions:

▶ How are your observations recorded? Are the forms and recording method that you use clear and organized?

▶ Have you recorded sufficient observations about each student to inform your instruction?

▶ Can you document change over time for a particular student? A group of students?

▶ Are you able to select specific teaching goals from *The Fountas & Pinnell Literacy Continuum* based on your observations?

▶ How often do you review and reflect on your observations?

Share your discoveries with the whole group.

Suggested Resources

Guided Reading: Responsive Teaching Across the Grades, Chapter 9, pages 209–221

The Fountas & Pinnell Literacy Continuum

MONTH 9

Gather together your observational assessments of one student's work across the year. Assess your present methods of reporting literacy progress on that student. Perhaps you have required forms to fill out; perhaps you have created your own forms for reporting progress. Bring copies of those forms to share with your colleagues. Working with a partner, use the following questions to examine each form and the assessments you have brought on one student:

- Does this form reflect a clear understanding of the literacy progress this student has made over the year?
- Does it create a summary of the student's literacy progress over the year that is understandable to families *and* the next year's teacher?
- Have you collected enough information to support your reflections?
- Does this form reflect your values and priorities as this student's teacher?
- Are some areas given more importance than others? Is that appropriate?
- What changes or additions would you make to reflect what this student has learned and what will continue to be a teaching priority?
- What should a comprehensive report look like, e.g., narrative, checklist, work samples, a combination?
- What feedback have you received in the past from families and classroom teachers about this reporting method?

Now look at grade 4 goals listed in *The Fountas & Pinnell Literacy Continuum* and *The Fountas & Pinnell Comprehensive, Phonics, Spelling, and Word Study Guide.* Could you use these resources to create a clearer report?

Share your thinking with the whole group. This should elicit a good discussion. Some of the group may want to return to this topic at a meeting over the summer to make revisions to your present reporting methods. Schedule that meeting and continue to work together to create a reporting method that reflects the important information that you have collected to relate to families and the next year's teacher.

Suggested Resources

The Fountas & Pinnell Literacy Continuum

The Fountas & Pinnell Comprehensive Phonics, Spelling, and Word Study Guide

MONTH 10

GOAL Reflect on your own professional learning growth this year, and set goals for next year

Meet with your colleagues to reflect upon and evaluate the professional learning activities that together you participated in throughout the year. Share how the activities and group discussions have influenced your teaching this year. Talk about the sessions that were most powerful and why. Talk about the least helpful aspects of the sessions. Brainstorm topics you would like to discuss in greater depth next year or new topics that you would like to include in your professional learning. Invite each teacher to plan one professional development session for the following year, and as a group, create a calendar that reflects your shared goals.

Book List

The following is a complete list of books, alphabetized by title, in the grade 4 collections of *Fountas & Pinnell Classroom*.

Cautions and recommendations: A level is a teacher's tool, but should not be used as a label for students. A book's level of difficulty is a resource for you; use the levels identified below for independent reading and book club titles to help guide student choice. Fountas & Pinnell do not advocate labeling the classroom library.

21st Century: Mysteries of Deep Space
Author: Paris, Stephanie
NONFICTION/EXPOSITORY, Level V

3, 2, 1 . . . Bungee! The Science Behind the Jump
NONFICTION/EXPOSITORY, Level U

Abby Takes a Stand
Author: McKissack, Patricia C.
FICTION/HISTORICAL, Level Q

Abel's Island
Author: Steig, William
FICTION/ANIMAL FANTASY, Level T

Able to Play: Overcoming Physical Challenges
Author: Stout, Glenn
NONFICTION/BIOGRAPHY, Level U

Action Jackson
Author: Greenberg, Jan & Sandra Jordan
NONFICTION/BIOGRAPHY

Ada Lovelace and Computer Algorithms
Author: Labrecque, Ellen
NONFICTION/BIOGRAPHY, Level Q

All-Star Joker, The
Author: Kelly, David A.
FICTION/REALISTIC, Level N

Alone in the Arctic: Can Science Save Your Life?
Author: Bailey, Gerry
HYBRID/NARRATIVE, Level P

Alone on the Ocean
NONFICTION/NARRATIVE, Level T

Althea Gibson, the Tiger of Tennis
NONFICTION/BIOGRAPHY, Level S

Amaterasu: Return of the Sun
Author: Storrie, Paul D.
FICTION/FOLKTALE, Level V

Amazing Women
Author: Jenner, Caryn
NONFICTION/BIOGRAPHY, Level U

Amazon Basin
Author: Reynolds, Jan
NONFICTION/NARRATIVE

Amazon Rainforest
Author: Rice, William B.
NONFICTION/EXPOSITORY, Level O

America's Champion Swimmer: Gertrude Ederle
Author: Adler, David A.
NONFICTION/BIOGRAPHY

Amusement Parks: Perimeter and Area
Author: Irving, Dianne
NONFICTION/EXPOSITORY, Level R

Anansi and the Box of Stories
Author: Krensky, Steven
FICTION/FOLKTALE, Level N

Ancient China: 305 BC
Author: Slepian, Curtis
NONFICTION/EXPOSITORY, Level V

Andy Russell, NOT Wanted by the Police
Author: Adler, David
FICTION/REALISTIC, Level N

Animal Architects
Author: Bradley, Timothy
NONFICTION/EXPOSITORY, Level P

Animals Helping with Healing
Author: Squire, Ann O.
NONFICTION/EXPOSITORY, Level T

Animals Nobody Loves
Author: Simon, Seymour
NONFICTION/EXPOSITORY, Level R

Anyone But Me
Author: Krulik, Nancy
FICTION/FANTASY, Level M

Apothecary's Apprentice, The
FICTION/FANTASY, Level V

Are Crop Circles Real?
Author: Lassieur, Allison
NONFICTION/EXPOSITORY, Level Q

Around the World
Author: Phelan, Matt
FICTION/HISTORICAL, Level U

As Long as the Rivers Flow
Author: Loyie, Larry
HYBRID

Asha and the Jewel Thief
FICTION/REALISTIC [MYSTERY], Level T

Astro Outlaw, The
Author: Kelly, David A.
FICTION/REALISTIC, Level N

Astronomers Through Time
Author: Greathouse, Lisa E.
NONFICTION/BIOGRAPHY, Level S

At Home in a Coral Reef
Author: Spilsbury, Louise & Richard
NONFICTION/EXPOSITORY, Level R

Attack of the Bullfrogs
Author: Shea, Therese
NONFICTION/EXPOSITORY, Level Q

Bad Kitty School Daze
Author: Bruel, Nick
FICTION/ANIMAL FANTASY, Level P

Bags Full of Ashes: A Folktale from Mexico
FICTION/FOLKTALE, Level R

Ban All Cars!
NONFICTION/PERSUASIVE, Level S

Banana Blade
NONFICTION/NARRATIVE, Level Q

Barbed Wire Baseball: How One Man Brought Hope to the Japanese Internment Camps of WWII
Author: Moss, Marissa
NONFICTION/BIOGRAPHY

Barefoot Book of Earth Poems, The
Author: Nicholls, Judith. Ed.
FICTION/POETRY

Batcat and the Seven Squirrels
Author: Walters, Eric
FICTION/REALISTIC, Level M

Bathrooms to Remember
NONFICTION/EXPOSITORY, Level O

Bats in the City
NONFICTION/EXPOSITORY, Level R

Be Water, My Friend: The Early Years of Bruce Lee
Author: Mochizuki, Ken
NONFICTION/BIOGRAPHY

Beachcombing: Exploring the Seashore
Author: Arnosky, Jim
NONFICTION/EXPOSITORY, Level O

Bear Named Winnie, A
NONFICTION/NARRATIVE, Level R

Bear's Life, A
Author: Read, Nicholas
NONFICTION/NARRATIVE

Beast, The
FICTION/FANTASY, Level R

Beauty and the Beast
Author: Brett, Jan
FICTION/FAIRY TALE

Beaver Alert!
NONFICTION/EXPOSITORY, Level Q

Becoming Invisible: From Camouflage to Cloaks
Author: Mooney, Carla
NONFICTION/EXPOSITORY, Level U

Before He Was Babe
NONFICTION/BIOGRAPHY, Level S

Before It Wriggles Away
Author: Wong, Janet S.
NONFICTION/MEMOIR, Level O

Behind the Canvas: An Artist's Life
Author: Apodaca, Blanca, & Serwich, Michael
NONFICTION/EXPOSITORY, Level S

Being Teddy Roosevelt
Author: Mills, Claudia
FICTION/REALISTIC, Level O

Beowulf: Monster Slayer
Author: Storrie, Paul D.
FICTION/EPIC, Level V

Better Than You
Author: Ludwig, Trudy
FICTION/REALISTIC

BFG, The
Author: Dahl, Roald
FICTION/FANTASY, Level U

Bicycle Man, The
Author: Say, Allen
FICTION/HISTORICAL

Big and Bold Art
NONFICTION/EXPOSITORY, Level P

Big Bertha's Big Trip
NONFICTION/NARRATIVE, Level R

Big Fantastic Earth
Author: Green, Jen
NONFICTION/EXPOSITORY, Level U

Big Wheel, Big Worries
NONFICTION/NARRATIVE, Level S

Bizarre Animals
Author: Bradley, Timothy
NONFICTION/EXPOSITORY, Level T

Blackberries in the Dark
Author: Jukes, Mavis
FICTION/REALISTIC, Level N

Blazing Courage
Author: Milner Halls, Kelly
FICTION/REALISTIC, Level U

Bless This Mouse
Author: Lowry, Lois
FICTION/FANTASY

Blue Hill Meadows, The
Author: Rylant, Cynthia
FICTION/REALISTIC, Level M

Blue Ribbons
FICTION/REALISTIC, Level Q

Books, Beasts, and Blood: The Mystery of the Teacher's Pet
FICTION/REALISTIC (HUMOROUS), Level S

Bored in Space
FICTION/SCIENCE FICTION, Level U

Boy and a Jaguar, A
Author: Rabinowitz, Alan
NONFICTION/AUTOBIOGRAPHY

Boy and the Whale, The
Author: Gerstein, Mordicai
FICTION/REALISTIC

Boy Called Bat, A
Author: Arnold, Elana K.
FICTION/REALISTIC

Boy of a Thousand Faces, The
Author: Selznick, Brian
FICTION/REALISTIC, Level R

Boy Who Discovered Snowflakes, The
NONFICTION/BIOGRAPHY, Level R

Boy Who Invented TV, The
Author: Krull, Kathleen
NONFICTION/BIOGRAPHY

Boy Who Lived with Bears, The: A Native American Tale
FICTION/FOLKTALE, Level U

Boys Against Girls
Author: Naylor, Phyllis Reynolds
FICTION/REALISTIC, Level S

Brave Red, Smart Frog: A New Book of Old Tales
Author: Jenkins, Emily
FICTION/FAIRY TALE

Brothers in Hope: The Story of the Lost Boys of Sudan
Author: Williams, Mary
FICTION/REALISTIC

Buffalo Bird Girl: A Hidatsa Story
Author: Nelson, S. D.
NONFICTION/BIOGRAPHY

Buffalo Storm, The
Author: Applegate, Katherine
FICTION/HISTORICAL

Bug Builders
Author: Bradley, Timothy
NONFICTION/EXPOSITORY, Level Q

Building an Igloo
Author: Steltzer, Ulli
NONFICTION/EXPOSITORY, Level Q

Buildings in Disguise
Author: Arbogast, Joan Marie
NONFICTION/EXPOSITORY, Level V

Bunnicula Meets Edgar Allan Crow
Author: Howe, James
FICTION/ANIMAL FANTASY, Level Q

Button Down
Author: Ylvisaker, Anne
FICTION/HISTORICAL, Level T

Button Hill
Author: Bradford, Michael
FICTION/FANTASY, Level T

Capybaras After Dark
Author: Niver, Heather M. Moore
NONFICTION/EXPOSITORY, Level Q

Case of the Missing Flamingos, The
FICTION/REALISTIC (MYSTERY), Level Q

Cat and Mouse in a Haunted House
Author: Stilton, Geronimo
FICTION/ANIMAL FANTASY, Level O

Catching Air
NONFICTION/NARRATIVE, Level R

Cendrillon: A Caribbean Cinderella
Author: San Souci, Robert D.
FICTION/FAIRY TALE

Charles Foster: Life as a Badger
NONFICTION/NARRATIVE, Level U

© 2020 by Irene C. Fountas and Gay Su Pinnell from *Fountas & Pinnell Classroom System Guide, Grade 4*. Portsmouth, NH: Heinemann.   Grade 4 Book List

Charlie Bumpers vs. The Perfect Little Turkey
Author: Harley, Bill
FICTION/REALISTIC, Level O

Chicken Sunday
Author: Polacco, Patricia
FICTION/REALISTIC

China: Land of the Emperor's Great Wall
Author: Osborne, Mary Pope
NONFICTION/EXPOSITORY, Level S

Chocolate Fever
Author: Smith, Robert Kimmel
FICTION/FANTASY, Level O

Clara Barton: Angel of the Battlefield
Author: Hollingsworth, Tamara
NONFICTION/BIOGRAPHY, Level O

Click
Author: Miller, Kayla
FICTION/REALISTIC

Cliques, Phonies, & Other Baloney
Author: Romain, Trevor
NONFICTION/EXPOSITORY, Level T

Coley's Journey
NONFICTION/NARRATIVE, Level Q

Coming Clean
FICTION/REALISTIC, Level O

Could We Survive on Other Planets?
Author: Wood, Alix
NONFICTION/EXPOSITORY, Level R

Coyotes
Author: Gagne, Tammy
NONFICTION/EXPOSITORY, Level O

Crane Wife, The
Author: Bodkin, Odds
FICTION/FOLKTALE

Crawling with Creatures: Your Body's Friends and Enemies
NONFICTION/EXPOSITORY, Level P

Crow Call
Author: Lowry, Lois
FICTION/HISTORICAL

Crow's Secret
FICTION/FANTASY, Level O

Crown: An Ode to the Fresh Cut
Author: Barnes, Derrick
FICTION/REALISTIC

Curtain Went Up, My Pants Fell Down, The
Author: Winkler, Henry, & Oliver, Lin
FICTION/REALISTIC, Level O

Dad's Camera
Author: Watkins, Ross
FICTION/REALISTIC

Dad, Jackie, and Me
Author: Uhlberg, Myron
FICTION/HISTORICAL

Dam, The
Author: Almond, David
FICTION/HISTORICAL

Dance Like Starlight, A: One Ballerina's Dream
Author: Dempsey, Kristy
FICTION/REALISTIC

Dancing Bees and Other Amazing Communicators
Author: Lindeen, Mary
NONFICTION/EXPOSITORY, Level R

Dancing Home
Author: Ada, Alma Flor, & Gabriel M. Zubizarreta
FICTION/REALISTIC

Danger Zone
FICTION/REALISTIC, Level V

Daniel Kish: A Different Way to See
NONFICTION/BIOGRAPHY, Level Q

Day at Work with a Chemist, A
Author: Gaddi, Rosalie
NONFICTION/EXPOSITORY, Level T

Day at Work with a Geologist, A
Author: Letts, Amelia
NONFICTION/EXPOSITORY, Level S

Detecting Floods
Author: Ventura, Marne
NONFICTION/EXPOSITORY, Level R

Detecting Hurricanes
Author: Bell, Samantha S.
NONFICTION/EXPOSITORY, Level R

Detecting Tornadoes
Author: Ventura, Marne
NONFICTION/EXPOSITORY, Level R

Dewey the Library Cat: A True Story
Author: Myron, Vicki, & Witter, Bret
NONFICTION/NARRATIVE, Level R

Diaper Boy and the Axeman
FICTION/REALISTIC, Level Q

Different Kind of Baseball, A
NONFICTION/EXPOSITORY, Level S

Dingo
Author: Saxby, Claire
HYBRID

Dirt Bikes
Author: Lanier, Wendy Hinote
NONFICTION/EXPOSITORY, Level T

Discovering New Planets
Author: Jemison, Dr. Mae, & Rau, Dana Meachen
NONFICTION/EXPOSITORY, Level Q

DJ Focus
NONFICTION/BIOGRAPHY, Level T

Dog on the Run
NONFICTION/NARRATIVE, Level Q

Dolphins and Sharks
Author: Osborne, Mary Pope, & Boyce, Natalie Pope
NONFICTION/EXPOSITORY, Level Q

Domitila: A Cinderella Tale from the Mexican Tradition
Author: Coburn, Jewell Reinhart
FICTION/FAIRY TALE

Don't Know Much About the Solar System
Author: Davis, Kenneth C.
NONFICTION/EXPOSITORY, Level S

Dragon of Woolie, The
FICTION/FANTASY, Level R

Dragon Prince, The: A Chinese Beauty and the Beast Tale
Author: Yep, Laurence
FICTION/FAIRY TALE

Dragon Rider
Author: Funke, Cornelia
FICTION/FANTASY, Level V

Dream Park: The Head of the House
FICTION/FANTASY, Level R

Dream Park: The Pop Star
FICTION/FANTASY, Level R

Dream Park: The Soccer Star
FICTION/FANTASY, Level R

Dream Park: The Straight-A Kid
FICTION/FANTASY, Level R

Drita: My Homegirl
Author: Lombarnd, Jenny
FICTION/REALISTIC, Level T

Drones and Whales: Collecting Snot at Sea
NONFICTION/EXPOSITORY, Level S

Drowning of Villa Epecuén, The
NONFICTION/NARRATIVE, Level V

Dude, Where's My Spaceship?
Author: Greenburg, Dan
FICTION/FANTASY, Level P

Duke Kahanamoku and the Secret History of Surfing
NONFICTION/BIOGRAPHY, Level T

Dumpling Days
Author: Lin, Grace
FICTION/REALISTIC, Level Q

Dunderheads, The
Author: Fleischman, Paul
FICTION/REALISTIC

Durbin's Quest
FICTION/FAIRY TALE, Level U

Earthquake in the Early Morning
Author: Osborne, Mary Pope
FICTION/FANTASY, Level M

East-West House, The: Noguchi's Childhood in Japan
Author: Hale, Christy
NONFICTION/BIOGRAPHY

Edmund Hillary Reaches the Top of Everest
Author: Yomtov, Nel
NONFICTION/BIOGRAPHY, Level S

Eight Days: A Story of Haiti
Author: Danticat, Edwidge
FICTION/REALISTIC

Eight Dolphins of Katrina: A True Tale of Survival
Author: Coleman, Janet Wyman
NONFICTION/NARRATIVE

Election Madness
Author: English, Karen
FICTION/REALISTIC, Level N

Elephant Orphans
Author: Hibbert, Clare
NONFICTION/EXPOSITORY, Level R

Elephant Rescue: True-Life Stories
Author: Leaman, Louisa
NONFICTION/NARRATIVE

Emma Gatewood's Long Walk
NONFICTION/NARRATIVE, Level R

Emmanuel Yeboah's Incredible Ride
NONFICTION/BIOGRAPHY, Level T

Emmanuel's Dream: The True Story of Emmanuel Ofosu Yeboah
Author: Thompson, Laurie Ann
NONFICTION/BIOGRAPHY

Emperor and the Kite, The
Author: Yolen, Jane
FICTION/FOLKTALE

Engineering: Feats & Failures
Author: Paris, Stephanie
NONFICTION/EXPOSITORY, Level U

Ereth's Birthday
Author: Avi
FICTION/ANIMAL FANTASY, Level S

Everything for a Dog
Author: Martin, Ann M.
FICTION/REALISTIC, Level T

Extraordinary Education of Nicholas Benedict, The
Author: Stewart, Trenton Lee
FICTION/FANTASY, Level V

Eye to Eye: How Animals See the World
Author: Jenkins, Steve
NONFICTION/EXPOSITORY

Face to Face with Whales
Author: Nicklin, Flip & Linda
NONFICTION/EXPOSITORY

Fame and Glory in Freedom, Georgia
Author: O'Connor, Barbara
FICTION/REALISTIC, Level S

Families Through Time
Author: Dustman, Jeanne
NONFICTION/EXPOSITORY, Level N

Far North
Author: Reynolds, Jan
NONFICTION/NARRATIVE

Farmer Will Allen and the Growing Table
Author: Martin, Jacqueline Briggs
NONFICTION/BIOGRAPHY

Fatty Legs: A True Story
Author: Jordan-Fenton, Christy, & Pokiak-Fenton, Margaret
NONFICTION/MEMOIR

Fearless! Stunt People
Author: Cohn, Jessica
NONFICTION/EXPOSITORY, Level S

Fergal's Tale
FICTION/HISTORICAL, Level T

Field Guide (The Spiderwick Chronicles, Book 1), **The**
Author: DiTerlizzi, Tony & Holly Black
FICTION/FANTASY

Field of Gold, The
FICTION/FOLKTALE, Level Q

Finders Keepers
FICTION/REALISTIC, Level U

Finding Dinosaur Sue
NONFICTION/NARRATIVE, Level R

First Emoticon, The
NONFICTION/NARRATIVE, Level P

Fish for Sillibump: A Noodlehead Tale
FICTION/FOLKTALE, Level Q

Fishers: Then and Now
Author: Zamosky, Lisa
NONFICTION/EXPOSITORY, Level N

Flint Heart, The
Author: Paterson, Katherine & John
FICTION/FAIRY TALE

Floating School, A
NONFICTION/EXPOSITORY, Level O

Floodwaters
FICTION/REALISTIC, Level U

Flush!
NONFICTION/EXPOSITORY, Level U

Fly Away
Author: MacLachlan, Patricia
FICTION/REALISTIC

Fly High: The Story of Bessie Coleman
Author: Borden, Louise, & Kroeger, Mary Kay
NONFICTION/BIOGRAPHY

Follow the Moon Home: A Tale of One Idea, Twenty Kids, and a Hundred Sea Turtles
Author: Cousteau, Philippe, & Hopkinson, Deborah
FICTION/REALISTIC

Fools of Chelm, The
FICTION/FOLKTALE, Level Q

Footprints on the Moon
Author: Siy, Alexandra
NONFICTION/EXPOSITORY, Level U

Fractions = Trouble
Author: Mills, Claudia
FICTION/REALISTIC, Level M

Framed: A Swindle Mystery
Author: Korman, Gordon
FICTION/REALISTIC, Level V

Freedom Summer
Author: Wiles, Deborah
FICTION/HISTORICAL

From Garbage to Garden: How to Make Compost
NONFICTION/PROCEDURAL, Level O

From Heroes to Zeros: Outrageous Sports Cheaters
NONFICTION/EXPOSITORY, Level V

From Russia with Lunch
Author: Hale, Bruce
FICTION/FANTASY, Level R

From Terrifying to Electrifying: Extreme Adventures
NONFICTION/EXPOSITORY, Level R

Frozen Land
Author: Reynolds, Jan
NONFICTION/NARRATIVE

Full Court Pressure
Author: Gunderson, Jessica
FICTION/REALISTIC, Level U

Fungus Among Us, A
FICTION/SCIENCE FICTION, Level S

Gecko
Author: Huber, Raymond
HYBRID

Get Cooking
FICTION/REALISTIC [HUMOROUS], Level T

Ghosts
Author: Osborne, Mary Pope, & Boyce, Natalie Pope
NONFICTION/EXPOSITORY, Level O

Giant Squid
Author: Fleming, Candace
NONFICTION/EXPOSITORY

Gloria's Way
Author: Cameron, Ann
FICTION/REALISTIC, Level O

Glorious Flight, The: Across the Channel with Louis Blériot
Author: Provensen, Alice & Martin
FICTION/HISTORICAL

Gnome War, The
FICTION/FANTASY, Level Q

Goin' Someplace Special
Author: McKissack, Patricia
FICTION/HISTORICAL

Going Home: The Mystery of Animal Migration
Author: Berkes, Marianne
HYBRID/EXPOSITORY, Level R

Gold-Threaded Dress, The
Author: Marsden, Carolyn
FICTION/REALISTIC

Grain of Rice, A
Author: Pittman, Helena Clare
FICTION/FOLKTALE, Level P

Grandfather's Gamelan
FICTION/REALISTIC, Level T

Grandfather's Journey
Author: Say, Allen
FICTION/HISTORICAL

Graves Family, The
Author: Polacco, Patricia
FICTION/FANTASY

Great Escape, The: Animals That Glide
NONFICTION/EXPOSITORY, Level P

Great Pacific Garbage Patch, The
NONFICTION/EXPOSITORY, Level S

Great Pie Giveaway, The
FICTION/REALISTIC, Level Q

Great TV Blackout, The
FICTION/REALISTIC, Level P

Great White Sharks
Author: Markle, Sandra
NONFICTION/EXPOSITORY, Level P

Gross Fossils: The Secrets of Dinosaur Dung
HYBRID/EXPOSITORY/FANTASY, Level R

Growing Up in the Amazon
NONFICTION/BIOGRAPHY, Level S

GULP! A Journey Through Your Digestive System
NONFICTION/EXPOSITORY, Level U

Hachiko Waits
Author: Newman, Leslea
FICTION/REALISTIC

Hand to Heart: Improving Communities
Author: Cohn, Jessica
NONFICTION/EXPOSITORY, Level T

Hands Around the Library: Protecting Egypt's Treasured Books
Author: Roth, Susan, & Leggett, Karen Abouraya
NONFICTION/NARRATIVE

Hank Aaron, Brave in Every Way
Author: Golenbock, Peter
NONFICTION/BIOGRAPHY

Hansel and Gretel and the Haunted Hut
Author: Blevins, Wiley
FICTION/FAIRY TALE, Level M

Harmony Island
FICTION/REALISTIC, Level S

Hellen Keller: A New Vision
Author: Hollingsworth, Tamara Leigh
NONFICTION/BIOGRAPHY, Level Q

Heroes
Author: Mochizuki, Ken
FICTION/HISTORICAL

Himalaya
Author: Reynolds, Jan
NONFICTION/NARRATIVE

Honest-to-Goodness Truth, The
Author: McKissack, Patricia
FICTION/REALISTIC

Hoop Hustle
Author: Maddox, Jake
FICTION/REALISTIC

Houdini Box, The
Author: Selznick, Brian
FICTION/HISTORICAL

How Bicycles Changed the World
NONFICTION/EXPOSITORY, Level U

How Can We Reduce Household Waste?
Author: Pratt, Mary K.
NONFICTION/EXPOSITORY, Level Q

How Coyote Stole the Summer: A Native American Folktale
Author: Krensky, Steven
FICTION/FOLKTALE, Level N

How Snakes and Other Animals Taste the Air
Author: Rajczak, Kristen
NONFICTION/EXPOSITORY, Level R

Human Environmental Impact: How We Affect Earth
Author: Sawyer, Ava
NONFICTION/EXPOSITORY, Level V

Hundred Dresses, The
Author: Estes, Eleanor
FICTION/REALISTIC, Level P

Hunter Moran Digs Deep
Author: Giff, Patricia Reilly
FICTION/REALISTIC, Level R

I Survived the Destruction of Pompeii, AD 79
Author: Tarshis, Lauren
FICTION/HISTORICAL

I Survived the Japanese Tsunami, 2011
Author: Tarshis, Lauren
FICTION/REALISTIC, Level Q

BC *I Wish I Were a Butterfly*
Author: Howe, James
FICTION/FANTASY

IR *I Wonder Why Stars Twinkle and Other Questions About Space*
Author: Stott, Carole
NONFICTION/EXPOSITORY, Level P

IR *I'm Out of My Body... Please Leave a Message*
Author: Greenburg, Dan
FICTION/FANTASY, Level N

IR *Ice Dove and Other Stories, The*
Author: De Anda, Diane
FICTION/REALISTIC, Level M

GR *Iceberg Wrangler, The*
NONFICTION/NARRATIVE, Level Q

IRA *Imagine*
Author: Herrera, Juan Felipe
NONFICTION/MEMOIR

BC *In Her Hands: The Story of Sculptor Augusta Savage*
Author: Schroeder, Alan
NONFICTION/BIOGRAPHY

IRA *In Our Mothers' House*
Author: Polacco, Patricia
FICTION/REALISTIC

IRA *In the Swim*
Author: Florian, Douglas
FICTION/POETRY

IR *Incredible Bugs*
Author: Farndon, John
NONFICTION/EXPOSITORY, Level V

IRA *Insectlopedia*
Author: Florian, Douglas
FICTION/POETRY

GR *Inside the World of Medical Robots*
NONFICTION/EXPOSITORY, Level S

IR *Island of the Aunts*
Author: Ibbotson, Eva
FICTION/FANTASY, Level S

IR *It's Disgusting and We Ate It!: True Food Facts from Around the World and Throughout History*
Author: Solheinm, James
NONFICTION/EXPOSITORY, Level V

IRA *Ivan: The Remarkable True Story of the Shopping Mall Gorilla*
Author: Applegate, Katherine
NONFICTION/NARRATIVE

IR *Jack Adrift: Fourth Grade Without a Clue*
Author: Gantos, Jack
FICTION/REALISTIC, Level U

IR *Jack and the Bloody Beanstalk*
Author: Blevins, Wiley
FICTION/FAIRY TALE, Level M

IRA *Jalapeño Bagels*
Author: Wing, Natasha
FICTION/REALISTIC

GR *Jamal's Prize*
FICTION/REALISTIC, Level S

GR *Jason to the Rescue*
NONFICTION/NARRATIVE, Level T

GR *Jaylen Arnold: Life with Tourette's*
NONFICTION/NARRATIVE, Level Q

GR *Jim White's Discovery*
NONFICTION/NARRATIVE, Level Q

IRA *Journey*
Author: MacLachlan, Patricia
FICTION/REALISTIC

GR *Junkyard Art: The Sculptures of Bordalo II*
NONFICTION/BIOGRAPHY, Level Q

IRA *Junkyard Wonders, The*
Author: Polacco, Patricia
FICTION/REALISTIC

IRA *Kamishibai Man*
Author: Say, Allen
FICTION/REALISTIC

GR *Karma, the Dog Detective*
NONFICTION/NARRATIVE, Level P

BC *Keep On! The Story of Matthew Henson, Co-Discoverer of the North Pole*
Author: Hopkinson, Deborah
NONFICTION/BIOGRAPHY"

IR *Kindred Souls*
Author: MacLachlan, Patricia
FICTION/REALISTIC, Level Q

IRA *King for a Day*
Author: Khan, Rukhsana
FICTION/REALISTIC

BC *King's Equal, The*
Author: Paterson, Katherine
FICTION/FAIRY TALE

GR *Knights on Ice*
FICTION/REALISTIC, Level T

BC *Knucklehead: Tall Tales and Almost-True Stories of Growing Up Scieszka*
Author: Scieszka, Jon
NONFICTION/MEMOIR"

IRA *La Mariposa*
Author: Jimenez, Francisco
FICTION/REALISTIC

GR *Laughing All the Way*
FICTION/FANTASY [HUMOROUS], Level R

GR *Laughing Matter, A*
NONFICTION/EXPOSITORY, Level V

BC *Leon's Story*
Author: Tillage, Leon Walter
NONFICTION/MEMOIR

GR *Let the Games Begin!*
NONFICTION/EXPOSITORY, Level R

IR *Let's Talk About Race*
Author: Lester, Julius
NONFICTION/EXPOSITORY, Level P

GR *Libraries on the Move*
NONFICTION/EXPOSITORY, Level Q

IR *Life and Non-Life in an Ecosystem*
Author: Rice, William B.
NONFICTION/EXPOSITORY, Level T

IR *Life Cycle of a Butterfly, The*
Author: Kalman, Bobbie
NONFICTION/EXPOSITORY, Level P

IRA *Little Book of Sloth, A*
Author: Cooke, Lucy
NONFICTION/NARRATIVE

IR *Little Dead Riding Hood*
Author: Blevins, Wiley
FICTION/FAIRY TALE, Level M

GR *Living on the Edge*
NONFICTION/EXPOSITORY, Level U

IRA *Lizards, Frogs, and Polliwogs*
Author: Florian, Douglas
FICTION/POETRY

IR *Look Inside: Your Skeleton and Muscles*
Author: Williams, Ben
NONFICTION/EXPOSITORY, Level P

IR *Look Out for the Fitzgerald-Trouts*
Author: Spalding, Esta
FICTION/REALISTIC, Level T

GR *Looking at Snowflakes*
NONFICTION/EXPOSITORY, Level R

IRA *Lost Lake, The*
Author: Say, Allen
FICTION/REALISTIC

IRA *Lotus Seed, The*
Author: Garland, Sherry
FICTION/HISTORICAL

BC *Louis Sockalexis: Native American Baseball Pioneer*
Author: Wise, Bill
NONFICTION/BIOGRAPHY

IR *Love, Amalia*
Author: Ada, Alma Flor
FICTION/REALISTIC, Level R

GR *Lurking Deep Below: Lake Monsters*
NONFICTION/EXPOSITORY, Level Q

IRA *Ma Dear's Aprons*
Author: McKissack, Patricia
FICTION/HISTORICAL

GR *Made to Last: Building with Mud*
NONFICTION/EXPOSITORY, Level S

GR *Magic at the Castle: A Club for Young Magicians*
NONFICTION/BIOGRAPHY, Level U

BC *Magic Finger, The*
Author: Dahl, Roald
FICTION/FANTASY

GR *Magic Fountain, The: A Tale from Korea*
FICTION/FOLKTALE, Level R

IR *Magic Half, The*
Author: Barrows, Annie
FICTION/FANTASY, Level T

IR *Magic Pomegranate, The*
Author: Schram, Peninnah
FICTION/FOLKTALE, Level N

IR *Magic Thief, The: Found*
Author: Prineas, Sarah
FICTION/FANTASY, Level U

IRA *Magnificent Birds*
Author: Walker Books
NONFICTION/EXPOSITORY

GR *Mail Under the Sea*
NONFICTION/EXPOSITORY, Level N

GR *Making a Forest*
NONFICTION/EXPOSITORY, Level U

IR *Malted Falcon, The*
Author: Hale, Bruce
FICTION/FANTASY, Level R

IRA *Mammalabilia*
Author: Florian, Douglas
FICTION/POETRY

IRA *Mangoes, Mischief, and Tales of Friendship: Stories from India*
Author: Soundar, Chitra
FICTION/FOLKTALES

GR *Mareko the Chicken*
FICTION/REALISTIC, Level R

IR *Markets Around the World*
Author: Petersen, Casey Null
NONFICTION/EXPOSITORY, Level O

GR *Marooned on JaSama*
FICTION/SCIENCE FICTION, Level V

IRA *Mary Cassatt: Extraordinary Impressionist Painter*
Author: Herkert, Barbara
NONFICTION/BIOGRAPHY

GR *Mastodon Memorial School*
FICTION/FANTASY, Level N

IRA *Matchbox Diary, The*
Author: Fleischman, Paul
FICTION/REALISTIC

IR *May B.*
Author: Rose, Caroline Starr
FICTION/HISTORICAL, Level V

IRA *Me, Frida*
Author: Novesky, Amy
NONFICTION/BIOGRAPHY

IRA *Meet Danitra Brown*
Author: Grimes, Nikki
FICTION/POETRY

GR *Meet the Moviemakers*
NONFICTION/EXPOSITORY, Level T

BC *Midnight War of Mateo Martinez, The*
Author: Yardi, Robin
FICTION/FANTASY

IRA *Million Fish...More or Less, A*
Author: McKissack, Patricia
FICTION

GR *Miniature Margaret*
FICTION/FANTASY, Level U

IR *Miraculous Journey of Edward Tulane, The*
Author: DiCamillo, Kate
FICTION/FANTASY, Level U

GR *Mirrors on the Mountain*
NONFICTION/NARRATIVE, Level S

IR *Missing Marlin, The*
Author: Kelly, David A.
FICTION/REALISTIC, Level N

GR *MISSION: EARTH*
FICTION/SCIENCE FICTION, Level T

BC *Mission: Wolf Rescue*
Author: Jazynka, Kitson
NONFICTION/NARRATIVE

IR *Mistakes Were Made*
Author: Pastis, Stephan
FICTION/REALISTIC, Level Q

GR *Molly Mackerel McNo*
FICTION/FANTASY, Level S

IR *Money Through History*
Author: McManus, Lori
NONFICTION/EXPOSITORY, Level V

GR *Monster Chef, The*
FICTION/FANTASY, Level Q

IR *Most Endangered Animals In the World, The*
Author: Gagne, Tammy
NONFICTION/EXPOSITORY, Level O

IR *Mr. Chickee's Funny Money*
Author: Curtis, Christopher Paul
FICTION/FANTASY, Level U

BC *Mr. Lincoln's Way*
Author: Polacco, Patricia
FICTION/REALISTIC

BC *Mrs. Mack*
Author: Polacco, Patricia
NONFICTION/MEMOIR

IR *Murder, My Tweet*
Author: Hale, Bruce
FICTION/FANTASY, Level R

GR *My Brother the Dragon*
FICTION/REALISTIC, Level N

IR *My Life as a Book*
Author: Tashjian, Janet
FICTION/REALISTIC, Level S

IRA *My Name Is Sangoel*
Author: Williams, Karen Lynn, & Mohammed, Khadra
FICTION/REALISTIC

IR *My Son, the Time Traveler*
Author: Greenburg, Dan
FICTION/FANTASY, Level N

BC *Mystery of Meerkat Hill, The*
Author: Smith, Alexander McCall
FICTION/REALISTIC

IR *Mystery of the Missing Luck*
Author: Pearce, Jacqueline
FICTION/REALISTIC, Level O

IR *Natural Disasters: Violent Weather*
Author: Parker, Steve, & West, David
NONFICTION/EXPOSITORY, Level T

GR *Nature's Recycling Team*
NONFICTION/EXPOSITORY, Level S

Nenets, The: Reindeer Herders of Siberia
NONFICTION/EXPOSITORY, Level S

Never Trust a Cat Who Wears Earrings
Author: Greenburg, Dan
FICTION/FANTASY, Level N

New Shoes
Author: Meyer, Susan Lynn
FICTION/HISTORICAL

Niagra Falls, or Does It?
Author: Winkler, Henry, & Oliver, Lin
FICTION/REALISTIC, Level R

Night of the Gargoyles
Author: Bunting, Eve
FICTION/FANTASY

Night of the Living Worms
Author: Coverly, Dave
FICTION/ANIMAL FANTASY, Level Q

Night on Mount Entoto, A: A Folktale from Africa
FICTION/FOLKTALE, Level V

Noggin's New Broog
FICTION/FANTASY, Level O

Now Look What You've Done
Author: Pastis, Stephan
FICTION/REALISTIC, Level Q

Now You See Me
FICTION/FANTASY, Level P

Off to Class: Incredible and Unusual Schools Around the World
Author: Hughes, Susan
NONFICTION/EXPOSITORY, Level V

Ogre's Dinner, The
FICTION/FANTASY, Level S

Oh, Rats!: The Story of Rats and People
Author: Marrin, Albert
NONFICTION/EXPOSITORY, Level T

Old Is New Again: Textile Recycling
HYBRID/EXPOSITORY/REALISTIC, Level S

On the Wing
Author: Florian, Douglas
FICTION/POETRY

On the Wing
Author: Elliott, David
NONFICTION/POETRY

Once Upon a Time Machine
FICTION/SCIENCE FICTION, Level S

One Hen: How One Small Loan Made a Big Difference
Author: Milway, Katie Smith
FICTION/REALISTIC

One Plastic Bag: Isatou Ceesay and the Recycling Women of the Gambia
Author: Paul, Miranda
NONFICTION/NARRATIVE

Optical Illusions: Games for Your Brain
NONFICTION/EXPOSITORY, Level V

Other Side, The
Author: Woodson, Jacqueline
FICTION/HISTORICAL

Out to Lunch
Author: Krulik, Nancy
FICTION/FANTASY, Level M

Outrageous Outfits: History's Most Extreme Fashions
NONFICTION/EXPOSITORY, Level V

Parrots over Puerto Rico
Author: Roth, Susan L. &, Trumbore, Cindy
NONFICTION/NARRATIVE

Pecos Bill: Colossal Cowboy
Author: Tulien, Sean
FICTION/TALL TALE, Level O

Pelorus Jack: The Dolphin That Guided Ships
NONFICTION/NARRATIVE, Level Q

Persian Cinderella, The
Author: Climo, Shirley
FICTION/FAIRY TALE

Pickleball: From a Game to a Sport
NONFICTION/EXPOSITORY, Level O

Pigling: A Cinderella Story
Author: Jolley, Dan
FICTION/FAIRY TALE, Level R

Pink Lakes and Other Shocking Sights
NONFICTION/EXPOSITORY, Level Q

Place to Start a Family, A: Poems About Creatures That Build
Author: Harrison, David L.
NONFICTION/POETRY

Play Ball!
Author: Posada, Jorge, & Burleigh, Robert
NONFICTION/MEMOIR

Pleasing the Ghost
Author: Creech, Sharon
FICTION/FANTASY, Level V

Poppy and Rye
Author: Avi
FICTION/ANIMAL FANTASY, Level S

Potato Travels
NONFICTION/PROCEDURAL, Level S

Prairie Adventure of Sarah and Annie, Blizzard Survivors, The
Author: Figley, Marty Rhodes
FICTION/HISTORICAL, Level P

Princess Furball
Author: Huck, Charlotte
FICTION/FAIRY TALE

Promise, The
Author: Davies, Nicola
FICTION/REALISTIC

Radiant Child: The Story of Young Artist Jean-Michel Basquiat
Author: Steptoe, Javaka
NONFICTION/BIOGRAPHY

Rapping for Kids: Corey's Story
NONFICTION/BIOGRAPHY, Level P

Razia's Ray of Hope: One Girl's Dream of an Education
Author: Suneby, Elizabeth
NONFICTION/REALISTIC

Reach for the Stars: The Story of the Three-Year Swim Club
NONFICTION/NARRATIVE, Level T

Read Between the Lines
FICTION/REALISTIC [MYSTERY], Level Q

Reading the Sun
NONFICTION/EXPOSITORY, Level V

Reading the Wind
NONFICTION/EXPOSITORY, Level V

Real Batman, The
NONFICTION/BIOGRAPHY, Level R

Really Weird Sports
NONFICTION/EXPOSITORY, Level R

Red Butterfly: How a Princess Smuggled the Secret of Silk out of China
Author: Noyes, Deborah
FICTION/HISTORICAL

Reluctant Brownie, The
FICTION/REALISTIC, Level U

Remarkable Towns
NONFICTION/EXPOSITORY, Level U

Rescue & Jessica: A Life-Changing Friendship
Author: Kensky, Jessica, & Downes, Patrick
FICTION/REALISTIC

Revenge of the Dragon Lady
Author: McMullan, Kate
FICTION/FANTASY, Level P

Rhino Rescue!
Author: Meeker, Clare
NONFICTION/NARRATIVE

Rickshaw Girl
Author: Perkins, Mitali
FICTION/REALISTIC

Riley's Letter
FICTION/REALISTIC, Level P

Rising from the Desert: Building the Burj Khalifa
NONFICTION/NARRATIVE, Level U

Robin Hood: A Graphic Novel
Author: Shephard, Aaron, & Watson, Anne
FICTION/LEGEND, Level N

Rock Stars!
NONFICTION/EXPOSITORY, Level T

Rockslide
FICTION/REALISTIC, Level T

Rough-Face Girl, The
Author: Martin, Rafe
FICTION/FAIRY TALE

Roughing It
FICTION/REALISTIC, Level P

Rowan of Rin
Author: Rodda, Emily
FICTION/FANTASY

Royal Bee, The
Author: Park, Frances & Ginger
FICTION/HISTORICAL

Rumpelstiltskin
Author: Zelinsky, Paul O.
FICTION/FAIRY TALE

Ruth and the Green Book
Author: Ramsey, Calvin Alexander
FICTION/HISTORICAL

Sadako
Author: Coerr, Eleanor
FICTION/HISTORICAL

Sadako and the Thousand Paper Cranes
Author: Coerr, Eleanor
FICTION/HISTORICAL, Level R

Safe Haven for Raptors
NONFICTION/EXPOSITORY, Level V

Sahara
Author: Reynolds, Jan
NONFICTION/NARRATIVE

Sailing on the Edge
FICTION/REALISTIC, Level R

Saving Olive Basset
FICTION/REALISTIC, Level O

Savvy
Author: Law, Ingrid
FICTION/FANTASY, Level U

Science Behind Wonders of the Earth, The: Cave Crystals, Balancing Rocks, and Snow Donuts
Author: Leavitt, Amie Jane
NONFICTION/EXPOSITORY, Level T

Science of Sleep, The
NONFICTION/EXPOSITORY, Level U

Scraps Book, The: Notes from a Colorful Life
Author: Ehlert, Lois
NONFICTION/MEMOIR

Scumble
Author: Law, Ingrid
FICTION/FANTASY, Level U

Seal Garden, The
Author: Read, Nicholas
NONFICTION/NARRATIVE

Secret Kingdom, The: Nek Chand, a Changing India, and a Hidden World of Art
Author: Rosenstock, Barb
NONFICTION/BIOGRAPHY

Seeds That Fly, Float, and Explode
NONFICTION/EXPOSITORY, Level O

Seven Brothers, The: A Noodlehead Tale
FICTION/FOLKTALE, Level Q

Shadow Door, The
Author: Bannister
FICTION/FANTASY, Level S

Shape Me a Rhyme: Nature's Forms in Poetry
Author: Yolen, Jane
NONFICTION/POETRY

Shh! Wild Animals Sleeping
NONFICTION/EXPOSITORY, Level Q

Shorty
FICTION/REALISTIC, Level T

Shouldn't You Be in School?
Author: Snicket, Lemony
FICTION/FANTASY, Level V

Shredderman: Attack of the Tagger
Author: Van Draanen, Wendelin
FICTION/REALISTIC, Level R

Shredderman: Secret Identity
Author: Van Draanen, Wendelin
FICTION/REALISTIC, Level R

Sideways Stories from Wayside School
Author: Sachar, Louis
FICTION/FANTASY, Level P

Sign Painter, The
Author: Say, Allen
FICTION/REALISTIC

Silent Skies: When the Plane People Came
NONFICTION/NARRATIVE, Level V

Silly World Records . . . and How to Beat Them
NONFICTION/EXPOSITORY, Level N

Sinking In: The Truth About Quicksand
NONFICTION/EXPOSITORY, Level O

Sisters
Author: Telgemeier, Raina
NONFICTION/MEMOIR

Six Dots: A Story of Young Louis Braille
Author: Bryant, Jen
NONFICTION/BIOGRAPHY

Sloth, The: Living with Less
NONFICTION/EXPOSITORY, Level P

Smart Girl's Guide, A: Friendship Troubles
Author: Criswell, Patti Kelley
NONFICTION/EXPOSITORY, Level U

Snicker of Magic, A
Author: Lloyd, Natalie
FICTION/FANTASY, Level V

Snook Alone
Author: Nelson, Marilyn
FICTION/FANTASY

Soap Box Rosie
FICTION/HISTORICAL, Level S

Sootface: An Ojibwa Cinderella Story
Author: San Souci, Robert D.
FICTION/FAIRY TALE

Space Burritos
NONFICTION/EXPOSITORY, Level O

Space Rock Hunt, The
FICTION/REALISTIC, Level R

GR *Spaghetti Garden*
FICTION/REALISTIC, Level R

GR *Spy, The*
FICTION/REALISTIC, Level P

GR *Stand Tall*
FICTION/REALISTIC, Level T

GR *Star Power: The Story of Annie Jump Cannon*
NONFICTION/BIOGRAPHY, Level T

IR *Star Scouts*
Author: Lawrence, Mike
FICTION/FANTASY, Level V

IRA *Step Right Up: How Doc and Jim Key Taught the World About Kindness*
Author: Bowman, Donna Janell
NONFICTION/BIOGRAPHY

IR *Still Firetalking*
Author: Polacco, Patricia
NONFICTION/MEMOIR, Level O

IRA *Stitchin' and Pullin': A Gee's Bend Quilt*
Author: McKissack, Patricia
FICTION/POETRY

BC *Strange Place to Call Home, A*
Author: Singer, Marilyn
NONFICTION/POETRY

GR *Strange Story of Ketchup, The*
NONFICTION/EXPOSITORY, Level O

IRA *Strong to the Hoop*
Author: Coy, John
FICTION/REALISTIC

GR *Stunt Camp*
FICTION/REALISTIC, Level U

GR *Suiting Up for Space*
NONFICTION/EXPOSITORY, Level T

IR *Surprise Island*
Author: Warner, Gertrude Chandler
FICTION/REALISTIC, Level O

BC *Sweet Clara and the Freedom Quilt*
Author: Hopkinson, Deborah
FICTION/HISTORICAL

IR *Switch*
Author: Law, Ingrid
FICTION/FANTASY, Level U

BC *Sylvia & Aki*
Author: Conkling, Winifred
FICTION/HISTORICAL

IRA *Symphony of Whales, A*
Author: Schuch, Steve
FICTION/REALISTIC

GR *Taking Cover*
FICTION/REALISTIC, Level V

GR *Taking the Reins*
FICTION/HISTORICAL, Level R

IR *Tale of Despereaux, The*
Author: DiCamillo, Kate
FICTION/FANTASY, Level U

BC *Tale of the Mandarin Ducks, The*
Author: Paterson, Katherine
FICTION/FAIRY TALE

GR *Talking Bird, The: A Tale from China*
FICTION/FOLKTALE, Level O

GR *Talking in Crayon*
NONFICTION/MEMOIR, Level R

GR *Taming Jazz*
FICTION/REALISTIC, Level O

IR *Taste of Blackberries, A*
Author: Buchanan Smith, Doris
FICTION/REALISTIC, Level S

IRA *Tea with Milk*
Author: Say, Allen
FICTION/HISTORICAL

GR *Temple Grandin's Squeeze Machine*
NONFICTION/BIOGRAPHY, Level T

GR *Temptation*
FICTION/REALISTIC, Level U

GR *Terrible, Terrible Yips, The*
NONFICTION/EXPOSITORY, Level P

IRA *These Hands*
Author: Mason, Margaret H.
FICTION/HISTORICAL

GR *They Called Him Mr. Bones*
NONFICTION/BIOGRAPHY, Level R

IR *Thief in the Village and Other Stories of Jamaica, A*
Author: Berry, James
FICTION/REALISTIC, Level V

IR *Thing About Georgie, The*
Author: Graff, Lisa
FICTION/REALISTIC, Level T

IR *Three Good Deeds*
Author: Vande Velde, Vivian
FICTION/FANTASY, Level S

IR *Thunder Creek Ranch*
Author: Spreen Bates, Sonya
FICTION/REALISTIC, Level M

GR *Time to Remember, A*
NONFICTION/EXPOSITORY, Level S

IR *Tiny Creatures*
Author: Bradley, Timothy
NONFICTION/EXPOSITORY, Level S

GR *Tiny Horses, Big Jobs*
NONFICTION/EXPOSITORY, Level Q

IR *Titanic: Collision Course*
Author: Korman, Gordon
FICTION/HISTORICAL, Level T

IR *Titanic: S.O.S.*
Author: Korman, Gordon
FICTION/HISTORICAL, Level T

IR *Titanic: Unsinkable*
Author: Korman, Gordon
FICTION/HISTORICAL, Level T

IR *Tools and Treasures of the Ancient Maya*
Author: Doeden, Matt
NONFICTION/EXPOSITORY, Level T

GR *Tough Enough*
NONFICTION/MEMOIR, Level Q

BC *Train to Somewhere*
Author: Bunting, Eve
FICTION/HISTORICAL

GR *Treasure of Timbuktu, The*
NONFICTION/NARRATIVE, Level V

GR *Trinity's Robot*
FICTION/SCIENCE FICTION, Level Q

GR *Trouble*
FICTION/REALISTIC, Level O

GR *Trouble at Space Station 6*
FICTION/SCIENCE FICTION, Level S

GR *Trouble on the Trail*
FICTION/REALISTIC, Level P

GR *Truth About Super Strength, The*
NONFICTION/EXPOSITORY, Level S

IR *Truth of Me, The*
Author: MacLachlan, Patricia
FICTION/REALISTIC, Level Q

IRA *Tuck Everlasting*
Author: Babbitt, Natalie
FICTION/FANTASY

IRA *Twelve Dancing Princesses, The*
Author: Isadora, Rachel
FICTION/FAIRY TALE

IRA *Twelve Kinds of Ice*
Author: Obed, Ellen Bryan
NONFICTION/MEMOIR

BC *Twits, The*
Author: Dahl, Roald
FICTION/FANTASY

IRA *Uncle Jed's Barbershop*
Author: Mitchell, Margaree King
FICTION/HISTORICAL

BC *Uncle Willie and the Soup Kitchen*
Author: DiSalvo-Ryan, DyAnne
FICTION/REALISTIC

BC *Uncommon Traveler: Mary Kingsley in Africa*
Author: Brown, Don
NONFICTION/BIOGRAPHY

GR *Underwater Art*
NONFICTION/NARRATIVE, Level U

IRA *Upside Down Boy, The*
Author: Herrera, Juan Felipe
NONFICTION/MEMOIR

IR *Upside-Down Magic*
Author: Mlynowski, Sarah, Myracle, Lauren, & Jenkins, Emily
FICTION/FANTASY, Level O

GR *Village on Stilts, A*
NONFICTION/NARRATIVE, Level S

IR *Volcano Goddess Will See You Now, The*
Author: Greenburg, Dan
FICTION/FANTASY, Level N

GR *Vultures: Nature's Cleanup Crew*
NONFICTION/EXPOSITORY, Level Q

GR *Wacky Ways Some Foods Grow, The*
NONFICTION/EXPOSITORY, Level N

IR *Waiting for Normal*
Author: Connor, Leslie
FICTION/REALISTIC, Level V

GR *Wanted: Flesh-Eating Beetles*
NONFICTION/EXPOSITORY, Level T

GR *Watch Out! Animals with Surprising Defenses*
NONFICTION/EXPOSITORY, Level S

IR *Water Habitats*
Author: Kalman, Bobbie
NONFICTION/EXPOSITORY, Level N

IR *Wayside School Is Falling Down*
Author: Sachar, Louis
FICTION/FANTASY, Level P

IR *We Meet Again*
Author: Pastis, Stephan
FICTION/REALISTIC, Level Q

IR *Wedding Drama*
Author: English, Karen
FICTION/REALISTIC, Level N

IR *Wedding for Wiglaf?, A*
Author: McMullan, Kate
FICTION/FANTASY, Level P

GR *Welcome, Humans: A Visit to the Robot Hotel*
NONFICTION/EXPOSITORY, Level O

IRA *Weslandia*
Author: Fleischman, Paul
FICTION/FANTASY

IRA *What Are You Glad About? What Are You Mad About?*
Author: Viorst, Judith
FICTION/POETRY

GR *What Kind of Name Is Pickleball?*
NONFICTION/MEMOIR, Level O

IR *When Did You See Her Last?*
Author: Snicket, Lemony
FICTION/FANTASY, Level V

BC *When Jessie Came Across the Sea*
Author: Hest, Amy
FICTION/HISTORICAL

GR *Whirling on the Giant Wheel: Carly Schuna's Story*
NONFICTION/BIOGRAPHY, Level S

IR *Who Could That Be at This Hour?*
Author: Snicket, Lemony
FICTION/FANTASY, Level V

IR *Who Was Ferdinand Magellan?*
Author: Kramer, Sydelle
NONFICTION/BIOGRAPHY, Level T

IR *Who Was Jackie Robinson?*
Author: Herman, Gail
NONFICTION/BIOGRAPHY, Level P

IR *Who Was Marie Curie?*
Author: Stine, Megan
NONFICTION/BIOGRAPHY, Level V

IR *Whole New Ballgame, A*
Author: Bildner, Phil
FICTION/REALISTIC, Level T

GR *Wiley's Crop*
FICTION/TALL TALE, Level Q

IR *Willoughbys, The*
Author: Lowry, Lois
FICTION/FANTASY, Level U

BC *Wilma Unlimited*
Author: Krull, Kathleen
NONFICTION/BIOGRAPHY

GR *Wiping Woes: The History of Toilet Paper*
NONFICTION/NARRATIVE, Level S

GR *Wise Folk: A Book of Tales*
FICTION/FOLKTALES [SHORT STORIES], Level S

IR *Witches, The*
Author: Dahl, Roald
FICTION/FANTASY, Level R

IRA *Wolf Island*
Author: Read, Nicholas
NONFICTION/NARRATIVE

IRA *Wolves in the Walls, The*
Author: Gaimon, Neil
FICTION/FANTASY

IR *Wolves of Willoughby Chase, The*
Author: Aiken, Joan
FICTION/FANTASY, Level V

GR *Working in the Clouds: A City Window Washer*
NONFICTION/NARRATIVE, Level P

GR *World's Biggest Classroom, The*
NONFICTION/EXPOSITORY, Level Q

GR *Writing Words in the Sky*
NONFICTION/EXPOSITORY, Level R

IR *Year of the Baby, The*
Author: Cheng, Andrea
FICTION/REALISTIC, Level P

IR *Year of the Book, The*
Author: Cheng, Andrea
FICTION/REALISTIC, Level P

IR *Year of the Fortune Cookie, The*
Author: Cheng, Andrea
FICTION/REALISTIC, Level P

IRA *Yeh-Shen: A Cinderella Story from China*
Author: Ai-Ling, Louie
FICTION/FAIRY TALE

IR *Yellow House Mystery, The*
Author: Warner, Gertrude Chandler
FICTION/REALISTIC, Level O

GR *Young Bike Racers*
NONFICTION/EXPOSITORY, Level U

IR *Your Life as an Explorer on a Viking Ship*
Author: Troupe, Thomas Kingsley
HYBRID/EXPOSITORY, Level S

IR *Zita the Spacegirl: Far from Home*
Author: Hatke, Ben
FICTION/FANTASY, Level S

GR *Zooming to Zaragon*
FICTION/SCIENCE FICTION, Level V

Glossary

abbreviation Shortened form of a word that uses some of the letters: e.g., *Mr., etc., NY.*

academic language The language needed to be successful in schools and in other scholarly settings. Academic language is often used in classroom lessons, assignments, presentations, and books. Another term for academic language is academic vocabulary.

accented syllable A syllable that is given emphasis in pronunciation. See also *syllable, stress.*

acronym A word formed by combining the initial letter or letters of a group of words: e.g., *radar = ra*dio detecting *a*nd *r*anging.

adjective suffix A suffix put at the end of a word root or base word to form an adjective. See also *suffix.*

adjusting (as a strategic action) Reading in different ways as appropriate to the purpose for reading and type of text.

adventure / adventure story A contemporary realistic or historical fiction or fantasy text that presents a series of exciting or suspenseful events, often involving a main character taking a journey and overcoming danger and risk.

adverb suffix A suffix put at the end of a word root or base word to form an adverb. See also *suffix.*

affix A letter or group of letters added to the beginning or ending of a base or root word to change its meaning or function (a *prefix* or a *suffix*).

allegory A narrative with symbolic meaning, often personifying abstract ideas, told to teach or explain something.

alliteration The repetition of identical or similar initial consonant sounds in consecutive or nearby words or syllables.

alphabet book / ABC book A book that helps children develop the concept and sequence of the alphabet by pairing alphabet letters with pictures of people, animals, or objects with labels related to the letters.

alphabet linking chart A chart containing upper- and lowercase letters of the alphabet paired with pictures representing words beginning with each letter (*a, apple*).

alphabetic principle The concept that there is a relationship between the spoken sounds in oral language and the graphic forms in written language.

analogy The resemblance of a known word to an unknown word that helps you solve the unknown word's meaning. Often an analogy shows the relationship between two pairs of words.

analyzing (as a strategic action) Examining the elements of a text in order to know more about how it is constructed, and noticing aspects of the writer's craft.

animal fantasy A modern fantasy text geared to a very young audience in which animals act like people and encounter human problems.

animal story A contemporary realistic or historical fiction or fantasy text that involves animals and that often focuses on the relationships between humans and animals.

antonym A word that has the opposite meaning from another word: e.g., *cold* versus *hot.*

archaic word A word that is part of the language of the past and has specialized uses in language today.

assessment A means for gathering information or data that reveals what learners control, partially control, or do not yet control consistently.

assonance The repetition of identical or similar vowel sounds in stressed syllables in words that usually end with different consonant sounds.

autobiography A biographical text in which the story of a real person's life is written and narrated by that person. Autobiography is usually told in chronological sequence but may be in another order.

automaticity Rapid, accurate, fluent word decoding without conscious effort or attention.

ballad A type of traditional poem or tale, often recited or sung, and usually telling a story important to a particular region or culture. First handed down orally and later in writing, ballads usually feature a hero whose deeds and attributes have grown and become exaggerated over time.

base word A word in its simplest form, which can be modified by adding affixes: e.g., *read; reread, reading*. A base word has meaning, can stand on its own, and is easily apparent in the language. Compare to *word root*.

behavior An observable action.

biography A biographical text in which the story of a real person's life is written and narrated by another person. Biography is usually told in chronological sequence but may be in another order.

blend To combine sounds or word parts.

bold / boldface Type that is heavier and darker than usual, often used for emphasis.

book and print features The physical attributes of a text: e.g., font, layout, length.

callout A nonfiction text feature, such as a definition, a quote, or an important concept, that is highlighted by being set to one side of a text or enlarged within the body of the text.

capitalization The use of capital letters, usually the first letter in a word, as a convention of written language (for example, for proper names and to begin sentences).

categorization A structural pattern used especially in nonfiction texts to present information in logical categories (and subcategories) of related material.

cause and effect A structural pattern used especially in nonfiction texts, often to propose the reasons or explanations for how and why something occurs.

chapter book A form of text that is divided into chapters, each of which narrates an episode in the whole. Chapters in early reading books are short and often have titles.

choral reading Reading aloud in unison with a group.

chronological sequence A structural pattern used especially in nonfiction texts to describe a series of events in the order they happened in time.

circular story A fiction story in which a sense of completeness or closure results from the way the end of a piece returns to subject matter, wording, phrasing, or setting found at the beginning of the story.

clipped word A word formed from shortening another word: e.g., *ad (advertisement)*.

closed syllable A syllable that ends in a consonant: e.g., *lem*-on.

cognates Words that appear in different languages with very similar spellings and meanings.

comparative ending A suffix (e.g., *-er, -est*) put at the end of a base word to show comparison between or among two or more things.

compare and contrast A structural pattern used especially in nonfiction texts to compare two ideas, events, or phenomena by showing how they are alike and how they are different.

compound word A word made of two or more smaller words or morphemes: e.g., *play ground*. The meaning of a compound word is usually a combination of the meanings of the words it is made of or can be unrelated (or only distantly related) to the meanings of the combined units.

concept book A book organized to develop an understanding of an abstract or generic idea or categorization.

concept word A word that represents an abstract idea or name or a category of items. Categories of concept words include color names, number words, days of the week, months of the year, seasons, and so on.

concrete poetry A poem with words (and sometimes punctuation) arranged to represent a visual picture of the idea the poem is conveying.

conflict In a fiction text, a central problem within the plot that is resolved near the end of the story. In literature, characters are usually in conflict with nature, with other people, with society as a whole, or with themselves. Another term for conflict is *problem*.

connective A word or phrase that clarifies relationships and ideas in language. Simple connectives appear often in both oral and written language: e.g., *and, but, because*. Sophisticated connectives are used in written texts but do not appear often in everyday oral language: e.g., *although, however, yet*. Academic connectives appear in written texts but are seldom used in oral language: e.g., *in contrast, nonetheless, whereas*.

connotation The emotional meaning or association a word carries beyond its strict dictionary definition.

consonant A speech sound made by partial or complete closure of the airflow that causes friction at one or more points in the breath channel. The consonant sounds are represented by the letters *b, c, d, f, g, h, j, k, l, m, n, p, qu, r, s, t, v, w, y,* and *z*.

consonant blend Two or more consonant letters that often appear together in words and represent sounds that are smoothly joined, although each of the sounds can be heard in the word: e.g., *tr*im.

consonant cluster A sequence of two or three consonant letters: e.g., *tr*im, *ch*air.

consonant clusters and digraphs chart A chart of common initial or ending consonant clusters and digraphs paired with pictures of representative words.

consonant digraph Two consonant letters that appear together and represent a single sound that is different from the sound of either letter: e.g., she*ll*.

content (as a text characteristic) The subject matter of a text.

contraction A shortened form of one or more words. A letter or letters are left out, and an apostrophe takes the place of the missing letter or letters.

conventions In writing, formal usage that has become customary in written language. Grammar and usage, capitalization, punctuation, spelling, and handwriting and word-processing are categories of writing conventions.

counting book A book in which the structure depends on a numerical progression.

critiquing (as a strategic action) Evaluating a text based on the reader's personal, world, or text knowledge, and thinking critically about the ideas in the text.

cumulative tale A folktale in which story events are repeated with each new episode, giving them a rhythmic quality.

cursive A form of handwriting in which letters are connected.

decoding Using letter-sound relationships to translate a word from a series of symbols to a unit of meaning.

description A structural pattern used especially in nonfiction texts to provide sensory and emotional details so that readers can determine how something looks, moves, tastes, smells, or feels.

dialect A regional variety of a language. In most languages, including English and Spanish, dialects are mutually intelligible; the differences are actually minor.

dialogue Spoken words, usually set off with quotation marks in text. Dialogue is an element of a writer's style.

diary A record of events and observations written in the first-person and kept regularly in sequential, dated entries.

diction Clear pronunciation and enunciation in speech.

dimension A trait, characteristic, or attribute of a character in fiction.

directionality The orientation of print (in the English language, from left to right).

distinctive letter features Visual features that make each letter of the alphabet different from every other letter.

draft An early version of a writer's composition.

drafting and revising The process of getting ideas down on paper and shaping them to convey the writer's message.

drawing In writing, creating a rough image (i.e., a sketch) or a finished image (i.e., a drawing) of a person, place, thing, or idea to capture, work with, and render the writer's ideas.

early literacy concepts Very early understandings related to how written language or print is organized and used—how it works.

editing and proofreading The process of polishing the final draft of a written composition to prepare it for publication.

editorial A form of persuasive nonfiction text in which the purpose is to state and defend an opinion, usually by an editor of a magazine, newspaper, or other media source.

endpapers The sheets of heavy paper at the front and back of a hardback book that join the book block to the hardback binding. Endpapers are sometimes printed with text, maps, or design.

English language learner A person whose native language is not English and who is acquiring English as an additional language.

epic A traditional tale or long narrative poem, first handed down orally and later in writing. Usually an epic involves a journey and a set of tasks or tests in which the hero triumphs. Generally the nature of the deeds and attributes of the hero have grown and become exaggerated over time.

essay An analytic or interpretive piece of expository writing with a focused point of view, or a persuasive text that provides a body of information related to a social or scientific issue.

exaggeration An overstatement intended to go beyond the truth to make something seem greater than it is.

expository text / expository nonfiction A nonfiction text that gives the reader information about a topic. Expository texts use a variety of underlying text structures such as description, temporal sequence, categorization, compare and contrast, problem and solution, and question and answer. Forms of expository text include reports, news articles, and feature articles.

fable A folktale that demonstrates a useful truth and teaches a lesson. Usually including personified animals or natural elements such as the sun, fables appear to be simple but often convey abstract ideas.

factual text See *informational text.*

fairy tale A folktale about real problems but also involving magic and magical creatures. Also called "wonder tales," fairy tales have been handed down through oral language over the years.

family, friends, and school story A contemporary realistic text focused on the everyday experiences of students of a variety of ages, including relationships with family and friends and experiences at school.

fantasy A fiction text that contains elements that are highly unreal. Fantasy as a category of fiction includes genres such as animal fantasy, fantasy, and science fiction.

feature article A form of expository text that presents information organized around a central theme or idea, or one particular aspect of a topic.

fiction Invented, imaginative prose or poetry that tells a story. Along with nonfiction, fiction is one of two basic genres of literature.

figurative language Language that compares two objects or ideas to allow the reader to see something more clearly or understand something in a new way. An element of a writer's style, figurative language changes or goes beyond literal meaning. See also *simile, metaphor, personification.*

fluency In reading, this term names the ability to read continuous text with good momentum, phrasing, appropriate pausing, intonation, and stress. In word solving, this term names the ability to solve words with speed, accuracy, and flexibility.

folktale A traditional fiction text about a people or "folk," originally handed down orally from generation to generation. Folktales are usually simple tales and often involve talking animals.

font In printed text, the collection of type (letters) in a particular style.

form A kind of text that is characterized by particular elements. Short story, for example, is a form of fiction writing that can be any fiction genre.

formal letter In writing, a functional nonfiction text usually addressed to a stranger, in which the form (for example, a business letter) follows specific conventions.

fractured fairy tale A retelling of a familiar fairy tale with characters, setting, or plot events changed, often for comic effect.

free verse A type of poetry with irregular meter. Free verse may include rhyme, alliteration, and other poetic sound devices.

friendly letter In writing, a functional nonfiction text usually addressed to friends and family that may take the form of notes, letters, invitations, or email.

functional text A nonfiction text intended to accomplish a practical task. Examples of functional texts include letters, lists, test writing, and writing about reading.

gathering seeds Collecting ideas, snippets of language, descriptions, and sketches for potential use in written composition.

genre A kind of category of text or artistic work or a class of artistic endeavor (including music, drama, and studio arts) that has a characteristic form or technique.

grammar Complex rules by which people can generate an unlimited number of phrases, sentences, and longer texts in that language. *Conventional grammar* refers to the accepted grammatical conventions in a society.

grapheme A letter or cluster of letters representing a single sound, or phoneme: e.g., *a, eigh, ay*.

graphic feature In fiction texts, graphic features are usually illustrations. In nonfiction texts, graphic features include photographs, paintings and drawings, charts, diagrams, tables and graphs, maps, and timelines.

graphic text A form of text with comic strips or other illustrations on every page. In fiction, a story line continues across the text; illustrations, which depict moment-to-moment actions and emotions, are usually accompanied by dialogue in speech balloons and occasional narrative description of actions. In nonfiction, factual information is presented in categories or sequence.

graphophonic relationship The relationship between the oral sounds of the language and the written letters or clusters of letters. See also *semantic system, syntactic system*.

Greek root A word root that comes from Greek. Many English words contain Greek roots. See also *word root*.

guide words The words at the top of a dictionary page to indicate the first and last word on the page.

haiku An ancient Japanese form of non-rhyming poetry that creates a mental picture and makes a concise emotional statement.

have a try To write a word, notice that it doesn't look quite right, try it two or three other ways, and decide which construction looks right; to make an attempt and self-check.

high fantasy A long, complex modern fantasy text characterized by the motifs of traditional literature—the hero, the hero's quest, the struggle between good and evil. High fantasy involves stories that take place in an alternative world alongside the real world, or where our world does not exist.

high-frequency words Words that occur often in the spoken and written language.

historical fiction A fiction text that takes place in a realistically (and often factually) portrayed setting of a past era. Compare to *realistic fiction*.

homograph One of two or more words spelled alike but different in meaning, derivation, or pronunciation: e.g., the *bat* flew away, he swung the *bat;* take a *bow, bow* and arrow.

homonym One of two or more words spelled and pronounced alike but different in meaning: e.g., we had *quail* for dinner; I would *quail* in fear. A homonym is a type of homograph.

homophone One of two or more words pronounced alike but different in spelling and meaning: e.g., *meat, meet; bear, bare.*

horror / horror story A fiction text in which events evoke a feeling of dread in both the characters and the reader. Horror stories often involve elements of fantasy, but they may also fit into the category of realism.

humorous story A realistic-fiction text that is full of fun and meant to entertain.

hybrid / hybrid text A text that includes at least one nonfiction genre and at least one fiction genre blended in a coherent whole.

idea development In writing, the craft of presenting and elaborating the ideas and themes of a text.

idiom A phrase with meaning that cannot be derived from the conjoined meanings of its elements: e.g., *raining cats and dogs.*

illustration Graphic representation of important content (e.g., art, photos, maps, graphs, charts) in a fiction or nonfiction text.

imagery The use of language—descriptions, comparisons, and figures of speech—that helps the mind form sensory impressions. Imagery is an element of a writer's style.

inferring (as a strategic action) Going beyond the literal meaning of a text and thinking about what is not stated but is implied by the writer.

inflectional ending A suffix added to a base word to show tense, plurality, possession, or comparison: e.g., dark-*er.*

infographic An illustration—often in the form of a chart, graph, or map—that includes brief text and that presents and analyzes data about a topic in a visually striking way.

informational text A nonfiction text in which a purpose is to inform or give facts about a topic. Informational texts include the following genres—biography, autobiography, memoir, and narrative nonfiction, as well as expository texts, procedural texts, and persuasive texts.

interactive read-aloud A teaching context in which students are actively listening and responding to an oral reading of a text.

interactive writing A teaching context in which the teacher and students cooperatively plan, compose, and write a group text; both teacher and students act as scribes (in turn).

intonation The rise and fall in pitch of the voice in speech to convey meaning.

irony The use of words to express the opposite of the literal meaning.

italic / italics A type style that is characterized by slanting letters.

journal See *diary.*

label A written word or phrase that names the content of an illustration.

label book A picture book consisting of illustrations with brief identifying text.

language and literary features (as text characteristics) Qualities particular to written language that are qualitatively different from those associated with spoken language: e.g., dialogue, setting, description, mood.

language structure See *syntax*.

language use The craft of using sentences, phrases, and expressions to describe events, actions, or information.

Latin root A word root that comes from Latin. Many English words contain Latin roots. See also *word root*.

layout The way the print and illustrations are arranged on a page.

legend In relation to genre, this term names a traditional tale, first handed down orally and later in writing, that tells about a noteworthy person or event. Legends are believed to have some root in history, but the accuracy of the events and people they describe is not always verifiable. In relation to book and print features, this term names a key on a map or chart that explains what symbols stand for.

letter See *friendly letter* and *formal letter*.

letter combination Two or more letters that appear together and represent vowel sounds in words: e.g, *ea* in *meat*, *igh* in *sight*.

letter knowledge The ability to recognize and label the graphic symbols of language.

letters Graphic symbols representing the sounds in a language. Each letter has particular distinctive features and may be identified by letter name or sound.

letter-sound relationships The correspondence of letter(s) and sound(s) in written or spoken language.

lexicon Words that make up language.

limerick A type of rhyming verse, usually surprising and humorous and frequently nonsensical.

lists and procedures Functional writing that includes simple lists and how-to texts.

literary devices Techniques used by a writer to convey or enhance the story, such as figures of speech, imagery, symbolism, and point of view.

literary nonfiction A nonfiction text that employs literary techniques, such as figurative language, to present information in engaging ways.

log A form of chronological, written record, usually of a journey.

long vowel The elongated vowel sound that is the same as the name of the vowel. It is sometimes represented by two or more letters: e.g., c*a*ke, *ei*ght, m*ai*l. Another term for long vowel is *lax vowel*.

lowercase letter A small letter form that is usually different from its corresponding capital or uppercase form.

lyrical poetry A songlike type of poetry that has rhythm and sometimes rhyme and is memorable for sensory images and description.

main idea The central underlying idea, concept, or message that the author conveys in a nonfiction text. Compare to *theme, message*.

maintaining fluency (as a strategic action) Integrating sources of information in a smoothly operating process that results in expressive, phrased reading.

making connections (as a strategic action) Searching for and using connections to knowledge gained through personal experiences, learning about the world, and reading other texts.

malapropism The replacement of a word with another word that sounds similar but has a different meaning, creating a humorous effect. Compare to *spoonerism*.

media Channels of communication for information or entertainment. Newspapers and books are print media; television and the Internet are electronic media.

memoir A biographical text in which a writer takes a reflective stance in looking back on a particular time or person. Usually written in the first-person, memoirs are often briefer and more intense accounts of a memory or set of memories than the accounts found in biographies and autobiographies.

mentor texts Books or other texts that serve as examples of excellent writing. Mentor texts are read and reread to provide models for literature discussion and student writing.

message An important idea that an author conveys in a fiction or nonfiction text. See also *main idea, theme*.

metaphor A type of figurative language that describes one thing by comparing it to another unlike thing without using the word *like* or *as*. Compare to *simile*.

modeled writing An instructional technique in which a teacher demonstrates the process of composing a particular genre, making the process explicit for students.

monitoring and self-correcting (as a strategic action) Checking whether the reading sounds right, looks right, and makes sense, and solving problems when it doesn't.

monologue A long speech given by one person in a group.

mood Language and events that convey an emotional atmosphere in a text, affecting how the reader feels. An element of a writer's style, mood is established by details, imagery, figurative language, and setting. Compare to *tone*.

morpheme The smallest unit of meaning in a language. Morphemes may be free or bound. For example, *run* is a unit of meaning that can stand alone (a free morpheme). In *runs* and *running*, the added *-s* and *-ing* are also units of meaning. They cannot stand alone but add meaning to the free morpheme. The *-s* and *-ing* are examples of bound morphemes.

morphemic strategies Ways of solving words by discovering meaning through the combination of significant word parts or morphemes: e.g., *happy, happiest; run, runner, running*.

morphological system Rules by which morphemes (building blocks of vocabulary) fit together into meaningful words, phrases, and sentences.

morphology The combination of morphemes (building blocks of meaning) to form words; the rules by which words are formed from free and bound morphemes—for example, root words, prefixes, and suffixes.

multiple-meaning word A word that means something different depending on the way it is used: e.g., *run—home run, run in your stocking, run down the street, a run of bad luck.*

multisyllable word A word that contains more than one syllable.

mystery / mystery story A special type or form of realistic or historical fiction or fantasy text that deals with the solution of a crime or the unraveling of secrets.

myth A traditional narrative text, often based in part on historical events, that explains human behavior and natural events or phenomena such as seasons and the sky.

narrative nonfiction A nonfiction text that tells a story using a narrative structure and literary language to make a topic interesting and appealing to readers.

narrative poetry A type of poetry with rhyme and rhythm that relates an event or episode.

narrative text A fiction or nonfiction text that uses a narrative structure and tells a story.

narrative text structure A method of organizing a text. A simple narrative structure follows a traditional sequence that includes a beginning, a problem, a series of events, a resolution of the problem, and an ending. Alternative narrative structures may include devices such as flashback or flash-forward to change the sequence of events or allow for multiple narrators. See also *organization, text structure,* and *nonnarrative text structure.*

news article A form of expository text that presents factual information about one or more events.

nonfiction Prose or poetry that provides factual information. According to their structures, nonfiction texts can be organized into the categories of narrative and nonnarrative. Along with fiction, nonfiction is one of the two basic genres of literature.

nonnarrative text structure A method of organizing a text. Nonnarrative structures are used especially in three genres of nonfiction—expository texts, procedural texts, and persuasive texts. In nonnarrative nonfiction texts, underlying structural patterns include description, cause and effect, chronological sequence, temporal sequence, categorization, compare and contrast, problem and solution, and question and answer. See also *organization, text structure,* and *narrative text structure.*

noun suffix A suffix put at the end of a word root or base word to form a noun. See also *suffix.*

novella A fiction text that is shorter than a novel but longer than a short story.

nursery rhyme A short rhyme for children, usually telling a story.

onomatopoeia The representation of sound with words.

onset In a syllable, the part (consonant, consonant cluster, or consonant digraph) that comes before the vowel: e.g., the *cr* in *cream.* See also *rime.*

onset-rime segmentation The identification and separation of the onset (first part) and rime (last part, containing the vowel) in a word: e.g., *dr-ip.*

open syllable A syllable that ends in a vowel sound: e.g., *ho*-tel.

organization The arrangement of ideas in a text according to a logical structure, either narrative or nonnarrative. Another term for organization is *text structure*.

organizational tools Book and print features that help to organize a text: e.g., table of contents, section title, sidebar.

orthographic awareness The knowledge of the visual features of written language, including distinctive features of letters as well as spelling patterns in words.

orthography The representation of the sounds of a language with the proper letters according to standard usage (spelling).

palindrome A word that is spelled the same in either direction: e.g., *noon*.

parody A literary text in which the style of an author or an author's work is imitated for humorous effect.

performance reading An instructional context in which the students read orally to perform for others; they may read in unison or take parts. Shared reading, choral reading, and readers' theater are kinds of performance reading.

peritext Decorative or informative illustrations and/or print outside the body of the text. Elements of the peritext add to the aesthetic appeal and may have cultural significance or symbolic meaning.

personal narrative A brief text, usually autobiographical and written in the first-person, that tells about one event in the writer's life.

personification A figure of speech in which an animal is spoken of or portrayed as if it were a person, or in which a lifeless thing or idea is spoken of or portrayed as a living thing. Personification is a type of figurative language.

persuasive text A nonfiction text intended to convince the reader of the validity of a set of ideas—usually a particular point of view.

phoneme The smallest unit of sound in spoken language. There are forty-four units of speech sounds in English.

phoneme addition To add a beginning or ending sound to a word: e.g., /h/ + *and*; *an* + /t/.

phoneme blending To identify individual sounds and then to put them together smoothly to make a word: e.g., /k//a//t/ = *cat*.

phoneme deletion To omit a beginning, middle, or ending sound of a word: e.g., /k//a//s//k/ - /k/ = *ask*.

phoneme-grapheme correspondence The relationship between the sounds (phonemes) and letters (graphemes) of a language.

phoneme isolation The identification of an individual sound—beginning, middle, or end—in a word.

phoneme manipulation The movement of sounds from one place in a word to another.

phoneme reversal The exchange of the first and last sounds of a word to make a different word.

phoneme substitution The replacement of the beginning, middle, or ending sound of a word with a new sound.

phonemic (or phoneme) awareness The ability to hear individual sounds in words and to identify particular sounds.

phonemic strategies Ways of solving words that use how words sound and relationships between letters and letter clusters and phonemes in those words.

phonetics The scientific study of speech sounds—how the sounds are made vocally and the relation of speech sounds to the total language process.

phonics The knowledge of letter-sound relationships and how they are used in reading and writing. Teaching phonics refers to helping children acquire this body of knowledge about the oral and written language systems; additionally, teaching phonics helps children use phonics knowledge as part of a reading and writing process. Phonics instruction uses a small portion of the body of knowledge that makes up phonetics.

phonogram A phonetic element represented by graphic characters or symbols. In word recognition, words containing a graphic sequence composed of a vowel grapheme and an ending consonant grapheme (such as *an* or *it*) are sometimes called a word family.

phonological awareness The awareness of words, rhyming words, onsets and rimes, syllables, and individual sounds (phonemes).

phonological system The sounds of the language and how they work together in ways that are meaningful to the speakers of the language.

photo essay A form of nonfiction text in which meaning is carried by a series of photographs with no text or very spare text.

picture book A form of illustrated fiction or nonfiction text in which pictures work with the text to tell a story or provide information.

planning and rehearsing The process of collecting, working with, and selecting ideas for a written composition.

play A form of dramatic text written to be performed rather than just read. A play will include references to characters, scenery, and action, as well as stage directions, and usually consists of scripted (written) dialogue between characters. Plays can be realistic fiction, historical fiction, or fantasy, and they might also include elements of special types of fiction such as mystery or romance.

plot The events, actions, conflict, and resolution of a story presented in a certain order in a fiction text. A simple plot progresses chronologically from start to end, whereas more complex plots may shift back and forth in time.

plural Of, relating to, or constituting more than one.

poetic text A fiction or nonfiction text intended to express feelings, sensory images, ideas, or stories.

poetry Compact, metrical writing characterized by imagination and artistry and imbued with intense meaning. Along with prose, poetry is one of the two broad categories into which all literature can be divided.

point of view The angle, or perspective, from which a fiction story is told, usually the first-person (the narrator is a character in the story) or the third-person (an unnamed narrator is not a character in the story).

portmanteau word A word made from blending two distinct words and meanings; e.g., *smoke* + *fog* = *smog*.

possessive Grammatical form used to show ownership; e.g., *John's, his.*

predicting (as a strategic action) Using what is known to think about what will follow while reading continuous text.

prefix A group of letters placed in front of a base word to change its meaning: e.g., *pre*plan.

principle In phonics, a generalization or a sound-spelling relationship that is predictable.

problem See *conflict*.

problem and solution A structural pattern used especially in nonfiction texts to define a problem and clearly propose a solution. This pattern is often used in persuasive and expository texts.

procedural text A nonfiction text that explains how to do something. Procedural texts are almost always organized in temporal sequence and take the form of directions (or "how-to" texts) or descriptions of a process.

propaganda One-sided speaking or writing deliberately used to influence the thoughts and actions of someone in alignment with specific ideas or views.

prose The ordinary form of spoken or written language in sentences and paragraphs and without the metrical structure of poetry. Along with poetry, prose is one of the two broad categories into which all literature can be divided. Prose includes two basic genres, fiction and nonfiction.

publishing The process of making the final draft of a written composition public.

punctuation Marks used in written text to clarify meaning and separate structural units. The comma and the period are common punctuation marks.

purpose A writer's overall intention in creating a text, or a reader's overall intention in reading a text. To tell a story is one example of a writer's purpose, and to be entertained is one example of a reader's purpose.

question and answer A structural pattern used especially in nonfiction texts to organize information in a series of questions with responses. Questions-and-answer texts may be based on a verbal or written interview, or on frequently arising or logical questions about a topic.

r-controlled vowel sound The modified or *r*-influenced sound of a vowel when it is followed by *r* in a syllable: e.g., *hurt*.

Reader's Notebook A notebook or folder of bound pages in which students write about their reading. The *Reader's Notebook* is used to keep a record of texts read and to express thinking. It may have several different sections to serve a variety of purposes.

readers' theater A performance of literature—i.e., a story, a play, or poetry—read aloud expressively by one or more persons rather than acted.

realistic fiction A fiction text that takes place in contemporary or modern times about believable characters involved in events that could happen. Contemporary realistic fiction usually presents modern problems that are typical for the characters, and it may highlight social issues. Compare with *historical fiction*.

related words Words that are related because of sound, spelling, category, or meaning. See also *synonym, antonym, homophone, homograph, analogy*.

report A form of expository text that synthesizes information from several sources in order to inform the reader about some general principles.

resolution / solution The point in the plot of a fiction story when the main conflict is solved.

rhyme The repetition of vowel and consonant sounds in the stressed syllables of words in verse, especially at the ends of lines.

rhythm The regular or ordered repetition of stressed and unstressed syllables in poetry, other writing, or speech.

rime In a syllable, the ending part containing the letters that represent the vowel sound and the consonant letters that follow: i.e., dr-*eam*. See also *onset*.

romance A special type of contemporary realistic or historical fiction text focused on the development of romantic (and sometimes sexual) attraction between characters.

root word See *word root*.

run-on sentence Two or more independent clauses that do not form a complete sentence because they are not joined correctly by punctuation and/or by a conjunction.

saga A long, sophisticated traditional tale or narrative poem.

satire Formerly, a fiction text that uses sarcasm and irony to portray and ridicule human failures. Like comedy, tragedy, and epic, satire was once a widely produced genre; it now appears in different forms or embedded within other genres.

schwa The sound of the middle vowel in an unstressed syllable (the *e* in *happen* and the sound between the *k* and *l* in *freckle*).

science fiction A modern fantasy text that involves technology, futuristic scenarios (or time travel to the past), and real or imagined scientific phenomena.

searching for and using information (as a strategic action) Looking for and thinking about all kinds of content in order to make sense of a text while reading.

segment To divide into parts: e.g., *to/ma/to*.

self-correcting Noticing when reading doesn't make sense, sound right, or look right, and fixing it when it doesn't.

semantic system The system by which speakers of a language communicate meaning through language. See also *graphophonic relationship, syntactic system*.

sentence complexity (as a text characteristic) The complexity of the structure or syntax of a sentence. Addition of phrases and clauses to simple sentences increases complexity.

sentence fragment A group of words written as a sentence but lacking some element—usually a subject or a verb—that would allow it to stand independently as a complete sentence.

sequel A form of literary work, typically a fiction text, that continues a story begun in a previous book. The central character usually remains the same, and new secondary characters may be introduced. Books with sequels are generally meant to be read in order.

series / series book A set of books that are connected by the same character(s) or setting. Each book in a series stands alone, and often books may be read in any order.

sets and subsets In relation to concept words, words that represent big ideas or items and words that represent related smaller ideas or items.

shared reading An instructional context in which the teacher involves a group of students in the reading of an enlarged text in order to introduce aspects of literacy (such as print conventions), develop reading strategies (such as decoding or predicting), and teach vocabulary.

shared writing An instructional context in which the teacher involves a group of students in the composing of a coherent text together. The teacher writes the enlarged text while scaffolding students' language and ideas.

short story A form of prose fiction that is focused on human experience as it is revealed in a series of interrelated events. Shorter and less complex structurally than novellas and novels, short stories use most of the same literary elements that are found in those forms.

short vowel A brief-duration sound represented by a vowel letter: e.g., the lal in *cat*.

Short Write A sentence or paragraph that students write at intervals while reading a text. Students may use sticky notes, note paper, or a reader's notebook to write about what they are thinking, feeling, or visualizing as they read. They may also note personal connections to the text.

silent *e* The final *e* in a spelling pattern that usually signals a long vowel sound in the word and that does not represent a sound itself: e.g., *make*.

simile A type of figurative language that describes one thing by comparing it to another unlike thing using the word *like* or *as*. Compare to *metaphor*.

solving words (as a strategic action) Using a range of strategies to take words apart and understand their meaning(s).

sources of information The various cues in a written text that combine to make meaning (e.g., syntax, meaning, and the physical shape and arrangement of type).

speech A form of expository, procedural, or persuasive text written to be spoken orally to an audience.

speech bubble A shape, often rounded, containing the words a character or person says in a cartoon or other text. Another term for *speech bubble* is *speech balloon*.

spelling patterns Beginning letters (onsets) and common phonograms (rimes), which form the basis for the English syllable. Knowing these patterns, a student can build countless words.

split dialogue Written dialogue in which a "*said* phrase" divides the speaker's words: e.g., "Come on," said Mom. "Let's go home."

spoonerism The switching of the first letters of words in a phrase, creating a humorous effect. Compare to *malapropism*.

sports story A contemporary realistic or historical fiction text focused on athletes and sports.

story-within-a-story A structural device occasionally used in fiction texts to present a shorter, self-contained narrative within the context of the longer primary narrative. See also *plot*.

strategic action Any one of many simultaneous, coordinated thinking activities that go on in a reader's brain. See *thinking within, beyond, and about the text*.

stress The emphasis given to some syllables or words in pronunciation. See also *accented syllable*.

style The way a writer chooses and arranges words to create a meaningful text. Aspects of style include sentence length, word choice, and the use of figurative language and symbolism.

suffix A group of letters added at the end of a base word or word root to change its function or meaning: e.g., hand*ful*, hope*less*.

summarizing (as a strategic action) Putting together and remembering important information, disregarding irrelevant information, while reading.

syllabication The division of words into syllables.

syllable A minimal unit of sequential speech sounds composed of a vowel sound or a consonant-vowel combination. A syllable always contains a vowel or vowel-like speech sound: e.g., *pen/ny*.

synonym One of two or more words that have different sounds but the same meaning: e.g., *high, tall*.

syntactic awareness The knowledge of grammatical patterns or structures.

syntactic system Rules that govern the ways in which morphemes and words work together in sentence patterns. This system is not the same as proper grammar, which refers to the accepted grammatical conventions. See also *graphophonic relationship, semantic system*.

syntax The way sentences are formed with words and phrases and the grammatical rules that govern their formation.

synthesizing (as a strategic action) Combining new information or ideas from reading text with existing knowledge to create new understandings.

tall tale A folktale that revolves around a central legendary character with extraordinary physical features or abilities. Tall tales are characterized by much exaggeration.

temporal sequence An underlying structural pattern used especially in nonfiction texts to describe the sequence in which something always or usually occurs, such as the steps in a process.

test writing A type of functional writing in which students are prompted to write a short constructed response (sometimes called *short answer*) or an extended constructed response (or *essay*).

text structure The overall architecture or organization of a piece of writing. Another term for text structure is *organization*. See also *narrative text structure* and *nonnarrative text structure*.

theme The central underlying idea, concept, or message that the author conveys in a fiction text. Compare to *main idea*.

thinking within, beyond, and about the text Three ways of thinking about a text while reading. Thinking within the text involves efficiently and effectively understanding what's on the page, the author's literal message. Thinking beyond the text requires making inferences and putting text ideas together in different ways to construct the text's meaning. In thinking about the text, readers analyze and critique the author's craft, the themes and ideas in the text, and literary elements.

thought bubble A shape, often rounded, containing the words (or sometimes an image that suggests one or more words) a character or person thinks in a cartoon or other text. Another term for *thought bubble* is *thought balloon*.

tone An expression of the author's attitude or feelings toward a subject reflected in the style of writing. Compare to *mood*.

tools As text characteristics, parts of a text designed to help the reader access or better understand it (table of contents, glossary, headings). In writing, references that support the writing process (dictionary, thesaurus).

topic The subject of a piece of writing.

traditional literature Stories passed down in oral or written form through history. An integral part of world culture, traditional literature includes folktales, tall tales, fairy tales, fables, myths, legends, epics, and ballads.

underlying structural pattern See *nonnarrative text structure*.

understandings Basic concepts that are critical to comprehending a particular area of content.

uppercase letter A large letter form that is usually different from its corresponding lowercase form. Another term for *uppercase letter* is *capital letter*.

verb suffix A suffix put at the end of a word root or base word to form a verb. See also *suffix*.

viewing self as writer Having attitudes and using practices that support a student's becoming a lifelong writer.

visual strategies Ways of solving words that use knowledge of how words look, including the clusters and patterns of the letters in words.

vocabulary Words and their meanings. See also *word meaning / vocabulary*.

voice The unique way that a writer uses language to convey ideas.

vowel A speech sound or phoneme made without stoppage of or friction in the airflow. The vowel sounds are represented by *a, e, i, o, u,* and sometimes *y*.

vowel combination See *letter combination*.

word A unit of meaning in language.

word analysis To break apart words into parts or individual sounds in order to parse them.

word boundaries The white space that appears before the first letter and after the last letter of a word and that defines the letter or letters as a word. It is important for young readers to learn to recognize word boundaries.

word-by-word matching Usually applied to a beginning reader's ability to match one spoken word with one printed word while reading and pointing. In older readers, the eyes take over the process.

word choice In writing, the craft of choosing words to convey precise meaning.

word family A term often used to designate words that are connected by phonograms or rimes (e.g., *hot, not, pot, shot*). A word family can also be a series of words connected by meaning (e.g., *baseless, baseline, baseboard*).

word meaning / vocabulary *Word meaning* refers to the commonly accepted meaning of a word in oral or written language. In education, *vocabulary* often refers to the words one knows in oral language and/or can read or write.

word origins The ancestry of a word in English and other languages.

word root A word part, usually from another language, that carries the essential meaning of and is the basis for an English word: e.g., *flect, reflect*. Most word roots cannot stand on their own as English words. Some word roots can be combined with affixes to create English words. Compare to *base word*. See also *Greek root, Latin root*.

word structure The parts that make up a word.

wordless picture book A form in which a story is told exclusively with pictures.

words (as a text characteristic) Decodability of words in a text; phonetic and structural features of words.

word-solving actions The strategies a reader uses to recognize words and understand their meaning(s).

writer's notebook A written log of potential writing topics or ideas that a writer would like to explore; a place to keep the writer's experimentations with writing styles.

References

Fountas, Irene C., and Gay Su Pinnell. 2018. *The Literacy Quick Guide.* Portsmouth, NH: Heinemann.

Use this reference tool to help you design effective literacy instruction for your classroom, school, or district.

———. 2017, 2011, 2008. *Fountas & Pinnell Benchmark Assessment Systems 1 and 2.* Portsmouth, NH: Heinemann.

Use this system to determine reading levels, gain specific information about reader's strengths and needs, and document progress over time.

———. 2017. *Guided Reading: Responsive Teaching Across the Grades,* Second Edition. Portsmouth, NH: Heinemann.

Use this book for help with teaching guided reading lessons. Learn how to select and introduce texts, teach during and after reading, and assess student progress.

———. 2015, 2014, 2009. *Leveled Literacy Intervention.* Orange System (Levels A–C, Kindergarten); Green System (Levels A–J, Grade 1); Blue System (Levels C–N, Grade 2); Red System (Levels L–Q, Grade 3); Gold System (Levels O–T, Grade 4); Purple System (Levels R–W, Grade 5); Teal System (Levels U–Z, Grade 6). Portsmouth, NH: Heinemann.

You can use these systems to align classroom teaching and intervention services. Leveled Literacy Intervention (LLI) *includes the professional book,* When Readers Struggle: Teaching That Works, *a program guide, lesson guides, a technology package, and fiction and nonfiction student books. The Lesson Guides provide specific help in implementing several lesson frameworks. The Guided Reading continuum is an integral part of lesson plans. The Orange system provides 110 lessons to be used with 110 different titles; Green includes 130 lessons and titles; Blue includes 120 lessons and titles; Red includes 192 lessons and 144 titles; Gold includes 192 lessons and 144 titles; Purple includes 204 lessons and 144 titles; and Teal includes 204 lessons and 144 titles. Each LLI system provides a complete range of resources, including children's books to support children who are struggling.*

———. 2014. *Fountas & Pinnell Select Collections.* Portsmouth, NH: Heinemann.

———. 2014. *Fountas & Pinnell Select Genre Sets.* Portsmouth, NH: Heinemann.

Use the PM Readers Collections *and* Genre Sets *organized according to their F&P Text Level Gradient™ within your classroom. Fountas & Pinnell Select Collections K–3 provides the classroom with books suitable for independent, guided, and take-home reading.*

———. 2013. "*Benchmark Assessment System 1* App." iTunes App Store. Portsmouth, NH: Heinemann.

———. 2013. "*Benchmark Assessment System 2* App." iTunes App Store. Portsmouth, NH: Heinemann.

————. 2013. "Fountas & Pinnell Universal Reading Record App." iTunes App Store. Portsmouth, NH: Heinemann.

These three Reading Record apps can be used as an efficient alternative to taking a reading record on paper. The Reading Record apps records the following student information: oral reading rate and accuracy rate, self-correction ratio rate, fluency score, and comprehension score. Use the apps to time the conference, calculate reading rates and ratios, save the record as a PDF, and sync the data to the Online Data Management System.

————. 2013. "*Leveled Literacy Intervention Blue* App." iTunes App Store. Portsmouth, NH: Heinemann.

————. 2013. "*Leveled Literacy Intervention Green* App." iTunes App Store. Portsmouth, NH: Heinemann.

————. 2013. "*Leveled Literacy Intervention Gold* App." iTunes App Store. Portsmouth, NH: Heinemann.

————. 2013. "*Leveled Literacy Intervention Orange* App." iTunes App Store. Portsmouth, NH: Heinemann.

————. 2013. "*Leveled Literacy Intervention Purple* App." iTunes App Store. Portsmouth, NH: Heinemann.

————. 2013. "*Leveled Literacy Intervention Red* App." iTunes App Store. Portsmouth, NH: Heinemann.

————. 2013. "*Leveled Literacy Intervention Teal* App." iTunes App Store. Portsmouth, NH: Heinemann.

Use the apps above for each Leveled Literacy Intervention *system. Each app provides the teacher with all of the Reading Records and texts specific to each system. Use the apps to complete Reading Records among your students in a paperless format, time the conference, calculate reading rates and ratios, save the record as a PDF, and sync the data to the Online Data Management System.*

————. 2013, 2011. *Reader's Notebook, K–2, 2–4, 4–8.* Portsmouth, NH: Heinemann.

Use the Reader's Notebook *to encourage reflection, inquiry, critical thinking, and dialogue about reading. The* Reader's Notebook *can be used to help students account for what they read through drawing and writing as they explore and convey their understanding.*

————. 2013. "*Sistema de evaluacion de la lectura* App." iTunes App Store. Portsmouth, NH: Heinemann.

Use this Reading Record App with your Spanish-speaking English language learners. This paperless Reading Record App, similar to the English version, records the following student information: oral reading rate and accuracy rate, self-correction ratio rate, fluency score, and comprehension score. Use the app to time the conference, calculate reading rates and ratios, save the record as a PDF, and sync the data to the Online Data Management System.

————. 2013, 2009, 2006. *The Fountas & Pinnell Leveled Book List, K–8, Volumes 1 & 2.* Portsmouth, NH: Heinemann.

Use these books and the leveled books website, fandpleveledbooks.com, with your studies of the Guided Reading continuum to analyze the characteristics of texts and select just-the-right book to use for guided reading.

———. 2013, 2009. *The Fountas & Pinnell Prompting Guide, Part 1, for Oral Reading and Early Writing, Spanish Edition.* Portsmouth, NH: Heinemann.

———. 2012, 2009. *The Fountas & Pinnell Prompting Guide, Part 1, for Oral Reading and Early Writing.* Portsmouth, NH: Heinemann.

———. 2012, 2009. *The Fountas & Pinnell Prompting Guide, Part 2, for Comprehension: Thinking, Talking, and Writing.* Portsmouth, NH: Heinemann.

———. 2012, 2009. *The Fountas & Pinnell Prompting Guide, Part 2, for Comprehension: Thinking, Talking, and Writing, Spanish Edition.* Portsmouth, NH: Heinemann.

The two tools listed above provide specific suggestions for language that you can use to teach, prompt for, and reinforce effective reading behaviors.

———. 2012. *The Fountas & Pinnell Genre Prompting Guide for Fiction.* Portsmouth, NH: Heinemann.

———. 2012. *The Fountas & Pinnell Genre Prompting Guide for Nonfiction, Poetry, and Test Taking, K–8.* Portsmouth, NH: Heinemann.

The Genre Prompting Guides *above are used to help guide students' inquiry toward explicit understandings of the characteristics of genres. Each prompting guide contains precise language for teaching readers how to focus their thinking and understanding of genres through inquiry.*

———. 2012. *Genre Study: Teaching with Fiction and Nonfiction Books.* Portsmouth, NH: Heinemann.

Use this professional resource with students to embark on an exploration into the study of genre.

———. 2012. *The Fountas & Pinnell Genre Quick Guide, K–8.* Portsmouth, NH: Heinemann.

This spiral-bound companion to Genre Study: Teaching with Fiction and Nonfiction Books *is designed to help you actively engage students in the exploration of texts so that they can notice and name genre characteristics and construct working definitions that guide their thinking as readers and writers.*

———. 2009. "Fountas & Pinnell Online Data Management Systems, Version 2." Portsmouth, NH: Heinemann.

Use the Fountas & Pinnell Online Data Management Systems to manage all of your assessment data.

———. 2008. *The Fountas & Pinnell Prompting Guides 1, 2, and Spanish Editions.* Portsmouth, NH: Heinemann. eBook.

The Prompting Guide eBook apps, available in English and Spanish, are suitable to use as ready-reference tools while working with students in several instructional contexts.

———. 2006. *Leveled Books, K–8: Matching Texts to Readers for Effective Teaching.* Portsmouth, NH: Heinemann.

Use this book and the leveled books website, fandpleveledbooks.com, with your studies of the Guided Reading continuum to analyze the characteristics of texts and select just-the-right book to use for guided reading.

———. 2006. *Teaching for Comprehending and Fluency: Thinking, Talking, and Writing About Reading, K–8.* Portsmouth, NH: Heinemann.

Use this book in your studies of the interactive read-aloud and literature discussions, shared and performance reading, and Guided Reading continuum to skillfully teach meaning making and fluency within any instructional context.

———. 2005. *Guided Reading: Essential Elements, The Skillful Teacher* (videotapes). Portsmouth, NH: Heinemann.

Use these videotapes with your studies in the Interactive Read-Aloud and Literature Discussion and Guided Reading continua. In the first part, "Essential Elements," watch guided reading lessons as they unfold to see how teachers introduce a text, support students as they read orally and silently, discuss text meaning, use "teaching points" to reinforce effective reading strategies, revisit the text to extend meaning, and conduct word work as needed. In part two, "The Skillful Teacher," observe the planning and organizing behind guided reading and learn how to meet the needs of individual readers. You'll discover how to group students, select books, plan book introductions, support word solving, teach comprehension strategies, develop fluency, and take running records.

———. 2005, 2001. *The Primary Literacy Video Collection: Guided Reading, Word Study,* and *Classroom Management.* Portsmouth, NH: Heinemann.

View these videos to see examples of classroom teaching and to learn how to create, organize, and manage a classroom environment that encourages and supports independent literacy learning.

———. 2001. *Guiding Readers and Writers: Teaching Comprehension, Genre, and Content Literacy.* Portsmouth, NH: Heinemann.

Use this book to explore and learn about the essential components of a quality upper-elementary literacy program.

McCarrier, Andrea, Gay Su Pinnell, and Irene C. Fountas. 2000. *Interactive Writing: How Language and Literacy Come Together, K–2.* Portsmouth, NH: Heinemann.

Use Interactive Writing *to support children's critical understanding of the writing process. In a step-by-step format, this book demonstrates how teachers can use interactive writing to teach a range of foundational literacy skills by sharing the pen with young writers.*

Pinnell, Gay Su, and Irene C. Fountas. 2018. *Literacy Beginnings: A Prekindergarten Handbook.* Portsmouth, NH: Heinemann.

A guide for supporting emerging readers, writers, and language users through play and exploration.

———. 2018. *The Fountas & Pinnell Phonics, Spelling, and Word Study System (Grades K, 1, and 2)*. Portsmouth, NH: Heinemann.

———. 2018. *The Fountas & Pinnell Word Study System (Grade 3)*. Portsmouth, NH: Heinemann.

———. 2019. *The Fountas & Pinnell Word Study System (Grade 4)*. Portsmouth, NH: Heinemann.

Use these lessons with your study of the Phonics, Spelling, and Word Study and Guided Reading continua, choosing lessons that align with your students' needs.

———. 2018. *Sing a Song of Poetry: A Teaching Resource for Phonemic Awareness, Phonics, and Fluency, Revised Edition (Grades K, 1, and 2)*. Portsmouth, NH: Heinemann.

Use these companions to the Phonics Lessons *series to utilize poetry to its full advantage to expand children's oral language capabilities, develop phonological awareness, and teach about the intricacies of print.*

———. 1998. *Word Matters: Teaching Phonics and Spelling in the Reading/Writing Classroom*. Portsmouth, NH: Heinemann.

This book will help you design and teach for effective word-solving strategies.

———. 2018. *Words That Sing: 100 Poetry Charts for Shared Reading, Pre-K–2*. Portsmouth, NH: Heinemann.

Use these poems for shared and choral reading to expand students' oral language abilities and provide opportunities to practice expressive and interpretive reading.

———. 2009. *When Readers Struggle: Teaching That Works*. Portsmouth, NH: Heinemann.

Use this volume to help you design and implement effective intervention programs for children in grades K–3 who have difficulty learning to read and write.